D0219560

Global Environmental Change

Global Environmental Change
Plants, Animals and Communities

Jonathan Graves
Department of Biology, University of York, UK

Duncan Reavey
Department of Zoology and Entomology,
University of Natal, South Africa

Longman

Longman
Longman Group Limited
Longman House, Burnt Mill, Harlow
Essex CM20 2JE, England
and Associated Companies throughout the world

© Longman Group Limited 1996

All rights reserved; no part of this publication may be
reproduced, stored in any retrieval system, or transmitted in
any form or by any means, electronic, mechanical,
photocopying, recording, or otherwise without either the prior
written permission of the Publishers or a licence permitting
restricted copying in the United Kingdom issued by the
Copyright Licensing Agency Ltd., 90 Tottenham Court Road,
London W1P 9HE.

First published 1996

British Library Cataloguing in Publication Data
A catalogue entry for this title is available from the British Library.

ISBN 0-582-21873-X

Library of Congress Cataloging-in-Publication data
A catalog entry for this title is available from the Library of Congress.

Set by 26 in 10 on 12pt Palatino
Produced through Longman Malaysia, GPS

Contents

How to use this book

Global warming is one of those fashionable areas of science that gets all sorts of people excited, whether tabloid journalists, pensioners in a bus queue, Calvin and Hobbes, even a few politicians. Sooner or later it will feature in television dramas, perhaps one day in great poetry. Though a few ask for more and more evidence that global environmental change is taking place, most accept that human activities are causing changes quite unlike any the earth has known before. Organisations that fund science have quickly realised this and the late 1980s and the 1990s have seen a huge research effort to explain the probable effects on our environment. The research continues, as we try to discover what rates of change can be tolerated if the ecosystems we know and use are to continue to exist.

In this book we introduce global environmental change and concentrate on its implications for plants, animals and biological communities. To do this we range widely through many different fields of biology. We include enough details from areas as diverse as cell biology, genetics, physiology and ecology to explain the basics of why global environmental change matters.

New, relevant research continues to be published at a spectacular rate, both in proceedings of conferences and in international journals. Use these to supplement what you find in this book. Newsworthy stories are covered in magazines like New Scientist and Scientific American. Useful, interesting and readable reviews and commentaries often appear in Trends in Ecology and Evolution ("TREE") and Ambio, occasionally in Nature and Science. The Annual Review series of journals often includes relevant material. Specialist journals have sprung up in recent years to deal with particular aspects of the subject. They include Global Environment Change (overviews on everything from policy and risk management to law and development issues) and Climate Change (mostly climatology). The sheer diversity of journals in which relevant articles appear is intimidating – even in this short book we include references to about 80 different journals.

To locate the newest references, use abstract journals like Biological Abstracts to search for keywords like GLOBAL WARMING, GREENHOUSE EFFECT, ELEVATED CO_2 and CLIMATIC CHANGE. If you have access to on-line searches, even better. Take care when selecting keywords, as some authors use different terms to mean the same thing. If you use an on-line search, careful use of the wildcard (*) can help. For example, CLIMAT* + CHANG* should find references to both CLIMATIC CHANGE and CHANGING CLIMATE.

Use the Science Citation Index to discover which recent papers refer to any particular paper from the past that you know about. Many of the references in this book are important studies frequently cited in new papers that are only now being published. If you use some of the references in this book in this way, the book becomes a resource that lets you explore the very latest thinking.

Jon Graves, York
Duncan Reavey, Pietermaritzburg

Acknowledgements

Our special thanks go to our families, friends and colleagues at York, Natal and further afield for their enthusiasm and support in all our activities. Our warmest thanks go to Anita de Brouwer, Margaret Simmons and to students in York and Natal who were a valuable source of ideas, feedback and impossible questions. The good news is that some of them will find the answers. Alex Seabrook at Longman warmed to our early ideas. Jo Whelan and Tina Cadle kept their cool during later stages.

We are grateful to the following for permission to reproduce copyright material:

Academic Press Ltd. for Fig. 6.4 and Fig. 6.6 (Moore, 1972); Copyright of American Association for the Advancement of Science reprinted with permission from Ex situ conservation of plant genetic resources, *Science* 253: 866–72 (Cohen *et al*, 1991); American Fisheries Society for Fig. 6.7 (After Coutant, 1990); Copyright by the American Geophysical Union for Fig. 1.1 Aspects of climate variability in the Pacific and the western Americas pp165–236 (Keeling *et al*, 1989); American Society of Ichthyologists and Herpetologists for Fig. 3.7 (Smith *et al*, 1983); Dr Lynne Barratt, Hunting and Aquatic Resources, University of York for Plate 6; Reprinted by permission of Blackwell Scientific Publications Inc. for Fig. 4.11 from *Conservation Biology* 2: 391–94 (Graham, 1988), Fig. 3.14 *Journal of Biogeography* 18: 371–383 (Lindenmayer *et al*, 1991); Blackwell Science Ltd. for Fig. 3.15b from *The Scientific Management of Temperate Communities for Conservation* (Thomas, 1991); CAB International for Fig. 3.4 (Warnes, 1985); Cambridge University Press for Fig. 3.5 from *Animal Physiology, Adaption and Environment* (Schmidt-Nielsen, 1979); Central Office of Information/NERC Centre for Population Biology, Imperial College, London for Plate 5; CSIRO Editorial Services for Fig. 2.8 (Slatyer & Morrow, 1977); Chris W. Dee for Plate 4; Dusenbury for Fig. 3.12 (Dusenbury, 1989); Dorling Kindersley Adult/Mr Richard Lewington for Fig. 3.15(a) from *The Butterflies of Britain and Ireland* (Lewington, 1991); Ecological Society of America for Fig. 3.13 (Menusan,

1935); U.S. Environmental Protection Agency for Fig. 5.5 EPA-230/5-89-053 (after Schmidtmann & Miller, 1989); Dr E. Fahrbach, Alfred Wegener Institute for Polar and Marine Research for Fig. 6.10; University of Hawaii Press for Fig. 3.3 (Howarth & Stone, 1990); Intergovernmental panel on Climate Change (IPCC) for Fig. 1.9 (IPCC, 1992); International Center for Living Aquatic Resources management for Fig. 6.1 (Jones, 1982); Macmillan Magazines Limited reprinted with permission from *Nature*, Fig. 1.8 Vostock ice core: A 160,000 year record of atmospheric Co^2 *Nature*, 329: 408–14 (Barnola *et al*, 1987), Fig. 3.20 Test size variation in *Globigerina bulloides* in responses to Quaternary Palaeoceanographic changes, *Nature* 275: 123–4 (Malmgren & Kennett, 1978), Fig. 3.22 Oscillating selection of Darwin's finches *Nature* 327: 511–13 (Gibbs & Grant, 1987), Fig. 3.23 Tibetan species of dung beetle from Late Pleistocene deposits in England, *Nature* 245: 335–36 (Coope, 1973); Minns & Moore, Fisheries and Aquatic Sciences, Bayfield Institute (After Minns & Moore, 1992); Dr. D. Pegg, Medical Crybiology Unit, University of York for Fig 3.8; The Physiological Society for Fig. 3.1 (Johnston & Jukes, 1966); Dr M.C. Press, Dept. of Plant and Animal Sciences, University of Sheffield for Plates 1–3; The Royal Meteorological Society for Fig. 5.3 Climate variation and the growth of crops, *Quarterly Journal* vol. 107 pp 749–774 (Montieth, 1981); Plenum Publishing Corporation for Fig. 4.8 Vegetation maps for eastern North America: 40,000 B.P. to the present, *Geobotany II* (Delcourt & Delcourt, 1981); The Royal Society of London for Fig. 3.24 *Philosophical Transactions* pp 22–23 B 344: 19–26: the response of insect faunas to glacial-interglacial climatic fluctuations (Coope, 1994); Royal Swedish Academy of Sciences for Fig. 6.8 (Goreau & Hayes, 1994); Society of Experimental Biology for Fig. 3.10 from *Symposia for the Society* (Cossins & Raymond, 1987); Springer-Verlag GmbH & Co. KG for Fig. 2.9 The nutritional status of plants from high altitude. A world-wide comparison, *Oecologia* 81: 379–91 (Korner, 1989), Fig. 3.2 Respiratory adaptations of a fossorial mammal the pocket gopher (*Thomomus bottae*), *Journal of Comparative Physiology* 78: 121–137 (Darden, 1972), Fig. 4.2 Competition among an assemblage of annuals at two levels of soil moisture, *Oecologia* 62, 196–98 (Bazzaz & Carlson, 1984), Fig. 4.3 Competition and patterns of resource use among seedlings of five tropical trees growth at ambient and elevated CO_2, *Oecologia*, 79: 212–22 (Reekie & Bazzaz, 1989), Fig. 6.10 Responses to Environmental Stress: *Ecological Studies* 88 (Fahrbach *et al*, 1991).

    Whilst every effort has been made to trace the owners of copyright material, in a few cases this has proved impossible and we take this opportunity to offer our apologies to any copyright holders whose rights we may have unwittingly infringed.

1 The atmosphere of the earth, past, present and future

Introduction

In 1991 the concentration of carbon dioxide (CO_2) in the atmosphere was estimated to be 355 parts per million (ppm), and increasing by about 1.8 ppm per year (Watson *et al.* 1992). The trend is best shown by measurements which started in the late 1950s, at Mauna Loa, Hawaii (Figure 1.1). The fluctuations seen on this graph are annual. In the northern hemisphere during the spring and summer CO_2 is taken up by photosynthesis and the concentration in the atmosphere falls. In the autumn respiration predominates, plants die back, decomposition is more active and so the concentration of CO_2 rises. These fluctuations betray the intimate link between the global regulation of CO_2 and the world's living things.

To understand how the processes of photosynthesis and respiration affect CO_2 concentration, we need to look at the chemical reactions involved.

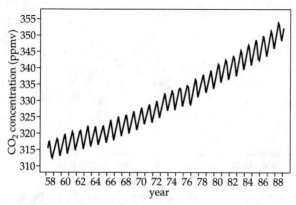

Figure 1.1   Monthly average CO_2 concentration in parts per million, observed continuously at Mauna Loa, Hawaii. (From Keeling *et al.* 1989).

Photosynthesis can be described by the following equation:

$$CO_2 + H_2O \xrightarrow{\text{light and chlorophyll}} CH_2O + O_2$$

Light is captured by pigments in plants and this energy is used to split water and incorporate CO_2 into carbohydrate (CH_2O). The carbohydrate is converted initially into glucose and starch and ultimately into a wide range of compounds.

Oxidative respiration is essentially the reverse process, taking carbohydrate and forming carbon dioxide and water, with the release of energy which can be used to fuel processes in the living cell:

$$CH_2O + O_2 \xrightarrow{\text{energy released}} CO_2 + H_2O$$

A longer-term record of the concentration of CO_2 in the atmosphere is available trapped in the ice caps. As snow falls air is trapped between the flakes; the snow is compressed into ice, but bubbles of the past atmosphere remain. Cores of ice have been drilled from ice sheets and the CO_2 concentration in the air bubbles measured.

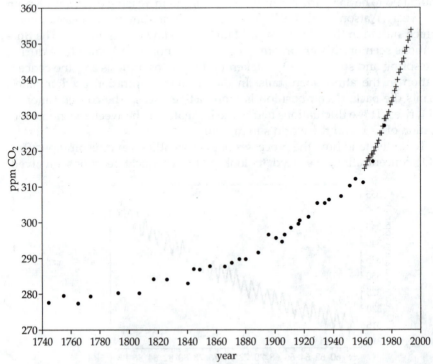

Figure 1.2 The increase in atmospheric CO_2 over the last 250 years. ●, measurements on air trapped in ice; +, direct measurements at Mauna Loa, Hawaii. (Data from UNEP 1991.)

Since the industrial revolution there has been an increase in the concentration of CO_2 in the atmosphere (Figure 1.2), with a particularly rapid rise since the 1940s. From this it has been inferred that it is human disruption of the natural biological and chemical interchange of carbon that is responsible for the increase. To understand why this has occurred and to predict future trends requires an understanding of a range of physical and biological processes.

Life on earth and the evolution of the atmosphere

Two gases, nitrogen and oxygen, constitute 98% of the earth's atmosphere. The other gases present are called trace gases, with argon the most abundant at a concentration of just under 1%. We are concerned with the next most abundant gas, CO_2, which is only present at a concentration of 0.035% (355 ppm), and some even scarcer gases such as methane, present at just 1.7 ppm (Table 1.1).

However, the earth's atmosphere has not always had this composition. In primeval times it was probably very similar to that emitted from modern-day volcanoes: mostly CO_2 and very little oxygen (Table 1.1). The water condensed to form oceans and CO_2 dissolved in the water, forming carbonates. Sulphur dioxide (SO_2) and other gases also dissolved but the nitrogen, being inert, accumulated in the atmosphere. Until 2 billion years ago there was no oxygen in the atmosphere. Evidence for this is that sediments of this era react chemically in an atmosphere containing oxygen and yet some show signs of atmospheric weathering. There is evidence for the presence of oxygen in sediments less than 1.8 billion years old. Thus at some time around 2 billion years ago oxygen started accumulating in the earth's atmosphere. Where did this oxygen come from?

The most primitive organisms require an anaerobic atmosphere. The evolution of blue-green algae-like organisms, able to photosynthesize, changed the atmosphere by the photosynthetic splitting of water into oxygen and hydrogen. The oldest rocks containing such photosynthetic organisms are

Table 1.1 The main gaseous constituents of the atmosphere and volcanic gases (%)

Gas	Atmosphere	Volcanic
Nitrogen	78	1
Oxygen	21	
Argon	0.93	
Carbon dioxide	0.035	12
Methane	0.00017	
Sulphur dioxide	variable	7
Water vapour	0–4	80

over 3 billion years old. The question remains, what happened in the interim 1 billion years before free oxygen occurred in the atmosphere? It is thought that in this period the large amount of ferrous iron dissolved in the oceans reacted with oxygen and was converted to ferric iron, which is insoluble and so sedimented out to form vast iron ore deposits. Eventually, all the ferrous iron was used up and so the excess oxygen started to accumulate in the atmosphere.

The existence of free oxygen in the atmosphere led to the formation of the ozone (O_3) layer due to photochemical reactions in the upper atmosphere. This layer helps to filter out some of the ultraviolet radiation from the sun. Radiation in the ultraviolet part of the spectrum is highly energetic, and thus can be damaging to living organisms. Prior to the development of this ultraviolet screen life was restricted to below water, where the damaging radiation was absorbed by a sufficient depth of water above. Thus with the development of the ozone layer the land became a much less harsh environment for life, and the evolution of organisms that could colonize the land soon followed.

The existence of free oxygen was also a prerequisite for another important step in the development of life, the evolution of oxidative respiration. This is much more efficient than anaerobic respiration and meant that life could evolve into a much wider range of forms occupying many different environments. The colonization of the land by plants increased the oxygen level further by photosynthesis and decreased erosion of the land surface. Much of the carbon fixed by the land plants did not decompose completely: the accumulation of organic matter led to the formation of deposits of oil, coal and shale, which are now used as fuel.

Clearly, the evolution of the earth's atmosphere has been intimately linked with the development of life on earth. Today both biological and geochemical processes are involved in maintaining its composition, but one species, humans, has now become so numerous that it is beginning to affect the composition of the atmosphere and shift it from its natural equilibrium.

Why is the concentration of CO_2 in the atmosphere increasing?

The burning of fossil fuels

Since prehistoric times people have burnt wood and other plant remains to produce heat and light. As wood became scarce in Europe in the 18th century, the use of coal became increasingly important. The demand for energy increased sharply during the industrial revolution to fuel the new industries and to provide for the domestic needs of a rapidly expanding urban population (Figure 1.3(a)). This demand was largely met by the increased use of fossil fuels, primarily coal.

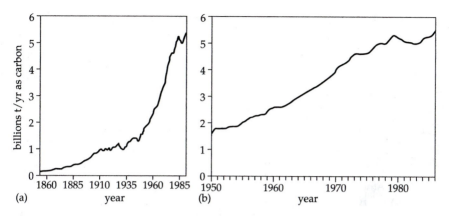

Figure 1.3 CO_2 emissions due to fossil fuel combustion (a) since 1860, (b) since 1950. (Data from UNEP 1991.)

Although the industrial revolution gathered pace in the early part of the 19th century, it was slow to develop and was very restricted geographically. Industrial activity has grown at an unprecedented rate since the last world war: as much coal has been consumed in the last 40 years as in all the rest of human history. As a consequence CO_2 production has increased rapidly during this period. Worldwide industrial development is one factor driving increased CO_2 production, but at the same time the world's population has increased from 3 billion in 1960 to over 5 billion in 1990, producing an ever-increasing demand for energy.

The link between industrial activity and CO_2 production can be clearly seen in Figure 1.3(b): oil prices increased in the early 1970s, when the cartel of oil-producing nations represented by OPEC increased the price, and then again in the early 1980s as a consequence of the Iran–Iraq war. Both were periods of global economic recession and were followed by a dip in the output of CO_2.

The countries responsible for industrial CO_2 emissions can be placed in three categories. The largest producers are the major industrialized developed nations in Europe, North America and the Pacific, followed by the populous developing economies such as China and India, and finally a group of largely agriculturally based economies with a small industrial base, such as much of Africa. The per capita CO_2 output is much higher in the countries in the first category (Figure 1.4), but interestingly North American and western European emissions of CO_2 have stabilized since the 1970s as a consequence of greater fuel efficiency, whereas output in eastern Europe and the developing countries has continued to rise. Figure 1.4 clearly indicates that many countries have a great capacity to increase CO_2 emissions in the future as their economies develop and their per capita usage of energy increases. Many countries attended the Earth Summit held in Rio de Janeiro in 1991, and agreed to take some initial steps towards regulating the emission of CO_2 into the atmosphere.

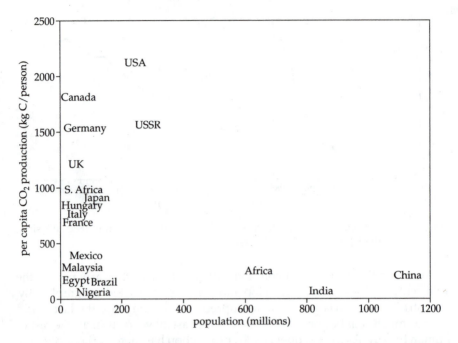

Figure 1.4   Per capita CO_2 production from fossil fuels and cement production by country or region versus population. The industrialized countries have a high per capita output of CO_2, whereas many populous developing countries produce much less CO_2 per capita. (Data from WRI 1990.)

Land use changes

The burning of fossil fuels is not the only way in which CO_2 can be released into the atmosphere: large amounts are also produced as a consequence of land use changes. In fact, it is only since about 1960 that emissions from fossil fuel combustion have become more important. Up until then the rise in the atmospheric concentration of CO_2 can be largely ascribed to deforestation, and agricultural changes leading to partial oxidation of soil humus, especially in North America. To date, approximately 320 billion tonnes (Giga-tonnes: Gtonnes) (measured as the carbon content only) of CO_2 have been released into the atmosphere: 120 Gtonnes by land use changes and 200 Gtonnes by fossil fuel burning.

Land use changes can release CO_2 into the atmosphere by causing the oxidation of carbon compounds in the vegetation or the soil. But some land use changes can also result in a net absorption of CO_2 from the atmosphere, if fixation of CO_2 via photosynthesis outweighs that lost by other processes. The burning of forests for the purpose of land clearance releases CO_2 rapidly into the atmosphere by combustion, whereas decomposition of felled trees releases CO_2 more slowly. On the other hand, if a parcel of land is abandoned the growth of vegetation may absorb CO_2 from the atmosphere over a period of years. Assessing the impact of land use changes therefore requires an analysis of how the amount of carbon incorporated in parcels of land changes over a long period.

Deforestation initially reduces the amount of carbon per unit area of land (carbon density) and there is a release of CO_2. If the forest is left to regenerate the carbon density will gradually recover, and it will act as a net sink for CO_2 as it does so. Eventually, all the CO_2 that was initially released may be reabsorbed via photosynthesis. If after deforestation the land is used for grazing or for growing crops, the carbon density will remain at a lower level and there will have been a net release of CO_2 into the atmosphere (see Plates 1–3).

An important consequence of deforestation is that there is often an increase in soil erosion, which exposes organic matter (humus and other undecomposed remains) in the soil to rapid oxidation. As a considerable proportion of the carbon resident in an area of land may be in the form of soil organic matter, this can be a very important source of CO_2. Furthermore, soil erosion and loss of nutrients often means that the original forest cannot re-establish, and instead a scrub with a much lower carbon density may be formed.

As indicated in Table 1.2, emissions of CO_2 due to land use changes are greatest for developing tropical countries with large forest reserves. This list contrasts strongly with those nations responsible for emissions by fossil fuel combustion. However, the estimated emission of CO_2 due to land use changes is only about 20% of the total.

The global carbon cycle

It is not easy to estimate each of the fluxes in the global carbon cycle. This is neatly illustrated by the fact that although between 5 and 7 Gtonnes of car-

Table 1.2 Estimates of carbon released by country in millions of tonnes

From industrial sources (1982)*		From land use changes (1989)†	
USA	1135	Brazil	454
USSR	901	Indonesia	124
China	413	Burma	83
Japan	226	Mexico	64
W. Germany	181	Thailand	62
UK	141	Colombia	59
Poland	112	Nigeria	57
France	111	Zaire	57
India	78	Malaysia	50
Italy	88	India	41

* Data from UNEP (1991)
† Data from Leggett (1990)

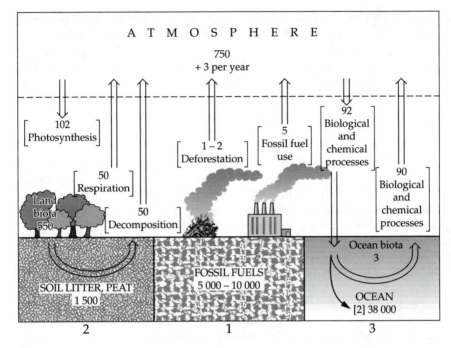

Figure 1.5   The global carbon cycle. All figures are in billions of tonnes of carbon (Gtonnes C). (After Schneider 1989.)

1. Large amounts of carbon are locked up as fossil fuels from which CO_2 is slowly being released by industrial activity, largely energy generation. The human-controlled flux of carbon into the atmosphere is estimated to be 5.7 Gtonnes C/year. Land use changes add a further 1.6 G tonnes C/year.

2. About 550 Gtonnes C are incorporated into surface vegetation. This is added to by photosynthesis. Much of this carbon is rapidly lost by the respiration of plants and animals and there is a slower loss via decomposition from the soil; some carbon may remain in the soil for a very long period. Terrestrial photosynthesis and respiration are assumed to be approximately balanced.

3. The marine carbon cycle is of a similar magnitude to that on land. The largest carbon sink is the ocean, which contains about 60 times as much as the air, mostly in the form of bicarbonate ions. The exchange of atmospheric carbon with the ocean occurs in two stages: the exchange of CO_2 with the warm surface waters and the movement of carbon from the surface waters to the deep ocean, where it may remain for long periods of time. The photosynthesis of phytoplankton is an important means of drawing CO_2 from the atmosphere. The mass of the ocean biota is much less than that on land. Nevertheless it is responsible for fixing about 40 Gtonnes of carbon through photosynthesis; though 36 Gtonnes is rapidly returned to the atmosphere via respiration.

Note there is a net loss into the oceans and the terrestrial biota of 2 Gtonnes each. It is not really known to what extent each acts as the 'missing sink', and these figures are arbitrary.

bon are released into the atmosphere each year as a result of fossil fuel burning and land use changes, only about half of this actually accumulates in the atmosphere. It is not known where the rest goes, but it has been proposed that the missing CO_2 is taken down into the deep ocean or that the northern forests are absorbing the extra.

The fluxes in the terrestrial biological system are more than an order of magnitude greater than those of human origin, therefore a small change in either the rate of photosynthesis or the rate of respiration, on a worldwide scale, might greatly alter the rate at which CO_2 accumulates in the atmosphere. Why might theses fluxes change in the future? An increased atmospheric concentration of CO_2 might lead to higher rates of photosynthesis and the incorporation of more carbon in the biosphere. A higher global temperature might increase the rate of respiration of many organisms, resulting in more CO_2 being returned to the atmosphere. These two processes are unlikely to neatly cancel; both will be discussed in more detail in later chapters.

In contrast to the terrestrial situation the exchange of CO_2 with the oceans is dominated by physical processes. CO_2 is more soluble in cold water: it therefore tends to dissolve in the cooler waters of the Arctic and is released in warmer waters. The ocean is normally stratified, with warmer (lighter) surface waters of about 100 m thickness on top of cooler (denser) deep waters. Only in the Arctic seas during the winter is this stratification destroyed, when the winter cooling of the surface water increases its density. The surface water then sinks with its enriched carbon content, slowly circulating via the deep ocean and not coming to the surface again for 500–1500 years.

Photosynthetic absorption of CO_2 is also a major contributor to the absorption of CO_2 by the oceans. Phytoplankton (small photosynthesizing organisms drifting in the sea) grow particularly in nutrient-rich upwellings, but also at lower density in the open ocean; their photosynthesis draws down CO_2 from the atmosphere into the surface layer of the ocean. When they die a proportion of plankton, and organisms further up the food chain, sink into the deeper ocean, delivering their carbon to the long-term repository of the abyss. Eventually, the long-term deep-water circulation will buffer the increase in the atmospheric CO_2, but only over timescales very long in human terms.

Attempting to extrapolate how the fluxes in the global carbon cycle might change in the future adds further uncertainty. Predicting how fast the concentration of CO_2 in the atmosphere will rise depends on both the scale of human activity and the response of the natural carbon cycle. Undoubtedly there will be an increase in CO_2 output as a consequence of growth in the world population and economic development. These factors will increase the demand for energy and cause further land use changes. The rate at which fossil fuels are burnt also depends on their availability and price, as well as the future development of alternative energy sources such as wind, solar and nuclear power. However, some of the greatest uncertainties lie in the reaction of the natural carbon fluxes, both oceanic and terrestrial: will photosynthesis increase as a consequence of the additional CO_2 in the atmosphere? How much will the oceans absorb and release? How might climate change feed back and increase or decrease these natural fluxes?

Consequences of the changes in atmospheric composition

The greenhouse effect

Radiation from the sun has a spectrum characteristic of a body at a temperature of 6000 Kelvin (K). As a consequence the radiation that reaches the earth is mostly at a short wavelength, in the visible region of the spectrum between 400 and 700 nm (Figure 1.6(a)). At the earth's surface radiation is absorbed, increasing the temperature of both land and ocean. The earth's surface then emits radiation, but with a spectrum characteristic of a much

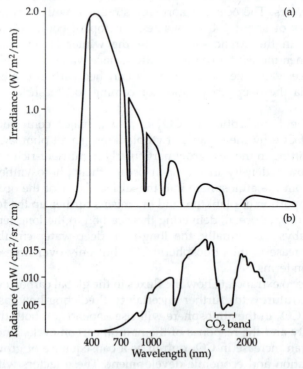

Figure 1.6 (a) The spectrum of sunlight at the earth's surface. (From Edwards and Walker 1983.) (b) The spectrum of the earth as taken from the Nimbus-4 satellite over the North African desert. (Adapted from NAS 1983.)

cooler body, on average about 283K (Figure 1.6(b)). This spectrum is richer in long-wave radiation in the red and infrared part of the spectrum. Some of the sun's radiation that reaches the earth's surface is also reflected. If we look down at the earth from a satellite in space the spectrum that reaches the satellite resembles the spectrum of a body at 283K, except for the fact that there are absorption bands in the infrared region. The most prominent of these are for water and CO_2. The radiation that these molecules absorb helps to increase the temperature of the earth. The greenhouse effect is not a controversial theory: it is a well proven fact. The insulation provided by the greenhouse gases is vital to the maintenance of life on earth, as without it global temperature would be 33°C cooler.

The world is constantly being warmed by solar radiation. On average the energy of the sun's radiation at the top of the earth's atmosphere is $1355\,W/m^2$ (the solar constant). The effect this has on the earth's climate is called solar forcing of the climate system. This varies from season to season and on longer timescales, as the sun's luminosity varies or the orbit of the earth around the sun alters. Some of this radiation is reflected back into space or absorbed in the atmosphere. At the earth's surface on a sunny day the incident energy would be about $1000\,W/m^2$. The greenhouse effect can be considered as an additional forcing factor, as it prevents some radiation from escaping. The increased forcing attributable to the addition of greenhouse gases by humans is $2.5\,W/m^2$. If the concentration of CO_2 in the atmosphere were to double, this forcing would increase to $4.3\,W/m^2$. An effective doubling of CO_2 – that is, changes in all greenhouse gases converted to the equivalent change in CO_2 – is predicted to occur in the first half of the next century, as a result of increased emissions of greenhouse gases.

The greenhouse gases

Water vapour is the most important greenhouse gas but its role as such is complicated by the fact that it forms clouds. Water vapour acts as a greenhouse gas absorbing radiation, but when it condenses into clouds it can either absorb long-wave radiation from the ground causing further warming, or reflect radiation from the sun causing a cooling effect. Which of these two predominates depends on the type of cloud and its height in the atmosphere.

Absorption of radiation somewhere in the infrared region is a property of a wide range of gas molecules, including CO_2, methane, chlorofluorocarbons (CFCs), nitrous oxide and sulphur dioxide, but of these CO_2 is the most important (Table 1.3). All of these gases are present in the atmosphere at a lower concentration than CO_2, but are much more potent as absorbers of infrared radiation.

The concentration of methane in the atmosphere is also rising as a consequence of human activity (Figure 1.7). It is produced by anaerobic respiration in a wide variety of environments, such as the stomachs of ani-

Table 1.3 Greenhouse gases and their contribution to radiative forcing during the 1980s. (From IPCC 1990)

Gas	Contribution to radiative forcing (%)	Annual rate of increase (%)
Carbon dioxide	55	0.5
Chlorofluorocarbons	24	5.6
Methane	15	0.9
Nitrous oxide	6	0.2

mals, swamps, paddyfields and waterlogged soils. A considerable amount is also produced during mining and oil/natural gas extraction. Methane is constantly removed from the atmosphere by reaction with hydroxyl (OH) radicals in the air and by the activity of soil organisms. About 530 million tonnes are produced annually. Of this 420 million tonnes are converted to CO_2 and CO by reaction with OH, a further 30 million tonnes are removed by soil bacteria, and 30 million tonnes are removed by other atmospheric reactions, leaving an increase of about 50 million tonnes per annum. Human population growth and agricultural development are increasing the production of methane, but recent figures reveal that the rate of accumulation in the atmosphere might be falling: it was approximately 20 parts per billion per year (ppb/year) in the late 1970s, but may have been as low as 10 ppb/year in 1989. As with CO_2, the interactions that regulate the concentration of methane in the atmosphere are complex and the future concentration does not only depend on how much is evolved by human activity. For further details on the sources and sinks of methane see Watson *et al.* (1992).

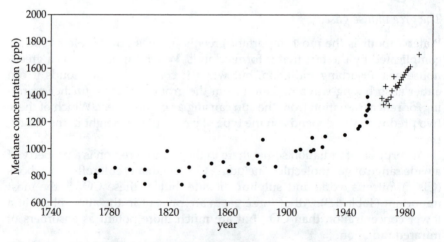

Figure 1.7   The increase in atmospheric methane over the last 250 years. ●, measurements on air trapped in ice cores; + direct measurements. (Data from UNEP 1991.)

CFCs are potent greenhouse gases (10 000–30 000 times more effective than CO_2), although they are present in only very small concentrations in the atmosphere. The damage these gases were inflicting upon the ozone layer was recognized by the signing of an international agreement, the Montreal Protocol (1987), which seeks to limit and eventually phase out their use in the medium term. Although CFC production is likely to fall as a result, they will be replaced by substitutes less damaging to the ozone layer but which over time will accumulate to higher concentrations and will have some effect. CFC concentration will continue to increase in the stratosphere for 5–10 years after production has stopped because of slow diffusion from the lower layers of the atmosphere. The role of CFCs as greenhouse gases is complicated because they simultaneously destroy ozone, which is also a greenhouse gas. Depletion of ozone contributes a negative radiative forcing, counterbalancing approximately 80% of CFC forcing over the decade of the 1980s. So, phasing out CFCs and replacing them with substitutes will have the unwanted side-effect of increasing greenhouse warming as ozone concentrations recover.

Although SO_2 is a greenhouse gas its accumulation in the atmosphere has probably had a net cooling effect. SO_2 released in the gas phase is converted to aerosol particles of sulphate, which may then grow by the formation of more sulphate, in both the gas and the liquid phases. These aerosol particles scatter and absorb short-wave (solar) radiation, but their influence on long-wave (infrared) radiation is less pronounced. Possibly more important than this direct effect on radiation is the fact that these particles are condensation nuclei for water vapour, and so influence the extent and nature of clouds. Recent estimates of the solar forcing caused by sulphate scattering over the northern hemisphere gave a figure of -1 W/m², compared to +2.5 W/m² for total trace gas forcing (Isaksen et al. 1992). In addition, their net effect via providing condensation nuclei for cloud formation is also negative. But the effect of sulphate tends to be localized: sulphate aerosols last for short periods, mostly in the troposphere (the lower atmosphere between 8 and 17 km altitude) and so will adjust rapidly to emission levels. Volcanic eruptions put sulphate into the stratosphere (the upper atmosphere above the troposphere and up to about 50 km altitude); the eruption of El Chichon in 1982 thus produced a cooling effect for several years, and this is likely to happen again as a consequence of the Pinatubo eruption in 1991. The lifetime of aerosol sulphate in the stratosphere is several years; particles eventually coagulate and are removed, principally by precipitation, after they have been used as condensation nuclei for water vapour. It has been suggested that a natural source of sulphate aerosols may be important in regulating the earth's climate (Charlson et al. 1987). Dimethylsulphide (DMS) is produced in large amounts by some marine phytoplankton, and could act in a feedback loop to stabilize temperature. Higher sea temperatures could lead to more DMS being produced: this increases cloud cover, reflecting solar radiation and thereby reducing temperature.

Although the greenhouse effect is an undoubted physical phenomenon the question of whether an enhanced greenhouse effect is causing global warming is still open. There are natural variations in the earth's climate over a range of timescales, and if a greenhouse warming trend exists it must be disentangled from these natural background changes.

Natural variations in climate

Milankovic cycles

The earth has gone through cycles of warming and cooling in the past: the last ice age ended about 15 000 years ago and we are currently in the middle of an interglacial period. But what causes these natural temperature fluctuations?

Evidently, one of the principal factors governing the earth's temperature is the amount of incoming solar radiation. Solar forcing of the climate does vary as a consequence of irregularities in the earth's movement through space. These cycles cause variations in the distribution of solar radiation through the year, although the total amount of radiation received remains approximately the same. There are three cycles:

1. Currently the earth is nearest the sun on its orbit during the northern winter, and furthest away from the sun in the summer. But in 11 000 years it will be reversed; this 22 000-year cycle is called the precession of the equinoxes.

2. The tilt of the earth's axis varies by 3° over a period of 41 000 years, and so summers and winters become more and less intense.

3. The shape of the earth's orbit around the sun also changes on a 100 000-year cycle.

These three cycles, called Milankovic cycles after the scientist who first proposed that they might be responsible for the ice ages, combine to produce an irregular but predictable variation in the amount of incoming solar radiation. However, the variation in solar forcing as a consequence of the Milankovic cycles is not large enough to directly account for the observed changes in the earth's climate. Therefore, when they were first proposed as a mechanism to explain ice ages, they were dismissed.

Past climate can be reconstructed from the concentration of the stable isotope ^{18}O in the shells of sea organisms. A large proportion of ^{16}O evaporates from the sea as it is lighter; if precipitation accumulates in ice at the poles the concentration of ^{18}O in the water increases. Therefore ^{18}O concentration in the shells is related to the volume of ice in the world. The advance and retreat of the world's glaciers can therefore be reconstructed from cores which contain shells laid down over long periods. There is a good correlation between climate and the Milankovic cycles, although over the last million years the dominant cycle has been over 100 000 years. But as the changes in solar radiation are not large enough to cause these changes in climate, other mechanisms have been proposed.

There is good evidence for a close relationship between the concentration of CO_2 in the atmosphere and these long-term climatic fluctuations. The Antarctic and Greenland ice caps contain ice that has been laid down year by year for hundreds of thousands of years. Cores have been drilled from these ice caps and the age of the ice can be calculated by a variety of techniques. The CO_2 concentration in the atmosphere at the time when the snow fell can be assessed from trapped bubbles of air. The temperature at which the snow fell can be inferred from the proportion of water containing deuterium, a heavy isotope of hydrogen. Water containing deuterium precipitates from clouds more rapidly than lighter water. This process is highly temperature sensitive, so the concentration of deuterium in snow is related to temperature. There is an excellent correlation between CO_2 concentration and temperature, as illustrated in the results from the Vostok core from Antarctica (Figure 1.8). One possibility is that changes in CO_2 concentration help amplify warming and cooling via the greenhouse effect. Alternatively, both the CO_2 and temperature fluctuations could be reacting to another force, such as changes in ocean circulation.

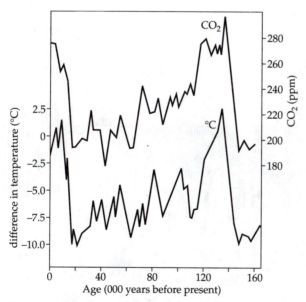

Figure 1.8 Changes in the concentration of CO_2 and temperature over the past 160 000 years. Reconstructed from the Vostok ice core, East Antarctica. (From Barnola *et al.* 1987.)

Recent changes in world temperature

The climate has changed significantly in historic times: the little ice age that lasted from about 1550 to 1850 was a period when the global climate was cooler and winters were particularly cold. The end was abrupt: it might have been due to a change in ocean circulation but it is also correlated with the increase in CO_2 in the atmosphere.

Since the 19th century there have been temperature data available from weather stations throughout the world, yet it is surprisingly difficult to compile an accurate picture of changes in world temperature over the last century (Jones and Wigley 1990). If a single weather station is considered, the local landscape is likely to have changed considerably with time as a consequence of industrialization and urbanization. This can greatly affect the local temperature. There may also have been changes in instrumentation, station location and time of day when measurements are taken, all of which may introduce additional errors. The data have been collated and allowance made for errors where possible, and the picture that emerges is illustrated in Figure 1.9. Overall there has been a worldwide warming of about 0.5°C since the end of the 19th century. During this time there have been two periods of rapid temperature increase, one between 1910 and 1930 and the other

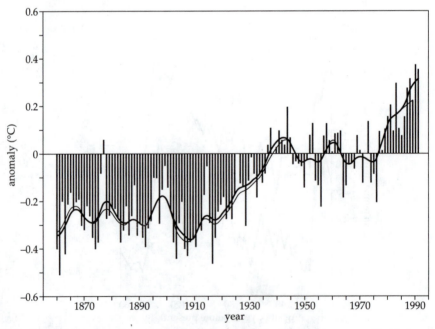

Figure 1.9 Combined land, air and sea surface temperature anomalies between 1861 and 1991, relative to the average temperature 1951–1980. (From IPCC 1992.)

between 1970 and the present. The 1980s was easily the warmest decade on record, containing six of the warmest years, and the trend has continued in 1991 and 1992.

However, the question remains as to whether or not this change in temperature has been caused by the accumulation of greenhouse gases in the atmosphere. Could the observed increase be due to a natural climatic variation (see Gribbin (1990) for an account of the controversy)? One argument is that it is a result of two factors, natural variation in the luminosity of the sun and volcanic activity. The luminosity of the sun changes in relation to sunspot activity, which has an 11-year cycle. This causes a 0.1% variation in luminosity which, if unbuffered by the oceans, could cause a temperature shift of 0.08–0.24°C over the cycle. Luminosity may vary on a longer timescale of 100 years or more, and is a proposed mechanism to account for historic cool and warm periods such as the little ice age. Volcanic activity throws dust into the upper atmosphere which reflects solar radiation and may thereby cause climatic variations. The problem with the argument is that even when both are considered they cannot account for the magnitude of the observed increase in temperature. Furthermore, it can be argued that some factors may be masking the true extent of the greenhouse effect. For example, the stable temperature period between 1940 and 1970 may be a consequence of increased cloudiness, particularly in the northern hemisphere. This could be due to SO_2 pollution from fossil fuel combustion, and there is evidence for increased cloudiness over the USA during this period. The conclusion of the Intergovernmental Panel on Climate Change (IPCC) scientific assessment was that there was a true increase in the world's temperature, but that this could not be unambiguously attributed to an enhanced greenhouse effect (IPCC 1990). Some estimates indicate that an unambiguous signal of global warming may take until 2020–2030 to emerge.

Predicting the climate of the future

The complexity of the earth's weather systems makes it difficult to predict future climatic trends. Computer models, called global circulation models (GCMs), are used to simulate the world's climate and predict future changes. The variables that drive these models include information concerning energy input from the sun and the gaseous composition of the atmosphere. The models then use equations describing the interaction of parts of the ocean–atmosphere system and basic physical laws (the conservation of mass, momentum and energy, the ideal gas law) to calculate temperature, pressure, wind speed, humidity, soil moisture etc. The world is simplified into a grid system, with points separated by several hundred kilometres horizontally and several kilometres vertically above the earth's surface. Calculations are done only at the intersections of the points. Some of the most powerful computers in the world are required to make the huge number of calculations required. A key test is whether these models have predicted the effects of past increases in greenhouse gases accurately: they predicted that the rise in CO_2 since preindustrial levels of 280 ppm should have caused a global warming of about 0.4–1.1°C. The actual warming, at 0.5°C, is towards the low end of this range.

One major problem with these models is that they do not take sufficient account of some of the possible feedback mechanisms which might act to amplify or dampen the greenhouse effect.

Higher temperatures may trigger any of the following:

Possible feedbacks amplifying the greenhouse effect

- A reduction in northern hemisphere snow cover and/or a melting of part of the Arctic ice sheet. This will reduce the earth's albedo (capacity to reflect solar radiation) thereby increasing temperature further.
- A release of methane currently locked in permafrost in the Arctic; this acts as a greenhouse gas.
- An increase in the rate of decomposition of organic matter in soils and peat, releasing additional CO_2 into the atmosphere.
- More evaporation leading to an increase in the concentration of water vapour in the atmosphere, which acts as a greenhouse gas.
- An increase in the rate of respiration in plants and animals releasing CO_2 currently resident in the living biota of the world.

Possible feedbacks decreasing the greenhouse effect

- More evaporation results in greater cloud cover, increasing the earth's albedo and thereby reducing the temperature.
- More evaporation increases polar precipitation of snow, which increases the earth's albedo.
- The increased concentration of CO_2 in the atmosphere stimulates photosynthesis globally, which sequesters more carbon in the biosphere.

The IPCC collated results from GCMs formulated by different research groups and concluded that the best estimate of the rise in global temperature that would occur if there was an equivalent doubling of CO_2 concentration was about 2.5°C, with a range between 1.5 and 4.5°C (IPCC 1990). The direct radiative effect of a doubling of CO_2 would produce a rise in temperature of about 1.2°C; any additional increase is due to feedbacks. But these models did not fully take into account the effect of the oceans, which tend to buffer the increase in temperature. Recent results from the new generation of coupled-atmosphere ocean models broadly confirm these earlier results (Gates *et al.* 1992), predicting a slightly lower average warming of 1.3–2.3°C for a doubling of CO_2. These rates are about 60% of what would be expected in the absence of the buffering of the oceans.

The predicted increase in global temperature may seem small, but this hides the impact that such a temperature rise might have. One way of appreciating this is to ask how much further south you might have to move to experience a similar change in temperature. For example, you would have to move from London to Nice in the south of France to experience a 3°C shift in average temperature. Furthermore, these figures represent the average change in global temperature; however, the change will not be evenly spread over the globe. The models predict that the increase in temperature will be least at the equator and increase towards the poles, especially in the northern hemisphere. This is partly caused by a feedback: the reduction in the ice cover in the northern hemisphere will reduce albedo and therefore amplify the warming effect.

Potentially more important than the average temperature increase is the increase in the likelihood of extreme events. If the average temperature is higher, the frequency of very hot days is likely to increase. For example, it has been estimated that a doubling of CO_2 would increase the number of days over 32°C in Atlanta, USA, from 17 to 53 a year. But a major obstacle to evaluating the impact of extreme events in the future is that the GCMs are still too coarse to make predictions on a regional scale. Two approaches have been used to circumvent this: fine-scale models are coupled to the global GCM, or statistical relationships between global and regional climate are used. As a consequence regional predictions are very uncertain. Overall there are indications that the frequency of storms might increase.

One climatic change that is fairly certain to occur if global temperature increases is an increase in the amount of precipitation: higher temperatures will result in more water vapour entering the atmosphere. However, GCM predictions about the regional distribution of the increased precipitation are very uncertain: there is only limited agreement between GCMs and this is not significant. There are likely to be areas that will experience increases, but also areas that will become drier. For example, some simulations have predicted drier summers in continental North America and parts of central Asia. Agriculture in these regions would undoubtedly suffer, which is important as they contain some of the major grain-growing areas of the world. Other predictions have indicated a future increase in precipitation in the mid-latitudes, coupled with a fall in the tropics. Interestingly, this is precisely the pattern that has occurred in the last two decades, contributing to the failure of harvests over several years in Sahel Africa. These events cannot be attributed to the greenhouse effect but do give an insight into the potential human consequences.

The possibility of a rise in sea level has attracted more media attention than almost any other aspect of global environmental change. There will certainly be thermal expansion of the oceans as the water temperature increases. However, it is the possibility that the polar ice caps might begin to melt that attracts the most attention. The melting of the Arctic ice would of course have no effect, as it is already floating on water. Melting of ice in mountain glaciers and surface ice and snow can only increase sea level by a relatively small amount, as there is a limited volume of water available. Most of the Antarctic is very cold, with an annual mean temperature of –50 to –60°C and a summer temperature of –20°C. It is therefore very unlikely that this will be affected by the projected temperature increase. Most estimates of the contribution of Antarctic melt to sea-level rise during the next century are low or even negative, as snowfall in Antarctica may increase. Some melting of the Greenland ice sheet may also make a small contribution. The IPCC estimates of sea-level rise by the year 2100 for the 'business-as-usual scenario' were as follows:

Best estimate	60 cm
Range	31–110 cm

Contributing factors

Thermal expansion	28–66 cm
Mountain	8–20 cm
Greenland	3–23 cm
Antarctic	-7–0 cm

The annual rate of sea-level rise is estimated to be about 6 mm/year. In the last 100 years sea level has already risen by 15 cm, but only half of this can be accounted for by thermal expansion and melting of mountain glaciers. Most communities should be able to cope with this, except in circumstances where local sea-level rise is greater due to land subsidence or in situations where sea level is already a problem. Bangladesh is a country already threatened by the sea: it is the victim of recurrent climate-related disasters which cause flooding. In such a situation it might be suspected that global sea-level rise would cause disaster, but it is not so simple. The coast of Bangladesh is constantly changing as vast amounts of silt are deposited by the three great rivers, the Ganges, the Brahmaputra and the Meghna. Together they carry 1.5–2.5 billion tonnes of sediment per year, much of which is deposited in the delta region, thereby raising the land level. But at the same time the crust subsides due to the additional weight, and the land level falls. Some argue that the effect of global sea-level rise will not even be noticed because these local changes are much larger. Probably in the case of Bangladesh the frequency of storms is of more concern than the gradual sea-level rise, to which people will adapt by occupying only suitable areas.

To understand the future that faces our world we have to take these predicted changes in its physical nature and try and interpret how the biosphere will respond. Indeed, the biosphere is an integral component which may act as a positive or negative feedback interacting with the physical changes. In this context it should be remembered that the largest fluxes of CO_2 in the global carbon cycle are biological processes.

References

Barnola JM, Raynaud D, Korotkevitch YS, Lorius C (1987) Vostok ice core: a 160 000-year record of atmospheric CO_2, *Nature* **329**, 408–14

Charlson RJ, Lovelock JE, Andreae MO, Warren SG (1987) Oceanic phytoplankton, atmospheric sulphur, cloud albedo and climate, *Nature* **326**, 655–61

Edwards G, Walker D (1983) C_3, C_4: *mechanisms, and cellular and environmental regulation, of photosynthesis*, Blackwell, Oxford

Gates WL, Mitchell JFB, Boer GJ, Cubasch U, Meleshko VP (1992) Climate modelling, climate prediction and model validation. In *Climate change 1992: the Supplementary Report to the IPCC Scientific Assessment*, eds. JT Houghton, BA Callander and SK Varney. Cambridge University Press, Cambridge, pp 97–134

Gribbin J (1990) An assault on the climate consensus, *New Scientist* 15 December, 26–31

IPCC (1990) *Climate change: the Intergovernmental Panel on Climate Change Scientific Assessment*, eds. JT Houghton, GJ Jenkins, JJ Ephraums. Cambridge University Press, Cambridge

IPCC (1992) *Climate change 1992: the Supplementary Report to the IPCC Scientific Assessment*, eds. JT Houghton, BA Callander and SK Varney. Cambridge University Press, Cambridge

Isaksen ISA, Ramaswamy, Rodhe H, Wigley TML (1992) Radiative forcing of climate. In *Climate change 1992: the Supplementary Report to the IPCC Scientific Assessment*, eds. JT Houghton, BA Callander and SK Varney. Cambridge University Press, Cambridge, pp 47–68

Jones PD, Wigley TML (1990) Global warming trends, *Scientific American* August, 66–73

Keeling CD, Bacastow RB, Carter AF, Piper SC, Whorf TP, Heimann M, Mook WG, Rouloffzen H (1989) A three-dimensional model of atmospheric CO_2 transport based on observed winds: 1. Analysis of observational data. In *Aspects of climate variability in the Pacific and the western Americas*, ed. DH Peterson, Geophysical Monograph 55, AGU, Washington DC, pp 165–236

Leggett J (ed) (1990) *Global warming: the Greenpeace Report*. Oxford University Press, Oxford

NAS (1983) *Changing climate: report of the carbon dioxide assessment committee*, National Academy of Sciences, National Academy Press, Washington DC

Schneider SH (1989) The changing climate, *Scientific American* September, 38–47

UNEP (1991) *Environmental Data Report 1989–90*, Basil Blackwell, Oxford

Watson RT, Meira Filho LG, Sanhueza E, Janetos A (1992) Sources and sinks. In *Climate change 1992: the Supplementary Report to the IPCC Scientific Assessment*, eds. JT Houghton, BA Callander and SK Varney. Cambridge University Press, Cambridge, pp 25–46

WRI (1990) *World resources 1990–1991. A report by the World Resources Institute*, ed. AL Hammond. Oxford University Press, Oxford

Further reading

IPCC (1990) *Climate change: the Intergovernmental Panel on Climate Change Scientific Assessment*, eds. JT Houghton, GJ Jenkins, JJ Ephraums. Cambridge University Press, Cambridge

Leggett J (ed) (1990) *Global warming: the Greenpeace Report*. Oxford University Press, Oxford

Mintzer IM (ed) (1992) *Confronting climate change, risks implications and responses*, Stockholm Environment Institute. Cambridge University Press, Cambridge

2 The impact of GEC on plants

Introduction

How will the biosphere respond to global environmental change (GEC)? Mankind is part of the biosphere and depends on it for survival, so this is a crucial question which needs to be addressed in order to formulate coping strategies. If the impact of GEC is likely to be severely damaging to the biosphere, this would be a strong argument to adopt strategies that may help prevent it. However, if GEC is inevitable strategies to help cope with the biological consequences need to be formulated. On a global scale the biosphere may act as a positive or negative feedback controlling the magnitude of GEC (see Chapter 1). The largest fluxes of CO_2 in the world are not directly controlled by man but are biological: photosynthesis is the largest flux of CO_2 out of the atmosphere and respiration its largest flux into the atmosphere. Increased plant growth, stimulated by both the increased CO_2 concentration and higher temperatures, could remove a substantial proportion of the CO_2 produced by human activity. Alternatively, higher temperatures may increase the rate of respiration and cause the release of additional CO_2.

On a smaller scale communities may be disrupted by GEC as plant and animal distribution changes in response to the increasing temperature, and as productivity is altered by CO_2 fertilization. Many communities are managed to produce food, timber, fibre and chemicals, and the impact of GEC on these industries may be profound. Understanding these potential changes must start with an appreciation of how individual plants and animals respond to environmental changes.

The effects of GEC on plants can be divided into two categories. First, even if the climate remains relatively stable the concentration of CO_2 in the atmosphere will continue to rise and this will directly affect the function of plants. Secondly, there are likely to be changes in temperature and precipitation which will also affect plants. However, the effects of climate and CO_2

cannot be entirely separated: changes in CO_2 will affect plant response to climate and vice versa. Quantitative and qualitative changes in primary production will influence the animal and microbial communities that depend on this productivity. The aim of this chapter is to provide detailed information on how plant function is affected by CO_2 and temperature. This will provide a foundation for the discussion of the possible impact of GEC on plant communities, both natural and agricultural.

Physiological effects of increased CO_2 concentrations on plants

Plant species may be classified into three types on the basis of the physiology of photosynthesis. Most plants operate what is called C_3 metabolism: this refers to the number of carbon atoms in the molecule produced as a consequence of fixing CO_2. There are two other groups of plants with fundamentally different photosynthetic processes, known as C_4 plants and crassulacean acid metabolism (CAM) plants. Photosynthesis is likely to increase most in C_3 plants.

Effect of CO_2 concentration on C_3 photosynthesis

As the concentration of CO_2 in the atmosphere increases the rate of photosynthesis may also increase, but not in direct proportion to CO_2 availability. In any particular situation, how much photosynthesis increases will depend not only on the concentration of CO_2 but on other factors that might limit photosynthesis. For example, photosynthesis is likely to increase more in a

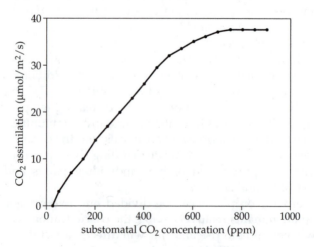

Figure 2.1   The effect of CO_2 concentration on the rate of photosynthesis in a potato leaf.

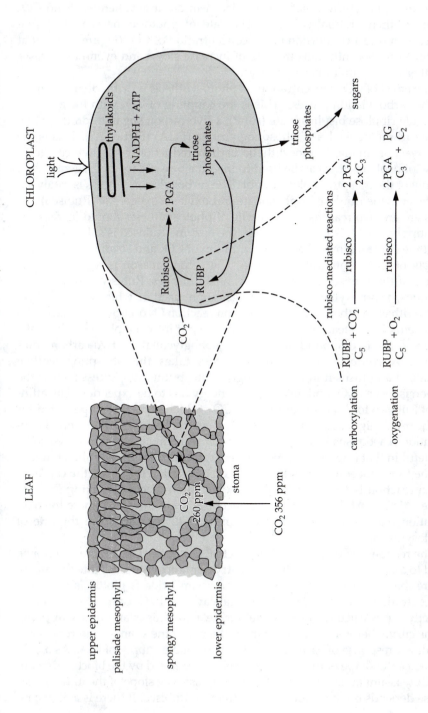

Figure 2.2 The photosynthetic carbon reduction cycle in a C_3 plant.

nutrient-rich environment than in a nutrient-poor environment. Consider an experiment in which a leaf is first placed in an atmosphere with no CO_2 which is then gradually added. The rate of photosynthesis will at first increase in direct proportion to the concentration of CO_2 (Figure 2.1), but at higher CO_2 concentrations the rate of increase slows and eventually ceases as other factors limit photosynthesis.

The effect of CO_2 concentration on photosynthesis is primarily influenced by the carboxylation process. This is the coupling of CO_2 with the acceptor molecule ribulose bisphosphate (rubP), a five-carbon sugar, to produce two three-carbon molecules of phosphoglycerate (PGA) (Figure 2.2). This is the first reaction in the photosynthetic carbon reduction cycle, which yields triose phosphates that can be used to manufacture sugars and regenerates a supply of the acceptor molecule rubP. The carboxylation process is catalysed by the enzyme ribulose bisphosphate carboxylase/oxygenase (Rubisco).

There are two reasons why the rate of photosynthesis should increase as the supply of CO_2 is increased. First, the enzyme Rubisco is substrate limited at the current atmospheric concentration of CO_2 and so an increase in the supply of CO_2 should alleviate this. The second reason is to do with the nature of the Rubisco enzyme. As its name implies, Rubisco catalyses two reactions, a carboxylation and an oxygenation reaction, which are in competition with each other. In the oxygenation reaction O_2 occupies the active site of the enzyme instead of CO_2, and rubP is split into one phosphoglycerate, a three-carbon compound and one phosphoglycollate, a two-carbon compound. A complex regeneration process takes the phosphoglycollate produced and turns it into phosphoglycerate, but in the process 50% of the carbon is lost as CO_2 and, in addition, energy has to be expended. The affinity of Rubisco for O_2 is lower than for CO_2, which is partly compensated for by the much higher concentration of O_2; nevertheless, the proportion of oxygenation reactions is low. The oxygenation reaction can be considered to be wasteful in that it loses CO_2, requires energy and uses up the rubP acceptor. As the CO_2 concentration at the site of carboxylation increases, the carboxylation reaction is favoured over the oxygenation reaction, making Rubisco more efficient. At the current CO_2 concentration in the atmosphere the oxygenation reaction of Rubisco results in a 30–40% reduction in the rate of photosynthesis.

The response of carbon assimilation to CO_2 supply (see Figure 2.1) can be used to assess aspects of the biochemistry of photosynthesis. Note that in the figure the rate of photosynthetic carbon assimilation is plotted against the concentration of CO_2 in the substomatal cavity (Ci). Ci cannot be measured directly but is calculated (see Panel for details). This is an important point, as the curve therefore factors out the influence of the stomata and represents the direct response of assimilation to the available supply of CO_2. As a consequence the shape of the curve is largely determined by the biochemistry of the CO_2 assimilation process in the chloroplast. The slope of the initial linear phase depends on the amount and activity of Rubisco. If there is a high con-

Calculating CO$_2$ concentration in the substomatal cavity (Ci)

According to Fick's Law of Diffusion

$$\text{Rate of diffusion} = \frac{\text{difference in concentration}}{\text{resistance}}$$

For the movement of water vapour from the inside of a leaf into the atmosphere we can define

$$E = \frac{ei - ea}{rw}$$

where E = rate of transpiration
        ei = water vapour concentration inside leaf
        ea = water vapour concentration in the air
        rw = resistance to water vapour transfer

thus

$$rw = \frac{ei - ea}{E}$$

E can be measured in a gas analysis system. ei can be determined if it is assumed that the humidity in the substomatal cavity is saturating: all we need to know then is the leaf temperature to be able to calculate the vapour concentration in saturated air at that temperature. ea can be measured by an appropriate sensor.

$$gw = \frac{1}{rw}$$

gw = conductance to water vapour transfer.

But water vapour diffuses 1.6 times faster than CO$_2$, so

$$gc = \frac{gw}{1.6} \quad \text{or} \quad rc = 1.6 \, rw$$

rc = resistance to CO$_2$ transfer
gc = conductance to CO$_2$ transfer (0.62 of H$_2$O conductance).

We can use this to calculate the substomatal concentration of CO$_2$. As with water vapour transfer we can define

$$rc = \frac{ca - ci}{A}$$

where A = rate of CO$_2$ assimilation by the leaf
        ci = substomatal concentration of CO$_2$
        ca = concentration of CO$_2$ in the air.

This can be rearranged to give

$$ci = ca - (rc \, A)$$

centration of Rubisco-active sites available the initial slope will be steep, whereas if there are few active sites available the slope will be shallow.

The rate of photosynthesis at CO_2 saturation is largely determined by the supply of rubP. In order for the concentration of rubP to be maintained, energy in the form of ATP (adenosine triphosphate) and reducing power in the form of NADPH (nicotinamide adenine dinucleotide phosphate) are required to run the photosynthetic carbon reduction cycle (see Figure 2.2). These molecules are produced by the absorption of energy from light in what are called the light reactions of photosynthesis. The curve illustrated was produced at an irradiance that saturates the light reactions, producing a maximum amount of ATP and NADPH. However, if the irradiance were lower the CO_2-saturated rate of photosynthesis would also be lower, as the supply of rubP would be restricted by the availability of ATP and NADPH. Furthermore, how much photosynthesis increases will depend on the balance between Rubisco activity and the capacity for the regeneration of rubP, both of which may vary between plant species and as a consequence of environmental conditions.

The effect of CO_2 on leaf water use

In many circumstances the growth of plants is limited by the availability of water. Plants can only draw water from the soil by constantly losing water from the leaves. This movement, called the transpiration stream, means that plants require a very large amount of water to grow. A typical C_3 plant will need to use 170 g of water to assimilate a single gram of CO_2. Therefore quite a short period without rain can often result in the drying of the soil and a reduction in plant growth. One of the most important consequences of growing plants in enriched CO_2 is that they become more efficient in the use of water. A doubling of the atmospheric concentration could theoretically lead to as much as a 75% increase in the amount of dry matter fixed per unit of water used by plants. Reviews of past experiments conducted under controlled conditions indicate that water use is reduced by about 30% when the concentration of CO_2 is doubled. To understand why this occurs the processes controlling water and CO_2 movement between the cells of the leaf and the outside atmosphere need to be considered.

For photosynthesis to proceed CO_2 must move from the air surrounding a plant leaf through the stomatal pores in the leaf epidermis into the substomatal cavity, and from there to the site of CO_2 incorporation in the chloroplast (Figure 2.3). This diffusion of CO_2 occurs down a concentration gradient. Along this gradient there are a series of barriers which the CO_2 molecule must cross, including the boundary layer of still air abutting the leaf surface and the cellular structures between the cell surface and the chloroplast stroma, where incorporation of CO_2 into sugars occurs. However, the greatest barrier to CO_2 movement is the stomatal aperture, and as a consequence the greatest fall in CO_2 concentration occurs across this barrier, from the bulk air where the CO_2 concentration is about 355 ppm to the substomatal cavity where, in C$_3$ plants, the concentration is typically 240 ppm. The changes in the concentration of CO_2 that occur along this gradient are usually calculated using a resistance model (see Panel). The total resistance to CO_2 diffusion depends on the size of the stomatal pores and the density of stomata on the leaf surface. The stomata also control the loss of water from the plant, and as a consequence the size of the stomatal pore is sensitive to the plant water status.

As discussed in the previous section the concentration of CO_2 in the substomatal cavity (Ci) is important in controlling the rate of photosynthesis. Ci also affects the stomatal aperture. In the dark the stomata are closed because of a high concentration of CO_2 produced by the respiration of the leaf cells. In the light the stomata open in response to the lowering of the CO_2 concentration through photosynthesis. There is also good evidence that in the light the stomatal aperture is adjusted to maintain the throughput of CO_2 at a rate just sufficient to ensure an adequate supply for photosynthesis. If the con-

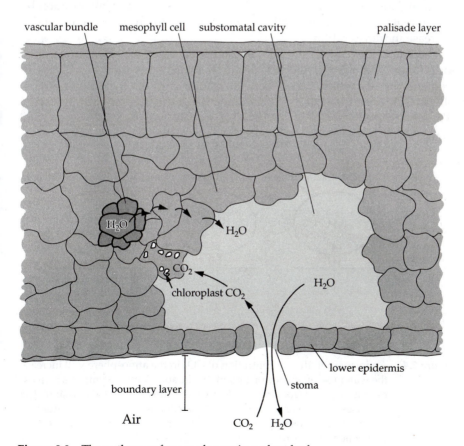

Figure 2.3   The pathway of gas exchange in a plant leaf.

centration of CO_2 in the atmosphere increases, the diffusion gradient between the air and the site of carboxylation in the chloroplast will increase. Therefore, CO_2 supply can be maintained at the same rate at a higher stomatal resistance. The important consequence of this is that if stomatal resistance increases, water loss from the leaf decreases, and so the plant is able to maintain photosynthesis but reduce water loss. The result is an increase in the water use efficiency (WUE), which is defined as:

$$WUE = \frac{carbon\ assimilated}{water\ transpired}$$

At one extreme, if the stomatal resistance is increased to maintain photosynthesis at a constant rate as the external concentration of CO_2 rises, there would be a considerable water saving and a rise in WUE (Figure 2.4). At the other extreme if stomatal resistance does not alter, the supply of CO_2 for carboxylation will increase and so the amount of carbon assimilated will go up markedly. As the loss of water would remain unchanged WUE would again increase. However, in most instances there will be partial compensation by the stomata and therefore both an increase in carbon assimilation and a decrease in transpiration.

There is evidence that stomatal resistance has increased in plants in historic times. A survey of old herbarium specimens revealed a decrease in stomatal density which was closely correlated with the increase in atmospheric CO_2 over the last 200 years since the industrial revolution started (Woodward 1987).

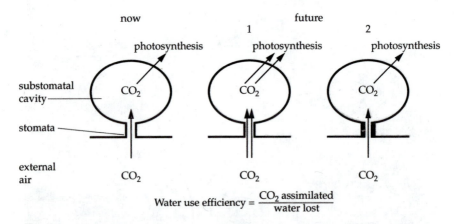

Water use efficiency $= \dfrac{CO_2\ assimilated}{water\ lost}$

Figure 2.4   An increase in the concentration of CO_2 in the atmosphere will increase the water use efficiency of a plant. In situation 1 photosynthesis increases but the stomata are unaffected; the amount of CO_2 assimilated increases but the amount of water loss remains unchanged. In situation 2 the stomata close, reducing assimilation to the same as before CO_2 enrichment; the amount of water lost is reduced but the same amount of carbon is assimilated.

CO$_2$ and plants with C$_4$ metabolism

Although there are considerably fewer C$_4$ species in the world (5% of the world's flora) some of them are among the most important agricultural crop plants, such as maize, millet, sorghum, sugar cane and tropical forage grasses. Because of their photosynthetic metabolism C$_4$ plants will benefit much less from enriched CO$_2$ than will C$_3$ plants.

C$_4$ metabolism can be split into two steps, a primary carboxylation which occurs in the mesophyll cells of the leaf, and a secondary carboxylation which occurs in the cells surrounding the vascular bundles (Figure 2.5). In the primary carboxylation step phosphoenolpyruvate (PEP), a three-carbon compound, acts as the acceptor molecule. This reaction is catalysed by the enzyme PEP carboxylase and produces oxaloacetate, a four-carbon compound (hence C$_4$). Oxaloacetate is converted to malate, which is transported out of the mesophyll cells and to the bundle sheath cells. Here malate is decarboxylated and the CO$_2$ produced combined with rubP via Rubisco, producing PGA, which enters the normal C$_3$ photosynthetic reduction cycle. Pyruvate is transported back to the mesophyll cells where it is used to regenerate more PEP.

Overall this system acts as a CO$_2$ pump ensuring a high concentration of CO$_2$ at the site of rubP carboxylation in the bundle sheath cells. This reduces photorespiration to nearly zero by increasing the CO$_2$ concentration so that it saturates the active sites of Rubisco. One of the most important points

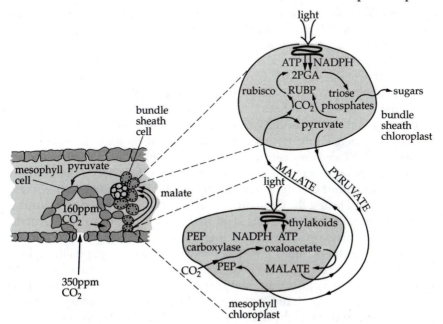

Figure 2.5   The morphology of the C$_4$ leaf and the C$_4$ photosynthetic carbon reduction pathway.

about this system is that PEP carboxylase has no competing oxygenase activity and a higher affinity for CO_2. To understand why this is important we need to consider what limits the rate of photosynthesis in C_3 plants in bright light. Under such conditions there will be a plentiful supply of energy but the rate of photosynthesis will be limited by the supply of CO_2 to Rubisco. As the concentration of CO_2 at the site of carboxylation falls in bright light, the low affinity of Rubisco for CO_2 and the competing oxygenase reaction limit the rate of carbon assimilation that can be achieved. This limitation is relaxed in C_4 plants by the presence of PEP carboxylase in the mesophyll cells. As a consequence the rates of photosynthesis in C_4 plants in bright light can be much higher than in C_3 plants.

A second consequence of the properties of PEP carboxylase is that Ci is usually much lower in photosynthesizing C_4 plants than in C_3 plants. C_4 photosynthesis is virtually saturated at 150 ppm Ci, whereas, in C_3 plants Ci is usually around 240 ppm. The ability to operate with a low Ci means that C_4 plants are more water use-efficient than C_3 plants, and as a consequence they are more common in drier habitats. An increase in atmospheric CO_2 will therefore have only a small effect in C_4 plants by increasing the concentration gradient between air and substomatal space. It will not markedly improve the efficiency of carboxylation in C_4 plants.

CO_2 and plants with crassulacean acid metabolism

Many succulent plants employ a third carboxylation process, called crassulacean acid metabolism (CAM) because it was first investigated in members of the Crassulaceae. It is not restricted to succulent plants but is most common in them. Although few CAM species are important agriculturally they compose approximately 10% of the world's flora. The striking feature of CAM metabolism is that it allows the plants to keep their stomata closed during the warm daylight hours, thereby minimizing water loss, which can be very important in hot arid environments. During the night the stomata of a CAM plant open, allowing CO_2 to diffuse in. In the mesophyll cells it is carboxylated by PEP carboxylase producing malate, which is transported to the large cell vacuoles where it is stored as malic acid. This accumulates in the vacuoles throughout the night. The supply of PEP is provided by the breakdown of starch. During the daylight the stomata shut and malic acid diffuses out of the vacuoles: it is converted to malate and thence to oxaloacetate, which is decarboxylated. The CO_2 is then carboxylated by Rubisco into the normal photosynthetic carbon reduction cycle. As with C_4 plants the primary carboxylating enzyme is PEP carboxylase, so the benefit of enriched atmospheric CO_2 may not be as great as with C_3 plants. A study of one of the few agriculturally important CAM species, the prickly-pear cactus, did show a 23% increase in dry weight when grown at 650 ppm CO_2 (Nobel 1991).

Effects of CO_2 on whole plant growth and development

Long-term effects of enriched CO_2

On the basis of physiology elevated atmospheric CO_2 should increase photosynthesis and improve WUE, especially in C_3 plants. However, we have so far been considering the situation where the concentration of CO_2 is varied over a short period of time. In order to affect the growth rate of plants, such increases in photosynthesis must be sustained over long periods. Only if this is true will increased photosynthesis act as a strong sink for CO_2 as the concentration in the atmosphere rises.

Often, when a plant is transferred from ambient CO_2 to an atmosphere enriched in CO_2 and kept there for a long period, the rate of photosynthesis increases initially but there is then a gradual fall to the original or an intermediate level, sometimes called downregulation of photosynthesis (Figure 2.6). Although this is common it does not happen in all plant species and a variety of responses to enriched CO_2 seem possible.

There is no single clear explanation of why this occurs, but it must be recognized that photosynthesis is a finely tuned process. For example, an increase in CO_2 concentration will disrupt the balance between carboxylation and the reactions associated with the capture and use of energy from light. The leaf might respond to this by changing the resources allocated to these parts of the photosynthetic process. A common observation is that the Rubisco activity and content are lower when plants are grown at elevated CO_2, which can reduce the rate of photosynthesis. For example, rice plants were grown at six CO_2 concentrations between 160 and 900 ppm. Rubisco

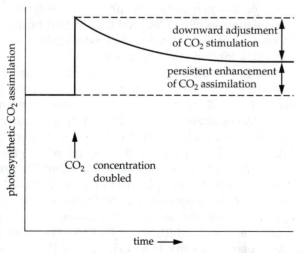

Figure 2.6   Often when leaves are exposed to CO_2 enrichment for a long period of time the initial enhancement in photosynthesis is not maintained.

activity declined steadily over this range, as did Rubisco content (Rowland-Bamford *et al.* 1991). On a leaf area basis activity decreased by 66% and Rubisco content by 32%. As Rubisco comprises a sizeable proportion of leaf protein this means that the total leaf protein content, and therefore the leaf nitrogen content, is lower.

A second mechanism which might affect the rate of photosynthesis in high CO_2 is the accumulation of excess carbohydrate in the leaves. The increased photosynthesis produces more carbohydrate, which has to go to somewhere in the plant to be used or stored. Such a destination is called a carbohydrate sink, such as growing primordia, seeds, storage organs etc. Sometimes an increased carbohydrate supply stimulates the production of new sinks, but if there is insufficient sink capacity carbohydrate can accumulate in the leaves. This may inhibit photosynthesis either by some sort of end-product feedback regulation or simply by starch accumulating to a concentration that causes damage to part of the photosynthetic system (Stitt 1991).

If downregulation of photosynthesis is a common response to increasing concentrations of CO_2 among plant species, the effect on plant productivity may be limited and any increase in the sequestration of carbon in the world's plants small. In this context, whether downregulation occurs in trees is of particular importance. Trees store large amounts of carbon in their wood for a long period of time and are therefore a major long-term sink in the global carbon cycle. Some experimental results indicate that downregulation does not occur under field conditions. In one of the few attempts to investigate tree growth under near-field conditions, sour orange trees rooted in soil were fumigated with air enriched in CO_2 for several years (Idso and Kimball 1991). Growth and photosynthesis were consistently higher throughout this period and there was no downregulation of either. The researchers contended that the downregulation so often observed may in part be an artefact of growing plants in containers that restrict root growth, leading to a build-up of carbohydrate and sink inhibition of photosynthesis.

In the above examples the rate of photosynthesis was measured at a high light intensity that induces a maximum rate of photosynthesis. However, many plants grow in the shade of others and many leaves on a single plant will be shaded by the leaves above. In low light the rate of photosynthesis is limited by the efficiency with which a leaf can convert radiant energy to chemical energy by fixing CO_2. This is called the quantum efficiency (or quantum yield) of photosynthesis, and is typically about 9% under ideal conditions. The quantum efficiency of photosynthesis is increased at higher CO_2 concentrations due to the suppression of the Rubisco oxygenation reaction. At low light intensities the amount of Rubisco present is not as important as the efficiency with which it can fix CO_2. Therefore, quantum efficiency is not particularly sensitive to any changes in Rubisco concentration that might occur as a consequence of downregulation. There is evidence that even after years of fumigation with enriched CO_2 the stimulation of quantum efficiency persists (Long and Drake 1991). Thus even if downregulation of photosynthetic capacity occurs photosynthesis will still be increased when a plant or leaf is growing under light-limiting conditions.

The plant carbon budget

Plant growth is a subtle process: an increase in the rate of photosynthesis need not lead to a significant increase in the overall growth rate of the plant. The growth form of a plant is probably as important as carbon assimilation in controlling its rate of growth. When a plant grows it takes CO_2 out of the atmosphere but only some of this is incorporated into long-lived tissues: as much as 40% of the carbon fixed may be used in respiration, and carbon may also be transported to symbionts, such as nitrogen-fixing bacteria or mycorrhizal fungi (Table 2.1).

The allocation of carbon to different organs such as roots, shoots, leaves and storage is known as partitioning. The balance of partitioning affects the rate of growth of a plant: for example, if a greater proportion of carbon is invested in the production of new leaf tissue then more CO_2 can be absorbed and the growth rate will be higher (if there are no other limiting factors). Furthermore, partitioning has important consequences for competition between plants and for agricultural productivity, where often only one part of the plant is harvested. Plants may compete below ground for water and nutrients or above ground for light. In nutrient-poor environments greater allocation to root growth may be of benefit, but as a consequence carbon assimilation through the leaves will be constrained. Alternatively, in a nutrient-rich environment capture of light is more important: plants that allocate more to leaf growth will be at an advantage and consequently the growth rates of species from such environments are faster.

The pattern of carbon allocation is often altered when plants grow in elevated CO_2, but there seems to be great variation in the response of different species. In some species there is an increase in the allocation of resources to root growth: for example, root dry weight and root length of soybean more than doubled when grown at 700 ppm CO_2 compared to plants grown at 350 ppm CO_2 after only 18 days of growth (Rogers *et al.* 1992), whereas the proportion of roots decreased in white clover (Ryle and Powell 1992). An

Table 2.1 The proportion of carbon assimilated by photosynthesis that is then allocated to different processes

Process	Percentage used
Growth	55
Root respiration	20
Shoot respiration	12
Mycorrhizal symbionts	7–10
Root exudation	5

increase in the proportion of roots has been reported in a number of herbaceous species but in relatively few cereals and tree species. Allocation of a greater proportion of carbon to roots can slow carbon uptake but will increase the volume of soil that a plant can exploit to remove water and mineral ions (Stulen and den Hertog 1993). The fact that different species change allocation patterns in different ways in response to high CO_2 might have important consequences for competitive interactions between species (see Chapter 4).

Increase in plant growth at high CO_2

Under conditions of non-limiting nutrient availability elevated CO_2 does appear to increase plant growth in a wide range of species, often by a considerable amount. Using a large number of observations made on agricultural yield in enriched CO_2 it was calculated that yield increased by 36% on average and by approximately 1% for every 10 ppm increase in the concentration of CO_2 (Kimball 1982) . A 10 ppm increase in the concentration of atmospheric CO_2 is currently occurring approximately every 6 years. The possibility that this will result in considerably increased agricultural yields is one of the potential benefits of environmental change (see Chapter 5). One important aspect of these observations is the great variability in the response of different species. The amount of variation is even greater in non-agricultural species, which have a wider range of growth characteristics than crop species. This is likely to affect interactions between coexisting species in many communities (see Chapter 4). For example, in a survey of 27 herbaceous species it was found that for a 190 ppm increase in CO_2 concentration the increase in growth varied from none to 55% for groups of species with different ecological characteristics (Hunt et al. 1991). One particular group of species which is likely to benefit less from CO_2 enrichment are those with C_4 metabolism. In most cases, when the growth of C_4 and C_3 species from similar habitats has been compared, the C_4 species were less affected by high CO_2.

CO_2 interactions with water and nutrient availability

Under non-agricultural conditions plant growth is often limited by factors other than CO_2 concentration, such as nutrient or water availability. Judging how enriched CO_2 will affect plant performance in suboptimal growing conditions needs some insight into the interactions between the availability of these vital resources and CO_2.

As discussed previously, enriched CO_2 will significantly increase the water use efficiency of plants by a combination of reduced stomatal resistance and increased photosynthesis. If the concentration of CO_2 doubles, both C_3 and C_4 plants should increase WUE by 30–40% if the stomata adjust to maintain a constant Ci. In addition, C_3 plants will increase photosynthesis by about 30%, whereas C$_4$ plants will show little change in photosynthesis. Thus in total C$_3$ plants could improve WUE by 75% but C$_4$ by only 35%. However, several other changes induced by enriched CO$_2$ need to be considered in order to evaluate the interaction between enriched CO$_2$ and water availability (Chaves and Pereira 1992). Elevated CO$_2$ may promote more rapid leaf growth, which will increase water use for the leaf canopy as a whole. This will counteract to some extent the reduction in transpiration rate caused by a CO$_2$-induced increase in stomatal resistance. High CO$_2$ grown plants sometimes have a greater proportion of roots, which will enable them to exploit a larger volume of soil and may delay the onset of symptoms of water stress, but might also cause more rapid drying of the soil. It is often found that the concentration of carbohydrates is higher in the leaves of high CO$_2$ grown plants. During water deprivation a high concentration of sugars can help protect against damage caused by desiccation.

If water use is reduced it can be argued that during the onset of drought the drying of the soil will be delayed and plant desiccation slowed. In a pot experiment water was withheld from the seedlings of two tree species for a period of 10 days (Tolley and Strain 1985). The seedlings were grown in three CO$_2$ regimes. In enriched CO$_2$ desiccation was delayed significantly in sweetgum but there was no significant difference between treatments for loblolly pine. This may point to an important difference in the reaction of the two species to enriched CO$_2$, but such an experiment provides a very simplified view of the situation that might occur under natural conditions; in particular, focusing on individual plants can be misleading. In another experiment the response of a canopy composed of many plants was investigated (Nijs et al. 1988). White clover was grown in a chamber system that allowed continuous monitoring of water and CO$_2$ exchange during the growing season. Leaf area development was faster at high CO$_2$ and therefore water use was initially greater, despite much higher stomatal resistance at high CO$_2$ and higher WUE. Total photosynthesis of the leaf canopy more than doubled over a 3-week period and there was a 16% increase in canopy transpiration, despite a decrease in transpiration per unit leaf area. The few studies which have combined long-term exposure to high CO$_2$ with water stress indicate that the relative increase in growth stimulated by enriched CO$_2$ is greater under water-stressed conditions than under non-stressed conditions (Chaves and Pereira 1992).

It is usually found that the nitrogen (N) content is lower in the leaves of plants grown in enriched CO$_2$. A combination of factors might contribute to this. As N is mostly incorporated in plant proteins the accumulation of carbohydrates in leaves grown at high CO$_2$ will cause a decrease in the proportion of N. But even if the proportion of N is expressed in relation to structural carbohydrates only, or on a leaf area basis, there is still usually a lower N concentration in enriched CO$_2$ grown leaves. A reduction in the concentration of Rubisco, which often occurs in response to prolonged growth at high CO$_2$, is likely to be mostly responsible for this. Rubisco is a large enzyme with a low affinity for CO_2 and so a considerable amount must be present in leaves for sufficient assimilation of CO_2 to occur. As a consequence Rubisco comprises about 20% of the protein in leaves. There may also be savings made by a reduction in the amount of other enzymes associated with photosynthesis as this is adjusted to the higher CO_2 availability. As a consequence the rate of photosynthesis per unit N will increase, improving the nitrogen use efficiency (NUE) of plants, which is defined as

$$NUE = \frac{Carbon\ assimilated}{Nitrogen\ used}$$

There is also a cost in terms of carbon in the maintenance and turnover of Rubisco and other proteins involved in photosynthesis. This reduces carbon loss through respiration and will also improve NUE. This means that for every unit of N available more carbon can be fixed by plants. Experiments performed in controlled environments indicate that plant growth is often enhanced at high CO_2, even when N availability is limiting. For example, in one experiment wheat plants grown in enriched CO_2 doubled their size irrespective of the N supply (Hocking and Meyer 1991). In contrast, several experiments have shown that the growth enhancement produced by CO_2 is reduced when phosphorus is limiting growth (see, for example, Conroy *et al.* 1990). However, evidence is accumulating that there is great variation in the response of different species to the combined effects of CO_2 and nutrient supply.

On a biosphere scale the change in NUE is important, as in many environments throughout the world N limits plant growth for part or all of the year. Thus an increase in this efficiency could increase the drawdown of carbon from the atmosphere. Also, a decrease in the N concentration in plant tissues will decrease the rate of decomposition of plant remains in the soil (see Chapter 4 for further details). Therefore, even in situations where nitrogen or water limit plant growth enriched CO_2 might still have significant effects on the performance of plants. The direct effects of CO_2 on carboxylation, WUE and NUE all point toward increased plant growth. However, there are still many problems in predicting the extent of growth enhancement, when it will occur during the growing season and which species will most benefit.

Temperature and plants

The species that inhabit the rain forests or savannah grasslands of the tropics are not the same as those found in northern Europe. Casual observation tells us that temperature is a major factor controlling the distribution of plants in the world. Future increases in temperature can therefore affect the distribution of plant species and, as a consequence, the distribution of animals that might be associated with them.

Temperature not only affects the distribution of plant species, it is also an important determinant of how a plant performs within its distribution range. How fast plants grow, how long they live, their susceptibility to disease and environmental extremes are all influenced by temperature. In order to understand the processes that might alter plant distribution an insight into how plant performance is affected by temperature is needed.

Factors controlling the temperature of plants

The temperature of vegetation may be very different from air temperature (Grace 1983). In cold climates leaves are often warmer than the air, whereas in hot climates they are cooler. This is a consequence of physical heat exchange processes, as plants cannot significantly alter temperature through metabolism. Certain wavelengths of solar radiation can be absorbed by the leaf and cause heating. Some radiation is also transmitted and reflected. Heat is also lost from the leaf by convection. Under still conditions, as the surface of the leaf heats and cools convection currents are generated in the air above the leaf, transporting heat away from the leaf surface. Convective heat exchange will be accelerated by turbulence in the air caused by wind.

Transpiration cools the leaf. The heat loss can be calculated as the rate of transpiration multiplied by the latent heat of vaporization of water. The rate of transpiration is determined by the concentration gradient for water diffusion and the resistance to this diffusion. Inside the leaf the air will be saturated with water vapour, whereas the vapour pressure of water outside the leaf is likely to be lower. Diffusion of water vapour can therefore occur from the leaf. The stomata are the principal resistance to water vapour transfer, so if the stomata shut transpiration will fall and leaf temperature rise. It is interesting to note that if enriched CO_2 in the atmosphere increases stomatal resistance, this will have the side-effect of increasing leaf temperature.

These considerations may be very important for plant survival at extreme temperatures. Plants in cool climates often have adaptations to maximize radiation absorption and those in hot climates can have high transpiration rates to cool the leaf (if water is available).

Temperature dependence of photosynthesis

Temperature is one of the most important environmental factors regulating the rate of photosynthesis. A plant will have an optimum temperature above and below which photosynthesis is restricted. Species which originate from different climatic conditions display a temperature dependence of photosynthesis related to their climate of origin (Figure 2.7).

From these temperature curves it can be inferred that modifications leading to an improvement in photosynthetic capacity at low temperatures decreases performance at high temperature, whereas if a species can perform well at high temperature it cannot do so at low temperature. There is

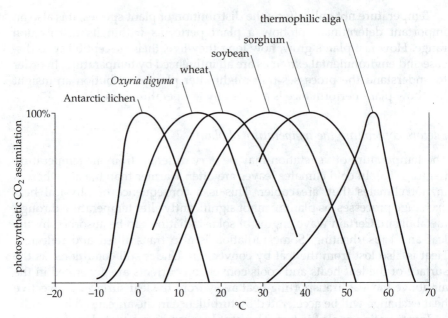

Figure 2.7   The effect of temperature on photosynthesis in species originating from different temperature environments. (After Larcher 1980.)

therefore considerable variation in temperature dependence among plant species. There can also be variation within a species. If populations from a single species are taken from habitats with different temperature regimes and grown under the same conditions, they can still show a difference in their temperature response related to where they came from.

One of the most comprehensive studies on this looked at the snow gum, a tree widely distributed in the colder areas of southeast Australia. In the mountains of southern New South Wales it occurs over a wide altitudinal range, from the valley bottoms through to the alpine timberline. Populations at different altitudes must encounter very different temperature regimes. Over this elevational range the species displays several morphological types which at one stage were classified as separate species. When individuals from different altitudes were grown under uniform conditions, the temperature optimum for photosynthesis could still be related to the altitude of origin (Slatyer 1977). Species that possess a great amount of genetic variation with respect to temperature may be more able to maintain their distribution range in response to increasing temperatures.

The temperature dependence curve of photosynthesis in a given species does not remain constant: it can change in response to changes in environmental temperature, a process called acclimatization (Slatyer and Morrow 1977). This is very useful, as in most habitats away from the equator the temperature varies considerably throughout the year. Figure 2.8 shows this for the snow gum tree, which alters the temperature optimum for photosynthe-

sis following the seasonal changes in the environment. This ability to accli-
matize is found in mature leaves and is not restricted to leaves that develop
at a particular temperature. It requires at least several days for significant
acclimatization to occur, and maximum change often does not occur for a
week or longer. Acclimatization to low temperatures probably involves
altering the capacity for the temperature-limited enzyme-mediated reactions
in photosynthesis, whereas high-temperature acclimatization may also
involve increased thermal stability.

The range of temperature regimes over which a species can successfully
maintain photosynthesis will depend on both the genetic variation within
the species (genotypic plasticity) and the degree to which individuals can
adjust photosynthetic physiology (phenotypic plasticity). For organisms
such as plants, which cannot adjust temperature, such plasticity may be particularly important in delimiting the temperature range over which the
species can survive.

The process of carboxylation is strongly affected by temperature. As we
have already considered, it is also affected by the concentration of CO_2 in the
atmosphere. Changing the concentration of carbon dioxide alters the temperature dependence of photosynthesis: an increase in the concentration of CO_2 of
200 ppm can increase the temperature optimum of photosynthesis by 5°C. In
order to understand why this occurs we need to look at how the operation of
the enzyme Rubisco alters with temperature. As temperature increases the
affinity of Rubisco for CO_2 falls, as does the solubility of CO_2. The affinity of
Rubisco for O_2 and the solubility of O_2 also falls, but not as fast, so that the proportion of oxygenation reactions increases. Therefore, as temperature increases
the amount of photorespiration increases. As a consequence of this, enriched
CO_2 stimulates photosynthesis more at higher temperatures. Calculations indicate that the effect of CO_2 enrichment is only slight below about 16°C (Long
1991). Two long-term studies have been carried out where natural vegetation
has been exposed to enriched CO_2 for several years. One of these was in a cool

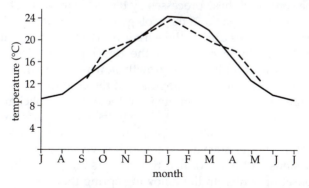

Figure 2.8   The effect of seasonal temperature changes in the environment (—) on
the temperature optimum (- - -) for photosynthesis in snow gum of
southeast Australia. (From Slatyer and Morrow 1977.)

tundra environment, where it was found that high CO_2 only stimulated photosynthesis for a short period at the start of the growing season (Tissue and Oechel 1987). In contrast, a study on a warm temperate salt marsh found that photosynthesis doubled, and that this enhanced rate was maintained (Arp and Drake 1991). The temperature of these two environments may play an important role in regulating the degree to which photosynthesis is stimulated by high CO_2. However, the results from these studies are also strongly affected by the nutrient availability in the two habitats (see Chapter 4 for details).

Temperature and plant growth

Everyday experience illustrates the importance of temperature in controlling plant growth. In temperate climates the winter is a period of dormancy for plants: many have shed their leaves and there is no evidence of growth occurring. This is not a consequence of a lack of resources, as most perennial plants will have abundant stores of carbohydrate available for growth, but it may be enforced by the cool temperature, which prevents the processes of cell division and expansion that must take place for growth to occur. In fact it is usually more complex. During the autumn, cooling temperatures and shortening days may trigger the onset of the dormant state. Often plants will then require a prolonged period of cold weather before they will grow in response to higher temperatures. As a consequence, a period of abnormally warm weather during the winter would not cause plants to grow. If growth did occur in midwinter the new young tissues produced would be killed by a subsequent change to cold weather. Once this chilling requirement is complete the plants again become sensitive to temperature, and growth will occur in response to the increased temperature during the spring.

The growth of plant tissue can be divided into two phases, cell division and subsequent cell expansion. Both processes are very sensitive to temperature, but cell expansion usually proceeds at lower temperatures than cell division. The control of these processes by temperature has a strong impact on the use of plants by man and the ecology of many plant species.

In temperate latitudes during the spring irradiance is high but temperature is low. Under these conditions the development of plants can be restricted by the direct limitation of growth slowing down the expansion of the plant canopy. The rate of development of the crop canopy in the spring is of critical importance in determining productivity in cool climates.

Many plant species that grow very early in the spring perform all the necessary cell division in the previous year, and only leaf expansion occurs in the spring. Thus species such as the bluebell have completed all the necessary cell divisions and have formed tiny flowers and leaves below ground before the onset of winter. In the following spring the cells expand as temperatures increase. This early expansion of the leaves ensures that the bluebell can take advantage of the bright light on the forest floor that occurs before the development of leaves on the trees above.

An increase in temperature, particularly during the winter, may therefore affect the length of this dormant season. The global circulation models (GCMs) predict that the temperature increase will be unevenly distributed throughout the year, with relatively higher temperatures in the winter. The contraction of the dormant period will depend on two factors, how warmer winter temperatures affect the dormancy mechanism and how soon cell division and expansion are released from temperature control in the spring. The consequences of increased winter temperatures are not easy to predict. For example, in the forests of the cool temperate regions of the world the timing of bud burst is important: if it occurs too early the developing buds may be killed by a late frost, but if it is too late a valuable portion of the short growing season is wasted. Timing is achieved by the buds requiring a period of chilling followed by a period of time above 0°C for the buds to develop. A computer model was used to predict the time of bud burst of trees in Finland for the global warming expected if atmospheric CO_2 doubles (Hänninen 1991). The increased temperatures stimulated earlier bud burst and therefore a longer growing season as expected, but warming also increased the number of warm winters, when bud burst occurred in midwinter and subsequent temperatures of less than minus 10°C caused frost damage. Thus by confusing the timing mechanism of plants warmer winters can lead to an increased risk of frost damage. However, probably the most important consequence of increased winter temperatures will be a lengthening of the growing season. In later chapters we will examine how this affects plant distribution and agricultural productivity.

Temperature and Arctic plants

Plants within a community will have adaptations in common that enable them to survive the temperature environment, whether it is hot, temperate or cold. In order to assess the implications of increased global temperature for any particular community these adaptations need to be considered. The GCMs predict that the temperature increase will not be evenly distributed over the surface of the earth, but will be greater further north. Thus, although global temperatures may only rise 2.4°C if the concentration of CO_2 doubles, Arctic temperatures might increase by as much as 8°C. The response of the Arctic vegetation and soil to such a large increase in temperature is important, as this region has in the past acted as a major sink for CO_2. Recent work indicates that warming in the Arctic will switch this region from being a net sink for CO_2 into a source (Oechel et al. 1993). Furthermore, the Arctic ecosystem may be severely damaged by such a large temperature increase. Some species may be driven to local extinction and others may invade the Arctic. In order to understand how the plants of the Arctic will respond to a temperature increase, we need to examine some of the adaptations Arctic plants have that enable them to survive in such a harsh environment.

It is often observed that plants growing in cool climates have a greater proportion of their material below ground than those from warmer climates.

Indeed, when plants are grown below their normal growth temperature the proportion of roots usually increases. One reason for this may be to maintain a balance between the assimilation of carbon above ground and the assimilation of water and inorganic nutrients below ground to maintain optimal growth. This is supported by the fact that these changes are often smaller when the nutrient status of the soil is high. Another factor which contributes to the generally high below-ground fraction in Arctic plants is that they tend to have well developed structures for the overwinter storage of carbohydrate. As the location cools there are fewer and fewer annual species in the flora until there are only one or two able to survive in the harshest environments. There is thus increasing reliance on vegetative propagation as a means of maintaining a population of plants. Sexual reproduction may only occur occasionally in particularly favourable growing seasons. Therefore, these species adopt a conservative strategy, investing a significant proportion of available resources in storage for the next season.

One way in which Arctic plants offset such a low proportion of above-ground tissue is by producing leaves that are capable of very high rates of photosynthesis. This also means that carbon assimilation is maximized during the short growing season available. As the conditions get cooler and the length of the growing season decreases there is an increase in the protein concentration in leaves coupled with an increase in carboxylation capacity. A survey of the nitrogen concentration of Arctic and alpine plants around the world revealed that as the length of the growing season decreased the concentration of nitrogen in the leaves increased (Figure 2.9). This occurs despite the fact that the nitrogen availability in soils from cool environments is often very low as a result of temperature limitation of the activity of soil organisms. Therefore higher temperatures will not only increase the length of the growing season but may also have an influence by altering the nutrient-mediated interaction between soils and plants in the Arctic.

Although higher temperatures might stimulate greater uptake of carbon from the atmosphere in Arctic plants it is also likely to greatly increase the respiratory loss of CO_2. Plants growing at low temperatures, in particular Arctic and alpine plants, show enhanced rates of respiration. This has been correlated with an increase in the respiratory capacity of mitochondria. In the summer the soil in the Arctic is cool, generally a few degrees above zero, often with a frozen layer not far below the surface. Under such cool conditions respiration will be restricted by temperature. The high respiratory capacity of plants growing under such conditions may be to ensure a sufficient energy supply for growth, turnover of cellular constituents and the uptake of inorganic nutrients. A consequence is that the rate of respiration is very sensitive to temperature (Figure 2.10). The growth and development of Arctic and alpine plants has been shown to be highly correlated with soil temperature, but what if the temperature increases markedly as predicted? A look at Figure 2.10 indicates that if temperature increased by 6°C, for example from 10°C to 16°C, the rate of respiration could almost double. As

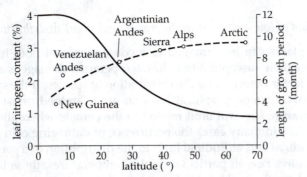

Figure 2.9 The nitrogen content of leaves (- - -) increases as the length of the plant growing season (—) gets shorter. The data are for herbaceous plants all taken from high-altitude sites but from different latitudes. (From Korner 1989.)

Arctic plants have a large proportion of their body below ground, an increase in soil temperature of 6°C would have a very strong effect on their carbon budget. There would be a large increase in respiration as below-ground parts respired more rapidly, but it might not be possible for the photosynthesizing tissue above ground to compensate. This can deplete the plants' carbohydrate reserves and eventually cause death. However, such a calculation does not take into account that long-term exposure to higher temperatures may reduce the sensitivity of respiration to temperature.

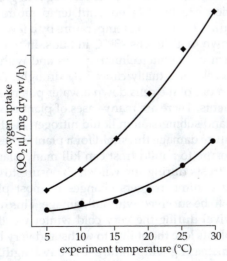

Figure 2.10 The effect of temperature on respiration in a southern species *Limonium binervosum* (●) and a northern species *Mertensia maritima* (♦). (From Crawford and Palin 1981.)

Mechanisms of low-temperature tolerance and plant distribution

Although plants can be damaged as a consequence of both high and low temperature their susceptibility to low-temperature damage is a much more important factor determining the distribution of species. If the species growing in a particular geographical location are examined, most will have a low-temperature survival limit related to the climate where they are growing (Table 2.2). In many cases the occurrence of damaging cold temperature sets a latitudinal and altitudinal limit to the distribution of a species. If global temperatures rise, in particular winter temperatures, these limits will be relaxed and species will be able to exploit new locations.

Plants that survive cold temperatures must possess a means of avoiding or tolerating low-temperature damage. Plants can be divided into three groups: chill-sensitive species, which are killed by temperatures below freezing; freeze-sensitive species, which are killed when ice forms in the tissues; and freeze-tolerant species, which can withstand ice in their tissues. Chill-sensitive plants are common in the tropics, where temperatures never fall below 0°C; the damage appears to be caused by changes in membrane structures within the cells, sometimes resulting in visible breakages. In freeze-sensitive plants when ice forms it does so within the cells causing disruption of cellular structures, particularly membranes. However, freezing never occurs at 0°C, as the content of a cell is not pure water and will as a consequence freeze at a temperature below zero. Cell sap freezes at temperatures between –1 and –5°C. Freezing may not occur at the freezing point of the cell sap owing to a process called supercooling. Ice crystal formation depends on the presence of suitable nuclei around which an ice crystal can begin to grow. If few are present crystal formation can be delayed until temperatures are well below freezing; this can reduce the freezing temperature by a few degrees C in most plant tissues and down to as low as –30°C in buds. In freeze-tolerant plants ice crystals only form in the intercellular spaces and within xylem vessels. Any damage to the cells is actually caused by drought. As the ice crystals grow water is drawn out of the cells down a water potential gradient, dehydrating the cell contents. There are many cases of plant tissues in midwinter being able to withstand submersion in liquid nitrogen at –196°C.

The low-temperature damage threshold for a plant varies during the year: in the summer exposure to a mild frost can kill many plants that normally survive very harsh frosts during the winter. Exposure to increasingly cool weather during the autumn triggers changes in most plants that enable lower temperatures to be survived without damage. This hardening process is essential for survival during the very cold winter weather (Figure 2.11). During the spring plants lose the ability to withstand very low temperatures in response to the increasing temperature and day length. Complete hardening can take several weeks to develop, but is lost more rapidly if there is a period of warmer weather. A late frost can therefore be particularly damaging. Alternatively an abnormally warm period of weather during the winter

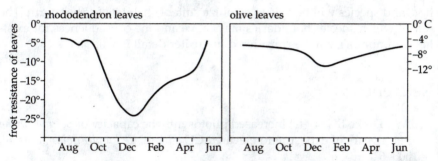

Figure 2.11 Gradual hardening of plant tissue to low temperature during the onset of winter. Olive trees are damaged as soon as ice is formed, even in the middle of winter when they are fully hardened to low temperature. In contrast, rhododendron can withstand ice formation in the leaves, but only in winter when they are frost hardened. (From Larcher 1980.)

can reduce the hardiness of tissues and a return to winter temperatures will cause damage.

Within the three major groups different species will be damaged at different temperature thresholds (see Table 2.2). In the northern hemisphere the northern distribution limit of many species can be correlated with the minimum winter isotherm at a particular temperature. It can be deduced from this that cold winter temperatures are likely to be the most important factor determining the northern distribution limit of such species. An increase in winter temperature will therefore release this constraint on species distribu-

Table 2.2 The low-temperature limits to leaf damage in plants from different climatic zones. (From Larcher 1980.)

Plants	°C for cold injury when hardened
Tropical	
Trees	+5 to -2
Forest undergrowth	+5 to -2
Subtropical	
Palms	-5 to -14
C_4 grasses	-1 to -3
Temperate	
Evergreen woody trees from regions with mild winters	-6 to -15
Winter deciduous trees	-25 to -40 *
Herbs	-10 to -20
Cold winter locations	
Evergreen conifers	-40 to -90
Broad-leaved trees	to -196 *
Herbs	-30 to -196 *

* Vegetative buds

tion, and species will be able to colonize suitable habitats further north. The rate at which species boundaries may move and the consequences for existing communities will be considered in greater detail in Chapter 4.

References

Arp WJ, Drake BG (1991) Increased photosynthetic capacity of *Scirpus olneyi* after 4 years of exposure to elevated CO_2. *Plant, Cell and Environment* **14**, 1003–6

Chaves MM, Pereira JS (1992) Water stress, CO_2 and climate change. *Journal of Experimental Botany* **43**, 1131–9

Crawford RMM, Palin MA (1981) Root respiration and temperature limits to the north–south distribution of four perennial maritime plants. *Flora* **171**, 338–54

Conroy JP, Milham PJ, Reed ML, Barlow EWR (1990) Increase in phosphorous requirements for CO_2-enriched pine species. *Plant Physiology* **92**, 977–82

Grace J (1983) Plant–atmosphere relationships. In *Outline studies in ecology*, eds. GM Dunnet, CH Gimmingham, Chapman and Hall, London

Hänninen H (1991) Does climatic warming increase the risk of frost damage in northern trees? *Plant, Cell and Environment* **14**, 449–54

Hocking PJ, Meyer CP (1991) Effects of CO_2 enrichment and nitrogen stress on growth and partitioning of dry matter and nitrogen in wheat and maize. *Australian Journal of Plant Physiology* **18**, 339–56

Hunt R, Hand DW, Hannah MA, Neal AM (1991) Response to CO_2 enrichment in 27 herbaceous species. *Functional Ecology* **5**, 410–421

Idso SB, Kimball BA (1991) Downward regulation of photosynthesis and growth at high CO_2 levels. No evidence for either phenomenon in three-year study of sour orange trees. *Plant Physiology* **96**, 990–2

Kimball BA (1982) *Carbon dioxide and agricultural yield. An assemblage and analysis of 430 prior observations*. WCL Report 11, US Water Conservation Laboratory, Phoenix, Arizona

Körner C (1989) The nutritional status of plants from high altitude. A worldwide comparison. *Oecologia* **81**, 379–91

Larcher W (1980) *Physiological plant ecology*, Springer Verlag, Berlin

Long SP (1991) Modification of the response of photosynthetic productivity to rising temperature by atmospheric CO_2 concentrations: has its importance been underestimated? *Plant, Cell and Environment* **14**, 729–39

Long SP, Drake BG (1991). Effect of the long term elevation of CO_2 concentration in the field on quantum yield of photosynthesis of the C_3 sedge *Scirpus olneyi*. *Plant Physiology* **96**, 221–6

Nijs I, Impens I, Behaeghe T (1988) Effects of different CO_2 environments on the photosynthesis yield relationship and the carbon and water balance of white clover (*Trifolium repens* L. cv. Blanca) sward. *Journal of Experimental Botany* **40**, 353–9

Nobel PS (1991) Environmental productivity indices and productivity for *Opuntia ficus-indica* under current and elevated atmospheric CO_2 levels. *Plant, Cell and Environment* **14**, 637–46

Oechel WC, Hastings SJ, Vourlitis G, Jenkins M, Reichers G, Grulke N (1993) Recent change of Arctic tundra ecosystems from a net carbon dioxide sink to a source. *Nature* **361**, 520–3

Rogers HH, Peterson CM, McCrimmon JN, Cure JD (1992) Response of plant roots to elevated atmospheric carbon dioxide. *Plant, Cell and Environment* **15**, 749–52

Rowland-Bamford AJ, Baker JT, Allen LH, Bowes G (1991) Acclimation of rice to atmospheric carbon dioxide concentration. *Plant, Cell and Environment* **14**, 577–83

Ryle GJA, Powell CE (1992) The influence of elevated CO_2 and temperature on biomass accumulation of continuously defoliated white clover. *Plant, Cell and Environment* **15**, 593–9

Slatyer, RO (1977) Altitudinal variation in the photosynthetic characteristics of snow gum *Eucalyptus pauciflora* Sieb. ex Spreng. III. Temperature response of material grown in contrasting thermal environments. *Australian Journal of Plant Physiology* **4**, 301–12

Slatyer RO, Morrow PA (1977) Altitudinal variation in the photosynthetic characteristics of snow gum *Eucalyptus pauciflora* Sieb. ex Spreng. I. Seasonal changes under field conditions in the Snowy Mountains area of south-eastern Australia. *Australian Journal of Botany* **25**, 1–20

Stitt M (1991) Rising CO_2 levels and their potential for carbon flow in photosynthetic cells. *Plant, Cell and Environment*, **14**, 741–62

Stulen I, den Hertog J (1993) Root growth and functioning under atmospheric CO_2 enrichment. *Vegetatio* **104/105**, 99–115

Tissue DT, Oechel WC (1987) Response of *Eriophorum vaginatum* to elevated CO_2 and temperature in the Alaskan tussock tundra. *Ecology* **68**, 401–10

Tolley LC, Strain BR (1985) Effects of CO_2 enrichment and water stress on gas exchange of *Liquidambar styraciflua* and *Pinus taeda* seedlings grown at different irradiance levels. *Oecologia* (Berlin) **65**, 166–72

Woodward FI (1987) Stomatal numbers are sensitive to increases in CO_2 from preindustrial levels. *Nature* **327**, 617–18

Further reading

Gates DM (1993) *Climate change and its biological consequences*, Sinauer, Sunderland Massachusetts

Solomon AM, Shugart HH (eds) (1993) *Vegetation dynamics and global change*, Chapman & Hall, London

3 The impact of GEC on animals

Introduction

From the last chapter it is clear that an increase in atmospheric CO_2 will directly affect the ways in which plants function. Changes in temperature and rainfall will also have a considerable impact, but how do these same factors affect animals? This chapter examines the effects of CO_2 and temperature on the ways that animals work. It deals with basic animal physiology then considers ways in which animals are likely to be affected by changes at the scale predicted for GEC. Later chapters consider the interactions of animals with plants in natural and artificial ecosystems, and in aquatic ecosystems where different factors become important.

CO_2 and animals

Are animals likely to respond to higher CO_2 concentrations in as spectacular a way as plants (see Chapter 2)? To answer this, we need to consider the importance of CO_2 in the way animals function.

For animals CO_2 is a waste product of metabolism. It is produced when carbohydrates, lipids and proteins are oxidized step by step in cellular respiration:

carbohydrates

lipids   – digestion →   5C or 6C sugars   fatty acids   + O_2 – respiration →   smaller   + CO_2 + H_2O

proteins   amino acids   molecules

ADP + P_i ATP

It is also produced at the end of glycolysis when CO_2 is removed from pyruvic acid. It is not released as a product of anaerobic metabolic pathways.

CO_2 must be removed from the body in order for respiration to proceed. One reason is that a high CO_2 concentration changes the acid–base balance in the body. Even the smallest difference in pH affects metabolism, and in humans the pH is buffered precisely at between pH 7.36 and pH 7.45. The ultimate effect of high CO$_2$ on mammals is a condition called respiratory acidosis. In humans it occurs when the pH of the blood falls below pH 7.36.

Mechanisms to remove CO$_2$ from the animal rely on diffusion across surface tissues into the outside environment, or at least into the lungs of birds and mammals, from where CO$_2$-rich air is exhaled in breathing. Larger animals also require a circulatory system to move CO$_2$ to respiratory surfaces. CO$_2$ and O$_2$ molecules are similar in size, and so will diffuse at similar rates. Furthermore, CO$_2$ is produced and O$_2$ is used at similar rates. Not surprisingly, then, the same systems for inhalation/exhalation and circulation are used for the transport of O$_2$ and CO$_2$.

For O$_2$ transport, O$_2$ diffuses across the respiratory surface and usually combines with a respiratory pigment of the blood. Examples of pigments are haemoglobin (in the blood cells of most vertebrates and in the blood cells or plasma of many invertebrates) and haemocyanin (in the plasma of some molluscs and arthropods), but there are othersas well. The pigment increases the amount of O$_2$ that can be transported in the blood because of its affinity for O$_2$. At high O$_2$ concentrations the affinity is high. At low O$_2$ concentrations the affinity is low, and O$_2$ is released from the pigment to be available for use in cellular respiration. One factor that reduces the affinity of haemoglobin to O$_2$ is the amount of CO$_2$, and so CO$_2$ is part of the mechanism to release O$_2$ in tissues where it is required. One reason why CO$_2$ has this effect is that it reacts with water to form carbonic acid:

$$CO_2 + H_2O \rightleftharpoons \underset{\substack{\text{carbonic} \\ \text{acid}}}{H_2CO_3} \rightleftharpoons \underset{\text{bicarbonate}}{H^+ HCO_3^-} \rightleftharpoons 2H^+ + \underset{\text{carbonate}}{CO_3^{2-}}$$

This reduces the pH, which reduces the affinity of haemoglobin for O$_2$. CO$_2$ also reacts with $-NH_2$ groups on proteins in the blood plasma and on haemoglobin, and forms carbamino compounds:

$$\text{protein-N}\begin{smallmatrix}H\\\\H\end{smallmatrix} + CO_2 \rightleftharpoons \text{protein-N}\begin{smallmatrix}H\\\\COO^-\end{smallmatrix} + H^+$$

This reaction also reduces the affinity of haemoglobin for O$_2$.

The predominant form of CO$_2$ in the blood is HCO$_3^-$. There is 20 times as much of this as CO$_2$ and there are negligible amounts of CO$_3^{2-}$. As the proportion of CO$_2$ changes with respect to other dissolved gases, the proportions of different forms of CO$_2$ in the blood also change. CO$_2$ enters and leaves the blood in the CO$_2$ form because this diffuses across membranes much more quickly than any of the other forms. The change to and from CO$_2$ occurs in the red blood cells rather than the blood plasma because the enzyme carbonic anhydrase is present there, and also because deoxygenated haemoglobin facilitates the formation of HCO$_3^-$. The same enzyme is also present in the epithelial cells of the lung capillaries, allowing a rapid change to CO_2 at the site where CO_2 leaves the body.

Mammals adjust their rate of O_2 and CO_2 transfer by two mechanisms: by adjusting the rate and/or volume of breathing, and by adjusting the rate of blood flow and its distribution throughout the body and at the respiratory surface. Flows of air and blood are closely regulated so that adequate O_2 and CO_2 transfer is maintained. The rate and depth of breathing in mammals are affected by many different factors, including emotional state, sleep, changes in temperature and light and the need to speak. Not surprisingly, O_2 and CO_2 have an important influence. Even though O_2 is essential for the body, the main factor that controls ventilation for terrestrial animals is CO_2. Add CO_2 to inhaled air and ventilation of mammals and birds increases (Figure 3.1).

The reason why O_2 is not used as the basis for regulation is that there is rarely ever a shortage of O_2. The animal cannot respond to low O_2 levels only after they become critical, because the parallel increase in CO_2 will become dangerous long before then. In other words, a decrease in O_2 from 21% to 16% is not a problem, but an increase in CO_2 to 5% is very harmful to most species. Therefore, CO_2 is the basis of regulation.

Chemoreceptors for O_2 and CO_2 are present in the carotid body (off the carotid arteries) and aortic body (close to the aorta) of mammals, and similar structures are present in a variety of forms in birds and amphibians. The chemoreceptors send messages to the respiratory centre of the brain. The response to a rise in CO_2 levels is almost immediate, and an increased rate of breathing can be maintained for as long as CO_2 levels are high.

Excess CO_2 can arise from two sources, the first being metabolic processes. However, increased ventilation normally operates very precisely to maintain a constant concentration of CO_2 in the blood even during exercise, and so CO_2 from this is not usually a problem. The second source is the air

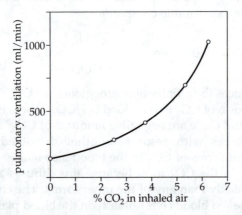

Figure 3.1   The effect of increased CO_2 in inhaled air on ventilation in chickens. (From Johnston and Jukes 1966.)

that is breathed. This causes more of a difficulty. If levels of CO$_2$ in the air are high, increased ventilation brings yet more CO$_2$ to the body rather than expelling it, and other mechanisms are required to prevent CO$_2$ build-up. One is buffering in the blood and tissues. Another response to high CO$_2$ is renal adjustment, in which NH$_4^+$, Cl$^-$, Na$^+$ and K$^+$ are excreted. Exchange of HCO$_3^{2-}$ and Cl$^-$ across cell membranes is one important mechanism for adjusting pH within cells: HCO$_3^{2-}$ enters the cell as Cl$^-$ leaves, the HCO$_3^{2-}$ combines with H$^+$ to form CO$_2$ and H$_2$O, and the CO$_2$ diffuses out of the cell, thus removing the acid. In shore crabs, high environmental CO$_2$ inhibits the HCO$_3^{2-}$ – Cl$^-$ exchange, so that the removal of metabolically produced CO$_2$ is reduced and salt balance is adversely affected.

Needless to say, gas exchange is achieved by very different mechanisms for invertebrates. In insects it is controlled by opening or closing spiracles which, when they are open, allow O$_2$ and CO$_2$ to diffuse along tracheal tubes into and out of the body. During periods of activity, when there is a greater need for O$_2$, the spiracles open wider and more frequently. A high CO$_2$ concentration in the insect's haemolymph is one stimulus which causes spiracle muscles to relax and the spiracles to open. An atmosphere of 2% CO$_2$ keeps all spiracles open and 3% CO$_2$ keeps them open wide. Each spiracle responds independently. Open spiracles mean that water loss is dramatically increased to harmful levels. However, a higher concentration of CO$_2$ is required to open the spiracles if the insect is already dehydrated; this minimizes the amount of water that is lost.

Aquatic animals, for example some diving mammals, do not rely so strongly on the small changes in CO$_2$ that are so important in regulation by terrestrial animals. The aquatic environment is considered in detail in Chapter 6.

The effects of CO$_2$ outside normal concentrations

Although higher levels of CO$_2$ than normal will stimulate changes in gas exchange, concentrations that are higher still could cause damage. Hypercapnia is a general term for symptoms caused by harmful levels of CO$_2$. Symptoms in mammals include:

- increased ventilation (though the ventilation rate returns to normal when the chemoreceptors for CO$_2$ become conditioned to higher CO$_2$ levels);
- constriction of pulmonary arteries;
- reduced contraction of heart muscles;
- fall in blood pressure;
- excess of potassium in the blood.

What concentrations are harmful? One set of government regulations on indoor air quality states that the level of CO$_2$ should not exceed 0.1%. However, in a study of bars and nightclubs in Vancouver, this recommendation was exceeded in every location sampled (Collett *et al.* 1992). Presumably the nightlife continued regardless. Air breathed by submarine crews contains around 0.9% CO_2 and 17% O_2 and does not cause significant stress. However, the performance of divers is impaired at levels of 6% CO_2.

Animals in high CO_2 environments

High levels of CO_2 are not restricted to artificial environments. Examples that occur naturally are given in Table 3.1. Much higher levels occur in a few extreme environments. For example, animals straying into the natural but extreme environments close to volcanic flues are rapidly overcome by a CO_2 concentration of 80%, and the ground can be littered with animal remains.

Some species spend almost all their lives underground in burrows sealed off from the outside world. Levels of CO_2 and O_2 in these sealed environments are spectacularly different from those outside. For example, CO_2 concentrations in burrows of the pocket gopher, a small North American mammal, range from 0.6% to 3.8% and O_2 concentrations range from 20.5% to 15.5% (Darden 1972). Do mammals like these respond to CO_2 levels in the same way as mammals in the open air?

One way of illustrating the response of animals to CO_2 levels is by measuring the amount of air inhaled per minute. The responses of a selection of mammals are shown in Figure 3.2. These data suggest that gophers are exceptional in their response to high CO_2. Gophers and other underground mammals share several physiological characteristics:

- low metabolic rate, which may reduce the requirement for gas exchange;
- very low ventilation rate at atmospheric CO_2 levels (perhaps 40% lower than above-ground species), increasing dramatically in high CO_2;
- slow heart rate, increasing dramatically if O_2 becomes dangerously low;
- high red blood cell count facilitating O_2 exchange;
- high O_2 affinity in blood, giving better O_2 transport;
- tissue activity despite high CO_2 and low O_2;
- high levels of myoglobin in skeletal muscle, facilitating O_2 diffusion from the blood.

Table 3.1   Natural variation in CO_2 levels

Environment	CO_2 level
Cavity within fig	up to 10%
Within caves	up to 6%
Interior of bee hives	0.2-6%
Overwintering chambers below bark	'high'
Warm, moist soils	3-5%
Soil covered by ice and snow	'high'
Interior of termite nests	0.5-5.2%
Burrows of mammals	0.5-4.8% (higher after active digging)

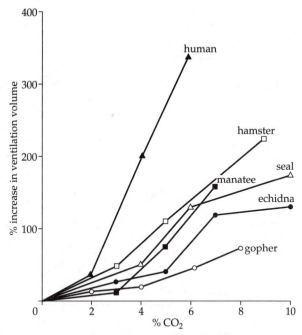

Figure 3.2   Responses of six mammal species to different CO$_2$ concentrations in the air. The seal and manatee are aquatic species. The echidna is a terrestrial species that spends much of its time burrowing for food. The gopher is sealed in subterranean burrows for most of its lifetime. (From Darden 1972.)

The reduced response seems to be due to some sort of alteration of the sensory system to the extreme CO$_2$ levels.

More is known about physiological adaptations of soil invertebrates. In some soil types, soil animals show several adaptations to high CO$_2$. These include low metabolic rate, a better buffering capacity of the haemolymph and regulation of the balance between acids and bases. Such adaptations allow species to thrive whatever the level of CO$_2$. One species of collembolan (a primitive insect group) tolerates CO$_2$ concentrations of up to 35%. Other collembolans living close to the ground surface are more sensitive to CO$_2$ and a concentration of 1.7% CO$_2$ can be fatal.

Caves can contain high levels of CO$_2$. A striking example of zonation within a cave system is illustrated in Figure 3.3 and is due to the size and location of the entrance, the shape and size of the passage, and high levels of moisture and organic matter. CO$_2$ builds up at the bottom of this cave because it is heavier than air and because there is no air flow. O$_2$ concentrations are low because decaying organic matter is being oxidized by microorganisms, and this is the main source of CO$_2$ in the caves.

As well as spectacular morphological adaptation, cave animals are likely to show physiological adaptations to the unusual atmosphere, but so far

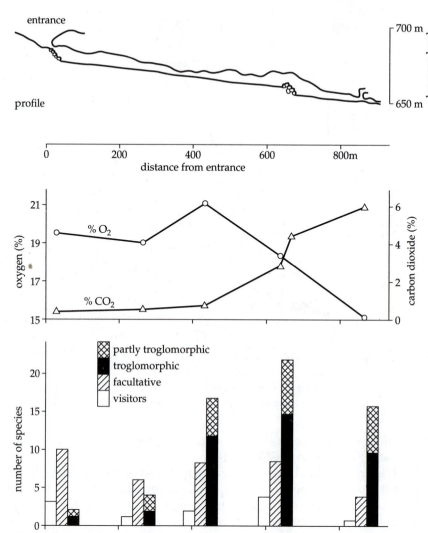

Figure 3.3   Profile, atmosphere and larger invertebrates in Bayliss Cave, Queensland. In this study, invertebrates are categorized as *troglomorphic:* obligate cave species showing extreme adaptations to life in caves (e.g. loss or reduction of eyes, wings, pigments; different body shape; longer appendages) (17 species); *partly troglomorphic:* species with less extreme adaptations to life in caves (7 species); and *facultative:* facultative permanent residents (21 species); *visitors:* temporary visitors (6 species). (After Howarth and Stone 1990.)

there have been few studies to explain features such as their characteristically low metabolic rate.

Animals making use of variation in CO$_2$ levels

As well as large natural differences in CO$_2$ among habitats, there is often small-scale variation in space and time.

Some animals can detect this variation precisely, and for insects in particular it has interesting implications. CO$_2$ receptors are present in all major insect groups, for example on the antennae of bees and ants, on the maxillary palps and antennae of flies, and on the maxillary and labial palps of beetles. Their apparent absence in other groups is probably because no one has looked.

CO$_2$ is an important cue for the activities such as host seeking, mating and even ventilation of the nests of insects (Nicolas and Sillans 1989). In many cases high CO$_2$ is an indicator of the presence of a possible food source, for example decaying plant or animal matter. Species such as wireworms (click beetle larvae) that feed on decomposing material respond to a CO$_2$ source up to 20 cm away and are sensitive to CO$_2$ concentration differences of 0.002–0.003% over a distance of 1 cm. Plant feeders use CO$_2$ gradients to locate plant roots in the same way. The mechanism is adequate for generalists that make use of whatever roots are present, but probably not specific enough for specialists searching for particular plant species; their search mechanism is likely to involve other plant metabolites too. These examples are mostly confined to below ground, where the environment is stable and concentration gradients are able to persist.

CO$_2$ is also an important cue to hosts for blood-sucking flies such as mosquitoes and tsetse. The source of this CO$_2$ is exhalation. Exhaled air contains around 4–5% CO$_2$, and a level 0.01–1% higher than the background level will persist close to the host. It is most likely to be an important cue midway through the host detection process. Host-specific odours are probably the best initial cue from long distances, and visual cues are probably more effective at close range. Alternatively, a higher CO$_2$ level could stimulate an increase in flight activity and increase the chance of encounters with a potential host. For mosquitoes, take-off is stimulated by a CO$_2$ concentration of 0.03% above that of the environment. Landing is stimulated by the presence of CO$_2$ so long as lactic acid (a second cue to a host) is present in low concentrations (Eiras and Jepson 1991).

There is some evidence that levels of CO$_2$ could also be a cue for females searching for a site for oviposition. Adult Japanese pine beetles are attracted at the same time that CO$_2$ is released from the trunks of possible hosts (Kobayashi et al. 1984). However, most insects have precise requirements for oviposition and CO$_2$ alone is unlikely to be a specific enough cue.

One of the most complex sets of responses to CO$_2$ is shown by fig wasps pollinating figs. Wasp eggs are laid in the ovaries of the figs. Wasp larvae and fig embryos develop alongside each other inside the cavity of the fig. The larvae develop into adult wasps inside the cavity, where their behaviour is linked closely to the CO_2 concentration, which can reach 10%. So long as it remains above 3–4%, females are inactive. However, males are active and mate with the females. After fertilizing the females, the males bore holes in the cavity wall and the cavity fills with air from outside. The females become active at this lower CO_2 concentration, then follow a decreasing CO_2 gradient and leave the fig through the holes. The females then search for new fig flowers in which to lay eggs, taking with them pollen from the plant in which they developed.

Abnormally high CO_2 levels can induce responses that return CO_2 levels to normal. One example is the response of honey bees to high CO_2 in the hive. CO_2 is maintained at around 1–3%. Honey bees do not have the ability to differentiate CO_2 concentrations more precisely than this. If the CO_2 concentration increases, the number of bees showing fanning behaviour also increases. Fanning is a behavioural response by bees to increase the air flow in the hive. In one study CO_2 was pumped into a small experimental hive. As the CO_2 concentration rose from 0.5% to 8%, the number of fanning bees increased from five to around 150 (40% of the colony). When pumping stopped, the CO_2 concentration was reduced by fanning to near normal levels within 6 minutes (Seeley 1974).

Will the predicted global increase in CO_2 have any significant effects on animals?

The preceding sections considered ways in which CO_2 concentration affects animal biology and how changes in concentration can be important cues. Now, with this background information, we can ask if the predicted doubling of atmospheric CO_2 concentration will have any significant direct effects.

The answer is clear. If humans in submarines live in 0.9% (9000 ppm) CO_2, beehives are maintained at up to 1–3% (10 000–30 000 ppm) CO_2 and non-specialized soil insects survive in up to 1.7% (17 000 ppm) CO_2, a rise in atmospheric CO_2 from 355 to 700 ppm is small enough to be insignificant.

What about animals that use tiny differences in CO_2 concentration as cues? Biting flies and root feeding larvae respond to an *increase* in CO_2, not to the absolute *concentration*. This may be due to adaptation in the CO_2 receptors or to habituation in the central nervous system. For stable flies, this habituation takes place very rapidly. Whereas an increase in CO_2 evokes an immediate response as soon as the stimulus is detected, there is no significant response at all after 2 or 3 minutes if the high CO_2 is maintained (Figure 3.4).

The answer here is just as clear. A doubling in atmospheric CO_2 over a timescale of decades will have no effect on mechanisms like this that habituate to new levels of CO_2 in minutes. Furthermore, the changes in

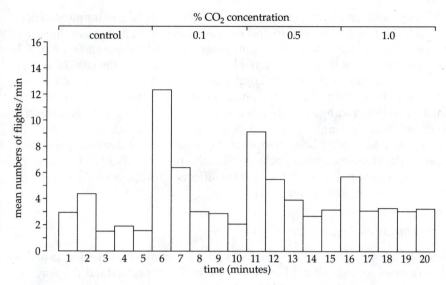

Figure 3.4 Mean number of flights per minute by stable flies *Stomoxys calcitrans* exposed to increasing CO_2 levels. (From Warnes and Finlayson 1985.)

background CO_2 are tiny compared to the natural variations which will continue to exist and continue to form a cue to animal behaviour. However, the indirect effects of an increase in CO_2 on the food plants of animals are likely to have a considerable impact. These plant–animal interactions are considered in Chapter 4.

Temperature and animals

Chapter 2 showed that temperature has a profound influence on the growth and reproduction of plants and that changes in temperature will affect productivity, timings and distribution. The rest of this chapter briefly examines ways in which temperature affects animals at a variety of levels – metabolism and cell biology, physiology, ecology and behaviour – to see how these aspects of animal biology might be affected by predicted changes in temperature. The four possible general responses of any species to environmental change – changes in distribution, tolerance, evolution and extinction – will then be considered to see which are likely.

Animal activity is restricted to temperatures that range from –1.86°C in Antarctic seas to around 55°C in hot springs, although some can survive more extreme temperatures in an inactive state. Each species has its own preferred temperature range between these two extremes. Some species thrive across a wide range of temperatures, others are restricted to a narrow range, and the range can change with time of year, developmental stage and conditioning.

Many animals are at the same temperature as their environment. These are **ectotherms**, and warm up and cool down with their surroundings. For these animals, body temperature and environmental temperature are usually the same unless they use external heat sources such as the sun. However, others can maintain a very different temperature by generating their own metabolic body heat. These are **endotherms**. Endotherms (mammals and birds) are buffered against changes in their surrounding temperature, but even so, outside temperature still determines how much energy must be spent on maintaining body temperature, what food is available, and ultimately distribution and abundance. Ectotherms are influenced in a much more fundamental way. Temperature affects growth and development, behaviour and reproductive success.

Temperature and animal physiology

Body temperature has an enormous impact on many physiological processes. We need to understand how if we are really to understand the ways in which animals are influenced by environmental change – and the ways they can respond. In general, higher temperatures accelerate most processes. One indicator of metabolic activity is O_2 consumption, and this usually increases by 2–3 times for every 10°C rise in temperature. This exponential increase is illustrated in Figure 3.5. However, above a particular temperature O_2 consumption no longer increases as rapidly and, at a higher temperature still, a lethal temperature is reached and death occurs.

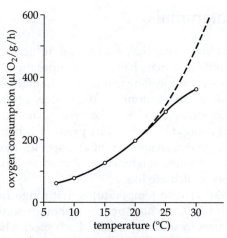

Figure 3.5 O_2 consumption at different temperatures for the Colorado beetle. The dashed line shows what would be expected if metabolic activity were to have continued to increase exponentially instead of falling off at high temperatures. (From Schmidt-Nielsen 1979.)

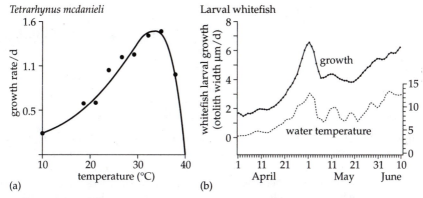

Figure 3.6   Effect of temperature on (a) development rate of early nymphs of a bug, *Tetrarhynus mcdanieli* (from Logan *et al.* 1976) and (b) on growth rate of larval whitefish. Growth was estimated by measuring daily growth rings of otoliths (ear bones) of fish caught on 11 June. (From Eckmann and Pusch 1989.)

The same pattern is found for a wide range of physiological processes. The growth rate of ectotherms, a result of many of these processes operating together, is greater at higher temperatures (Figure 3.6).

Several factors could contribute to malfunction or death from high temperature, perhaps in combination:

• The function of proteins and nucleic acids depends on their maintaining specific conformations (i.e. three-dimensional structures). The structures are held together by weak interactions within and between large molecules. Usually if one link is broken the other links break too. However, this **denaturing** can often be reversed. Denaturing can be affected by temperature or, in other words, the level of thermal energy. An increase in thermal energy increases the vibration of bonds between atoms, affecting bond lengths and bond angles. Hydrogen bonds, van der Waal interactions and salt bridges will vibrate more. Once a critical number of bonds are broken at any one time, the rest break and the structure breaks down. A temperature increase of only a few degrees can be sufficient to cause this.

• Temperature can affect the **synthesis** of proteins. Figure 3.7 shows the pathway by which several newly synthesized polypeptide strands are folded into a protein. The protein itself is stable over a wide range of temperatures. However, some of the stages in folding require the temperature to be within narrower limits.

• Different metabolic processes respond to temperature changes in different ways, so the normal **biochemical balance** could be disrupted.

• The animal's increasing O_2 demand at higher temperatures might not be satisfied.

• Biological membranes are the boundaries of cells and organelles. They regulate ion transport; cell recognition; receptor-mediated processes in which

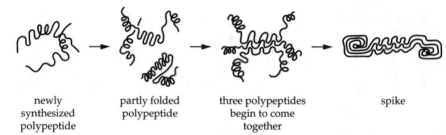

| newly synthesized polypeptide | partly folded polypeptide | three polypeptides begin to come together | spike |

Figure 3.7   The folding pathway of a protein that forms the tail spike of a bacterio-phage (a virus that infects bacteria) of *Salmonella*. Folding takes place in several stages. In some strains folding does not proceed beyond an inter-mediate stage because the folding process is temperature dependent and environmental temperature is not correct. (From Smith *et al.* 1984.)

substances bind to specific surface receptors before being brought into the cell; and energy transduction, and are a barrier to diffusion. Membranes are described as a 'fluid mosaic' in which proteins are sealed within a lipid bilayer (two layers of lipids, hydrophilic on the outsides, hydrophobic within) or attached to the bilayer, usually on one side or the other depend-ing on the function. Temperature affects the **fluidity of the membrane**, which changes from a gel phase to a liquid-crystalline phase as tempera-ture increases by several degrees. The membrane only functions in the liquid-crystalline phase. The temperature of the transition depends on many factors, including the proportions of different lipids that are present and their characteristics (e.g. polarity, chain lengths). At a higher tempera-ture still, the liquid-crystalline phase becomes disordered and the membrane too permeable. When cholesterol is also present, as it is in many membranes, it maintains the organization of the membrane at a higher tem-perature. When higher proportions of unsaturated fatty acids are present in the membrane lipids, the liquid-crystalline phase is maintained at a lower temperature. The activity of most enzymes present in the membrane is crit-ically dependent on the membrane fluidity. If they are to function, the membrane proteins must remain sealed in the bilayer and maintain their conformation. A change in the membrane fluidity to the gel phase could cause aggregation – and reduced activity – of the proteins.

Low temperatures could also reduce performance and lead to death. One rea-son is that metabolic activity could drop to a critically low level. One study of tropical fish showed death at 10°C was caused by low temperature depress-ing the respiratory centre of the brain, causing a reduction in gill ventilation and leading to lack of O_2. At the level of cells, one result of cold shock is a change in the permeability of membranes, causing a change in the balance of cations, escape of contents of the cell and entry of materials that would not normally penetrate the cell membrane. The reasons are that cold shock caus-es the membrane lipids to gel so that the fluid mosaic is disrupted, and that proteins are inactivated because of a slow drift in their conformation.

If the temperature drops to freezing, damage can be even more severe. Ice crystals at the cell surface cause mechanical damage to the cell. Furthermore, solutions outside the cell can also change markedly. Solutes in water become more concentrated when part of the water changes to ice, and this could cause osmotic stress on the cell. Between 64% and 75% of water leaves the cell and the cell shrinks, damaging the membrane and disrupting its func-

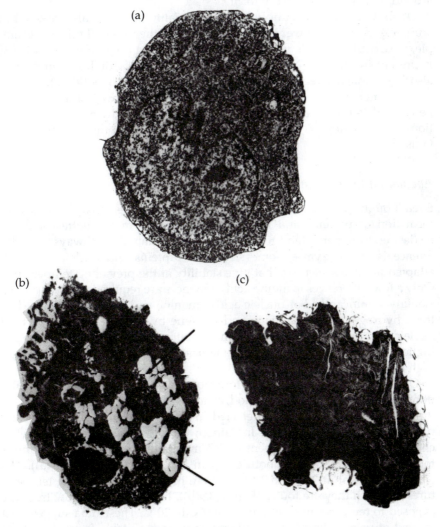

(a)

(b)   (c)

Figure 3.8   Effect of freezing on cells. (a) Chinese hamster connective-tissue cell before freezing. (b) Rapid cooling induces ice cavities (as shown by arrows) and survival does not occur. (c) In contrast, 10 minutes at –26°C before cooling to –80°C allows cellular shrinkage, the absence of obvious intracellular ice and high survival. Approximate magnification ×5400. (Courtesy of Dr David Pegg, Medical Cryobiology Unit, University of York.)

tion (Figure 3.8). If freezing also occurs within the cell, organelles could experience these same stresses.

However, many animals can endure temperatures below freezing by avoiding freezing. One mechanism to avoid damage is supercooling. Water and aqueous solutions can cool to well below their freezing points without freezing taking place, so long as there are no nuclei of ice or other material around which ice will rapidly form.

Other animals are simply freeze tolerant: the animals freeze, but antifreeze chemicals lower the freezing point of their body fluids. For example, a particular peptide which reduces the freezing point of water by 0.4°C is present in mussels. NaCl at concentrations 40–70% higher than normal also has a major effect. Most Antarctic fish have glycopeptide antifreezes which somehow prevent tiny nuclei of ice from forming. Fish in cold temperate waters only use antifreezes as necessary – in midwinter, the blood of flounders contains 3% peptide antifreeze. At the end of the summer it contains none.

Adaptation to temperature

Even though temperature changes of only a few degrees can disrupt the conformation of proteins and nucleic acids, animals in the hottest and the coldest environments tend to have the same metabolic pathways. The difference is that enzymes, some structural proteins and nucleic acids are adapted to have structures that give stability at the prevailing temperature. Only a few differences in amino acid sequences are required to affect protein stability significantly. For nucleic acids, guanine and cytosine are linked by three hydrogen bonds, adenine and thymine by only two. In the parts of nucleic acid molecules involved in maintaining the conformation, there is a higher proportion of guanine–cytosine base pairs in organisms that live at high temperatures.

One way of detecting different forms of enzymes is by using high-resolution electrophoresis. By this method, changes in the frequencies of alleles for different enzymes have been detected in rainbow trout. Which alleles are present depends on latitude. In rainbow trout, one form of the acetylcholinesterase enzyme is present in fish maintained at 2°C, another form is found in fish at 17°C, and both occur in fish at 12°C (Figure 3.9(a)). The enzymes present at 2°C and 17°C operate most efficiently at the temperatures in which they are found (Figure 3.9(b)). In the wild, rainbow trout are exposed to temperatures ranging from 0°C to 20°C. These data suggest that instead of using a large variety of enzymes, each suitable for a given temperature, the trout only use two, which are present together at intermediate temperatures. Changes in the forms of different enzymes happen quickly enough for animals to keep up with seasonal changes in temperature because the turnover time of most enzymes is fairly rapid. Each enzyme molecule may exist for a few weeks.

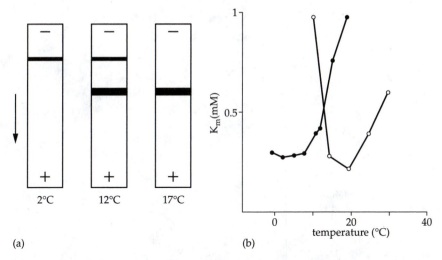

(a)   (b)

Figure 3.9 Temperature and the enzyme acetylcholinesterase of rainbow trout. (a) Electrophoresis results for acetylcholinesterase from fish acclimated in the laboratory to different temperatures. The bands indicate distance moved by the enzyme along a gel in response to the electric current. Different forms of the enzymes have different electric charges and/or masses, so they move different distances. Two different forms of the enzyme are present in fish at 12°C.

(b) Activities of different forms of the enzyme. K_M is the Michaelis constant, an indication of the behaviour of the enzyme. A low value indicates that most of the enzyme is attached to its substrate in an enzyme–substrate complex. A high value indicates that less is attached to its substrate. The activity of the enzyme depends on the proportion that is attached to its substrate: more complexing means greater activity. Here, the lowest K_M for the enzyme taken from fish kept at 2°C (●) is at 2°C, so its effectiveness is greatest at this temperature. The lowest K_M for the enzyme from fish kept at 17°C (○) is at 20°C. (From Clarke 1987.)

The chemical composition of membranes is regulated to maintain the fluidity of the bilayer so that the membrane continues to function. Figure 3.10 demonstrates different membrane properties in fish moved from a warm to a cool environment. The membrane becomes less fluid and its function could be impaired. However, given time, the fish become acclimatized to the cool conditions, membrane composition changes and fluidity increases. Similar homeostatic responses have been described for mammals and microorganisms. How the response is regulated is not clear.

Animals found in more constant environments or that maintain their own constant body temperature do not show such rapid acclimatization. Even so, populations of the same species in different environments have different membrane compositions from each other, each appropriate to the environ-

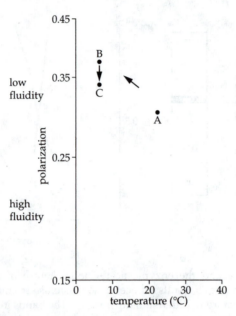

Figure 3.10   Membrane fluidity for goldfish. Fish kept at 25°C (A) were transferred
to 5°C and the membrane fluidity decreased (B). After 10-14 days at 5°C,
the fish had acclimatized and fluidity had increased (C). Membrane fluidity is quantified by inserting into the membrane a molecule which
rotates polarized light. The molecule's movements in the membrane
depend on the fluidity of the membrane and determine how the molecule rotates the light. Low polarization indicates more rotation of the
'molecular probe' and hence greater fluidity of the membrane. (From
Cossins and Raynard 1987.)

mental temperature. Whatever the compositions, the fluidity of the membrane is extraordinarily similar.

It is clear that many species have mechanisms to cope with a changing
environment which they use through the seasons. If adaptation is a change
in the proportions of particular forms of enzymes, then it is straightforward.
If animals can respond to seasonal changes over a few weeks, then environmental changes over several decades should not be a problem. More difficult
is to predict the response of species from thermally stable environments
where there are no seasonal changes to which they must respond. Movement
to another location where conditions are similar is perhaps more likely than
a physiological response.

Temperature and sex

Sex can be determined by temperature. The sex of turtles is determined by
the incubation temperature of the eggs: at higher temperatures embryos
develop faster and grow larger. For turtles, it is an advantage if the females

are large because it affects the number of eggs they lay. Size matters less to males. Sex is linked to temperature so that warmer temperatures produce females and cooler temperatures produce males. For alligators the situation is reversed: eggs incubated at <30°C develop into females and those incubated at 34°C produce males. Competition between males affects their success in reproduction and large size is an advantage, and so males are produced at higher temperatures. Intermediate temperatures over a narrow range produce both sexes.

How does temperature affect development to produce one sex or the other? In some species of frogs and toads, male and female sex chromosomes differ only slightly and individuals have the potential to be of either sex. Immatures develop as females at 10°C but as males at 27°C. 'Female' individuals switched from a cool to a warm environment gradually switch sex to become males. The temperature turns on and off the genes for hormones that control male and female characteristics.

The sex of the moth *Taleporia tubulosa* is determined by the temperature to which the egg is exposed. This species always has one sex chromosome (X) present in the egg as it matures. At 30°C, the sex chromosome is oriented so that it tends to remain in the egg during the divisions of meiosis. At 5°C it is oriented differently and tends to end up in the polar body, a cell which does not go on to produce offspring. This means that an egg can end up with (X) or without (O) the sex chromosome, depending on temperature. The egg is fertilized by a sperm that always carries a sex chromosome (X). The result of

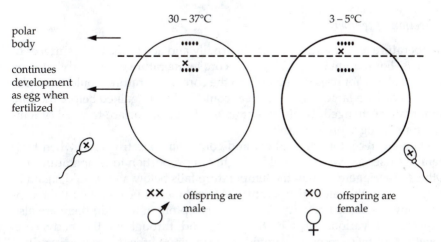

Figure 3.11 Sex determination in the moth *Taleporia tubulosa*. When eggs mature at a high temperature the sex chromosome (X) tends to remain in the developing egg during meiosis. At lower temperatures it tends to migrate into the polar body. The result, explained in the text, is more males at high temperatures and more females at low temperatures. (After Bacci 1965, based on Seiler 1920.)

fertilization is male (XX) or female (XO). Thus, at higher temperatures during egg maturation most offspring are male, and at low temperatures most
are female because temperature affects the migration of the sex chromosome
(Figure 3.11).

In each of these cases, males and females are both produced because:

• environmental temperatures fall between the two extremes;
• any environment has warmer and cooler parts, whether these are different
  parts of the same site or distant sites from which males and females come
  together to breed;
• there is variation among individuals in the critical temperature at which
  one sex or the other is triggered.

High temperature is also a cue for a switch from sexual to parthenogenetic
reproduction. Parthenogenesis is reproduction from a female gamete without fertilization by a male gamete. Low temperature triggers sexual
reproduction in zooplankton, inducing gamete production in some and
gonad development in others. Low temperature, when combined with the
changes in day length found in the autumn, cues sexual reproduction in
aphids. A reason for the switch is that sexual reproduction creates genetic
variation among offspring, which is likely to be an advantage in difficult
(cold) conditions. Parthenogenesis allows successful genotypes to increase
their numbers rapidly in good (warm) conditions. Thus a temperature
change could have a significant effect on the life histories of species that
already possess sexual and parthenogenetic life history pathways.

Detection of temperature

Temperature receptors are present internally and across the body surfaces of
animals. For mammals and birds, the core temperature of the body must be
kept constant. Yet responding only to the core temperature would be inade-
quate because a large amount of heat could be lost or gained before the core
temperature changed. Using receptors on the body surface to warn of temperature changes prevents this.

Different receptors detect heat and cold. Some are triggered when temperature rises above a threshold, roughly in proportion to temperature rise.
Others are triggered when the temperature falls below a threshold, again in
proportion to the fall in temperature. At extremes of heat or cold the receptors show decreased activity. As well as receptors in the skin there are also
receptors at various sites in the brain and throughout the body core.
Together, all these receptors provide information to the thermostatic centres
in the brain, in particular in the hypothalamus. Physiological responses of
mammals to heat include sweating, panting and increased blood flow to the
skin. Responses to cold include the generation of heat and reduced blood
flow to the skin. An additional response of fish to heat is increased ventilation: this is because the metabolic rate of fish increases at a higher

temperature and more O_2 is needed. Heat receptors are present on the antennae, palps and tarsi of the legs of insects and cold receptors have also been found. Insect sense organs respond not just to temperature but also to the rate of temperature change.

How sensitive to temperature can animals be? Data exist for many different organisms. A species of nematode shows the greatest sensitivity, responding to a gradient of 0.001°C/cm, but even this is a thousand times less sensitive than what is theoretically possible for the structure of the thermal receptor. Mammals are less sensitive to temperature, and detect changes of 0.1°C or more.

Behavioural responses to temperature

As well as physiological responses to changes in temperature, animals can respond by their behaviour, avoiding unfavourable conditions or seeking more favourable ones. Locusts adjust their posture and position to ensure that they gain heat from the sun. Some caterpillars move into the sun when their temperature is below optimal and move into the shade when it is above. Others construct silk tents or tie leaves, creating structures that increase the temperature of their immediate environment.

Animals use temperature gradients as cues for movement around their environment. Nematodes use patterns of soil temperature that change throughout the day to find their way to particular depths in the soil to locate plant roots. The behavioural rule is to move in the direction of temperatures that are a few degrees higher than that to which they are acclimatized. Because of changes in the temperatures at different soil depths at different times of day, nematodes tend to move to a particular depth however deep they start out (Figure 3.12).

In the same way, subterranean termites forage below the soil surface but move closer to the surface where objects cast a cool temperature shadow into the soil beneath. *Melanophila* beetles detect the heat of forest fires and use it as a cue to the location of burned trees, in which they lay eggs. Many parasites use the body heat of their hosts as a cue to their location, and heat is the main stimulus that induces probing of hosts by tsetse flies. Temperature differences between different water currents are used by fish to sense the direction of the currents (Westerberg 1984).

In all these cases, although climate change will increase temperatures, heterogeneity in temperatures within environments will remain. Thermal gradients will still exist even though the background temperature could be 2°C higher. Thus higher temperatures should present no problems to species that respond to temperature cues.

Animals also use temperature sensors to gain other information about their environment. The rate of heat loss from an animal depends on the material with which it is in contact. Wood conducts heat slowly; rock conducts heat ten times faster. Animals can use temperature sensors to detect

soil surface

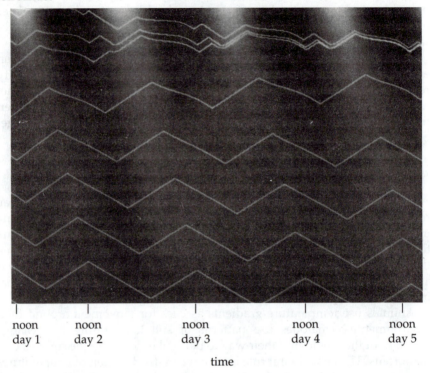

noon   noon   noon   noon   noon
day 1   day 2   day 3   day 4   day 5

time

Figure 3.12 A computer model to show nematode movements in soil over 4 days. Temperature is indicated by colour: the darker the shade, the cooler the temperature. The white lines show the positions of 'model' nematodes. The nematodes start at different depths. The behavioural rule of the nematode is to move towards a temperature which is several degrees higher than its acclimation temperature. The result is that, whatever depth they start out at, these nematodes move to a specific depth. Perhaps this is the best depth at which to locate host roots. (From Dusenbery 1989.)

conduction of heat and identify the material. This method of sensing can be used whatever the temperature.

Many activities of ectotherms only take place once a threshold temperature has been reached. These include insect flight, and activities that depend on flight including mate location, oviposition (Figure 3.13), feeding on nectar, evading predators and dispersal. A temperature increase will have a significant effect, possibly increasing overall reproductive success. Excessive temperatures, however, could cause heat stress and decrease activity and longevity.

Temperature and lifecycles

Temperature affects the growth rate of animals that do not maintain a stable body temperature. If animals grow faster, they could mature and produce

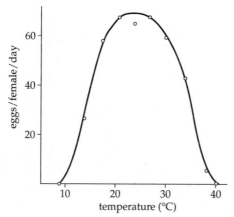

Figure 3.13   Effect of temperature on the rate of oviposition by the bean weevil *Bruchus obtectus*. (From Menusan 1935.)

offspring more quickly. They could also reach a larger size and, as a consequence, produce more or larger offspring. Both possibilities could increase fitness (i.e. the relative contribution of the genotype to the next generation when compared to the contributions of other genotypes).

A consequence of a faster growth rate is that extra generations could be fitted into the year, at least in theory. Whether it is possible depends on the environmental cues used by animals to trigger different stages in their life history. Like plants, some animals have determinate growth patterns and undergo an obligatory dormant stage at a particular point in the lifecycle. Others are more flexible, and these are the ones that are likely to be influenced by climate change. Some insects squeeze in an extra generation in years when conditions are good, and probably use temperature or photoperiod as a cue to indicate whether sufficient time is likely to be available. Many species have two or three generations each year in warmer regions and just one in cooler areas. In both cases, an extra generation could increase the total population by the end of the season – and increase fitness. On the other hand, extra generations may fail if there is not sufficient time to complete development to the normal dormant stage.

Sometimes other constraints are just as influential as climate in determining life history patterns. One intriguing illustration is an Arctic caterpillar *Gynaephora groenlandica*, for which a single generation lasts about 14 years. Larval development takes so long because feeding is limited to just 3–4 weeks per year. Caterpillars begin to hibernate in late June, even though suitable food is available throughout July. The reason is that peak activity of parasitoids that attack the caterpillars is in July, and they do not attack hibernating caterpillars. Thus this species trades feeding opportunities for parasitoid avoidance. So, even if temperatures increase as dramatically as predicted for the Arctic, other constraints could limit the ways species respond.

Temperature also affects how early in the year animals become active. A network of suction traps operated across Britain since 1965 has been used to monitor the phenology of aphids in relation to weather, especially winter temperature (Harrington *et al.* in press). Some species spend the winter as parthenogenetic adults and these fly earlier in the spring after milder winters. A 1°C increase in mean January and February temperature leads to the spring flight 2 weeks earlier. This means that aphid populations can reach large numbers earlier in the year. In unusually warm years, when temperatures have been close to those predicted for global warming, aphids have become active 6 weeks earlier than usual. The warm temperatures also mean less mortality and sublethal stress, less inhibition of movement, and a delay in the production of sexual individuals.

Seasonal changes in temperature can be an important cue to other lifecycle events too, including hatching of the eggs, initiation of courtship and egg laying.

If environmental conditions are difficult, reproduction can be delayed. Implantation of the embryo of the red kangaroo is delayed until environmental conditions make it almost certain that an adequate food supply will be available for the young. Maturation of the gonads of female grayling and meadow brown butterflies is delayed during summer drought when the host plant of the larvae is in poor condition (Garcia-Barros 1988). At least for the butterflies, this lifecycle adaptation allows the species to have wider distributions in Europe than related species.

Climate is one dominant factor affecting the abundance of animals. For ectotherms at least, a warmer temperature closer to the optimum is likely to increase numbers. Predicting what will happen in real life is not straightforward, because abundance is so strongly influenced by interactions with other organisms (see Chapter 4) and by abiotic changes happening at the same time.

Dormancy

If conditions are difficult for part of the year (due to cold and/or shortage of food and water), many animals opt out. One way is to pass the dead season in a dormant, resistant stage.

For several different groups of mammals (e.g. some marsupials, bats, shrews and rodents) body temperature and other physiological functions are drastically reduced for hours or weeks, but the animals return to normal body temperature by using heat produced internally. This torpor is simply an advanced form of thermoregulation that allows energy and water to be conserved. Body functions are drastically reduced – heart rate by 95%, O_2 consumption by 99% – and body temperature drops to within 2°C of environmental temperature. If the environmental temperature falls below a critical minimum, possibilities are:

• maintenance of the critical temperature by increased metabolism;

• death, if the body temperature drops below the critical minimum;
• arousal out of torpor and search for a better location.

The third is the most usual. Seasonal transitions between activity and torpor are regulated by a circannual rhythm (an internal body clock running on a cycle of a year) which is perhaps finely tuned by temperature, photoperiod or other environmental factors.

The great majority of temperate and high-latitude invertebrates survive winter cold in diapause, a state of dormancy when metabolic rate is extremely low. It is most frequently cued by photoperiod. Light stimulates the brain, which turns on neurosecretory cells to produce a diapause hormone or, in aphids, stimulates the cells directly. Photoperiod is a better cue than temperature because it allows the animals to anticipate changing conditions – if they wait for a drop in temperature it could be too late. Even so, high or low temperatures can induce, avert, intensify or accelerate diapause depending on species. Diapause is common in tropical insects too, governed by the same physiology and often regulated by photoperiod modified by temperature. There are a few cases where temperature is the sole controlling factor: flesh flies in East Africa and a parasitoid of *Drosophila* flies enter diapause when daytime temperatures drop below a threshold and terminate diapause when temperatures rise.

Nearly all insects are able to undertake diapause in only a single stage in the life history, and there is no flexibility. The exceptions are interesting. For example, some aphids can overwinter either as parthenogenetic adults or as diapausing eggs, which are more tolerant of cold. The proportion of each is related to temperature in the previous winter.

Predicted increases in temperature could mean that in some circumstances dormancy is no longer necessary, or that it lasts a shorter time. For endotherms, the energetic cost of dormancy – and possibly the risk of mortality – would be less in a warmer environment.

Migration

Migration is the second way to escape difficult environmental conditions. It is specialized behaviour that has evolved independently many times for the movement of individuals or populations from one region to another. One form is vertical migration. For example, the distribution of plankton at different depths changes dramatically during the course of a day. Vertical movements of planktonic copepods of the order of 10–100 m/h are cued by light levels, possibly for the avoidance of predators or for more efficient metabolism in cooler water after feeding. Vertical migration of invertebrates deeper into the soil is a seasonal response to winter cold or low humidity in the dry season. Vertical migration of birds up and down mountain sides is a response to change in weather conditions. For example, at least 16 species of montane forest birds, ranging from eagles to cuckoos, breed on Mount Oku,

Cameroon, in the dry season and move from montane forest to other habitats lower down the mountainside during the wet season (Plate 4).

Horizontal migration, often over vast distances on an annual cycle, is a response of many animal groups to the same kinds of seasonal changes in weather conditions and food availability. Migrations of terrestrial and marine mammals, fish, insects and birds are well known. The best studied are birds (Berthold 1993). Their usual cue for migration is the annual cycle of seasons and photoperiod. Differences from year to year are caused by weather processes (low- and high-pressure areas lasting a few days) and by heat exchange between oceans and the atmosphere (varying by several weeks each year). For birds, different triggering mechanisms can operate for different species:

- direct response to annual cycle (e.g. to photoperiod or start of monsoon rains), often linked to a circannual rhythm;
- the same, but with additional essential requirements (e.g. also requires the presence of a mate);
- the same, but modified by other factors (e.g. weather, presence of food);
- response to factors that reset the timing of migration (e.g. failure of first brood because of predation or destruction of the nest by a storm).

Present-day migration routes have developed since the end of the last glaciation and continue to change. Routes and destinations can vary from year to year, sometimes in response to climate changes that affect food supplies. During drought years, when suitable nesting habitat is not available, pintail ducks extend their migration northwards to the coastal plains of Alaska and successfully nest there.

Some species are very conservative in their migration patterns. The wheatear is a Palaearctic species which has extended its range west to Greenland and east to Alaska. From the Palaearctic, wheatears migrate south to Africa in winter. From Greenland and Alaska they also move vast distances to Africa each year, even though apparently suitable areas are very much closer. Other species show rapid, radical changes. For example, over the last 25 years central European populations of the blackcap have changed their migratory behaviour: the destination of their winter migration has changed from the Mediterranean to the British Isles. One possible reason is the reliability of food because of increased winter feeding of birds by people. Another is the avoidance of strong competition with other species in the Mediterranean. Another is the shorter winter days in more northerly latitudes, which stimulate an earlier return migration, earlier reproduction and the chance to choose the best habitats and to breed with other birds that have also returned early from Britain (Berthold 1993).

Current research is trying to establish the extent to which migration routes are genetically controlled, rather than the result of learning from other individuals or responding to cues from the environment. Work on the basic control of migration has been done in laboratory experiments indoors, where there are no environmental cues. Studies show that the most basic features of bird migration (e.g. when to start migrating, the direction in which to fly) are genetically controlled. This is not surprising for small, short-lived species that might only migrate twice in their lifetime. However, when cues are available birds adjust their migration behaviour in response to their environment: weather, wind, availability of food and the behaviour of other birds of the same species. Intriguing results have come from selection experiments on blackcap populations in which some individuals migrate and others do not. It took just three generations to turn a parent population of 75% migrants into a 100% migratory population, and 4–6 generations to turn it into an almost completely non-migratory population. This shows the extremely high potential for evolution of migratory behaviour and indicates how quickly migrating animals might adjust their behaviour in response to environmental change (Berthold *et al.* 1990).

Climate change could also disrupt the timing of migration. One study in Germany recorded the dates at which migrating birds passed a reference point during their autumn migration over a 21-year period. Nineteen of 28 passerines, which migrate short distances, migrated up to 10 days later in years when the onset of autumn weather was delayed by 5–6 days. These birds are likely to benefit from a longer period in their summer breeding grounds. A smaller proportion might migrate each year and an increasing proportion become resident in summer breeding grounds. Long-distance migrants did not show changes in timing. This makes sense, because they are less likely to be influenced by local conditions: their arrival south of the Sahara must coincide with seasonal rains and birds that arrive late are likely to be at a severe selective disadvantage (Gatter 1992).

Another problem is change in the synchrony between migrants and their food sources. Sanderlings and plovers migrate from South America to breed in the Arctic during the short northern summer, where adults and young feed on summer insects present in large numbers. Feeding on the route is essential. A regular feeding ground is Delaware Bay, where the birds feed on the eggs of horseshoe crabs. If the crabs lay earlier or later because of climate change, the migration could be seriously affected because of the absence of a suitable feeding area.

Climate change could eventually lead to a dramatic change in behaviour that affects resident as well as migratory species. A possible scenario is given in Table 3.2.

Temperature and distribution

How closely is the geographical distribution of a species related to temperature? One suggestion is that the limit of a distribution is set by the limits of an animal's physiology. For example, for endotherms that need to compensate for colder temperatures by generating more heat, metabolic rate can only be increased up to a physiological limit. If cold temperatures demand a

Table 3.2   Likely effects of climate change on the Eurasian–African bird migration system. (After Berthold 1993.)

- Milder winters will reduce mortality for residents, so numbers will increase.
- Favourable springs and summers will give earlier and better breeding conditions, so density will increase.
- Partial migratory species will become completely or almost completely resident as the resident part of the population increases.
- Short and medium distance migrants could migrate shorter distances or even remain on their summer breeding grounds all year round.
- Because of greater numbers of residents, migrants will be less able to establish territories on their return, leading to wider spread, possibly density regulation by reduced clutch sizes, and the loss of migratory behaviour for some species. The greatest impact will be on long-distance migrants that might not be able to change their behaviour quickly enough.
- Increased drought in the sub-tropics will lead to an increase in dry season migrations due to shortages of resources.

higher metabolic rate than is physiologically possible, the animal simply cannot exist in that location: death from hypothermia would occur.

This possibility has been tested for North American birds. If it were correct, limits of distributions would correlate closely with temperature isotherms along the whole length of the northern edge of their distribution. In practice, a close correlation exists for only four out of 50 species that were analysed; for these four species, metabolic rate is likely to vary by no more than 25% of their basal metabolic rate for birds found at different points along the length of their northern limit. For a further 21 species there is a looser correlation, with a variation of metabolic rate that is 25–50% of basal metabolic rate. But for more than half of the species, birds found at different points along their northern limit have very different metabolic rates from each other.

Another test is to compare the distributions of birds of different body sizes. Large species could extend further into colder climates than small species. The theoretical explanation is based on two general patterns:

- All birds can increase their metabolic rate above basal by a roughly similar factor (often guessed at around 2.5 ×, but probably more).
- Smaller animals have a higher basal metabolic rate than larger animals.

This should mean that small birds reach the physiological maximum metabolic rate at less cold temperatures than large birds. However, the data show that birds of all sizes occur in the coldest regions, suggesting that a limit to metabolic rate is not the deciding factor for most bird species (Repasky 1991).

The important point is that even though there are maximum and minimum temperature limits for survival, they do not give a useful indication of geographical distribution of animals. It is not possible to explain most distributions by temperature alone, though temperature must certainly have some influence. A whole range of other factors must be considered (Hoffmann and Blows 1994). These include:

• daily and seasonal patterns in climate;
• distribution of food plants or host animals;
• distribution of competitors and predators;
• patterns of dispersal and migration;
• features of the abiotic environment;
• characteristics of the habitat;
• barriers to movement, such as mountains or oceans;
• historical constraints on distribution.

One recent model, called BIOCLIM, has been developed by the CSIRO in Australia. It uses data for 24 different climatic variables of significance to insects to predict current distribution and future distributions in different environmental conditions. To show that the model works, it has been used to pinpoint likely locations for species that have not been recorded in an area before, and it is usually right. Often it is not 'average' conditions that matter, but extreme conditions such as prolonged drought or unusually high temperatures for a few days. For example, the northern limit of trout in New Zealand is determined largely by high winter temperatures which cause egg mortality. In the same way, low winter temperatures cause extremely high mortality of painted turtle hatchlings during their first winter. In one study close to the species' northern limit, only one hatchling survived the winter from 53 individuals in 10 different nests studied over two winters.

BIOCLIM has been used by Lindenmayer *et al.* (1991) in a study of Leadbeater's possum, a rare marsupial restricted to montane forests in Victoria, Australia. Twenty-four different climatic factors (Table 3.3) were estimated for each of the sites where possums occurred in order to work out the climatic requirements of the animal and create a 'bioclimatic profile' of the species. From these data, their potential distribution could be predicted. The possum is limited to sites that are within a narrow range of conditions. Maps of its current distribution and the distribution of suitable sites (Figure 3.14 (a)) are very similar. However, the distribution of sites with the same range of climatic conditions in 2050 will be much more restricted if climate predictions are correct (Figure 3.14 (b)). Implications for the conservation of rare species are discussed in Chapter 7.

One way of testing the importance of particular climatic factors is by physiological studies in conditions typical of those outside the usual distribution. Another way is by manipulation experiments in which animals are moved outside their usual range. Thimbleberry aphids, for example, moved north of their usual northernmost boundary, did not become established because the summer season was too short to allow them to produce a generation of sexual females able to lay overwintering eggs (Gilbert 1980).

Table 3.3 The 24 variables used in the BIOCLIM model. There is enough information here to describe usual conditions, extremes and seasonality. (From
Lindenmayer *et al.* 1991)

1	Annual mean temperature (°C)
2	Annual mean maximum temperature (°C)
3	Annual mean minimum temperature (°C)
4	Maximum diurnal temperature range (°C)
5	Mean temperature of the warmest month (°C)
6	Mean temperature of the coldest month (°C)
7	Mean seasonal range (index 5–index 6) (°C)
8	Isotherm seasonality (mean diurnal range/mean seasonal range)
9	Maximum temperature of the hottest month (°C)
10	Minimum temperature of the coldest month (°C)
11	Annual temperature range (index 9–index 10) (°C)
12	Mean temperature of the wettest quarter (°C)
13	Mean temperature of the driest quarter (°C)
14	Mean temperature of the warmest quarter (°C)
15	Mean temperature of the coldest quarter (°C)
16	Annual precipitation (mm)
17	Precipitation of the wettest month (mm)
18	Precipitation of the driest month (mm)
19	Annual precipitation range (index 17–index 18) (mm)
20	Seasonality index [index 19/(index 16/index 12)]
21	Precipitation of the wettest quarter (mm)
22	Precipitation of the driest quarter (mm)
23	Precipitation of the warmest quarter (mm)
24	Precipitation of the coldest quarter (mm)

Sometimes climate does not affect animals directly but instead affects
interactions with other species. The northern limit of the red fox in Eurasia
and North America has moved northwards in warmer periods in the last 100
years. The likely reason is that prey availability has increased because of
warmer summer temperatures, increasing the primary productivity which
determines prey numbers. At the same time the distribution of the Arctic fox
has contracted because it cannot compete with the red fox (Hersteinsson and
Macdonald 1992). These sorts of changes in biotic interactions are more difficult to test than changes in temperature or other aspects of climate. Again,
the most direct way is by manipulation experiments. They are also very difficult to predict for new climatic conditions.

One way to assess whether abiotic or biotic factors are the more influential is to examine important characteristics of populations. Caughley *et al.*
(1988) suggested three:

• population density;
• the intrinsic rate of population increase;

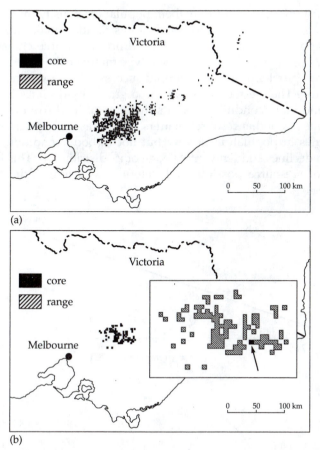

Figure 3.14 Current and predicted distributions of Leadbeater's possum. The species is restricted to Victoria, Australia. (a) Predicted current distribution using a bioclimatic profile of the species. (b) Predicted distribution in 2050 using the same bioclimatic profile and anticipated climate changes. The model identifies a 'range' of the species, which includes all sites within the minimum and maximum values of the bioclimatic profile, and a smaller number of 'core' areas which exclude sites with extreme conditions. (From Lindenmayer *et al.* 1991.)

- body condition, which can be described by fecundity or fertility or a collection of body measurements or an estimate of body fat (the kidney fat index correlates well with body fat reserves in mammals and is obtained by estimating the amount of adipose fat covering the kidney).

If each of these factors declines **gradually** towards the edge of the distribution, it is likely to be due to a climatic factor or another environmental factor. If there is a **sudden** drop in body condition and rate of population increase, it is possible that the animals have responded to changes in resources across their distribution by adjusting their population density, but that lack of resources beyond the extremes of their distribution make further adjustments impossible. If there is a sudden drop in all three characteristics, a sudden change in the vegetation or soil type might be the cause. Though this method has problems, it has been used successfully to examine two species of kangaroo. The western grey kangaroo gradually declines in population density and body condition towards the edge of its distribution, implying that climate or another resource matters. In contrast, the eastern grey kangaroo declines in population density but not in body condition, until body condition declines suddenly at the edge of its distribution. This implies that the limit of a resource, possibly food, determines the limit of the distribution.

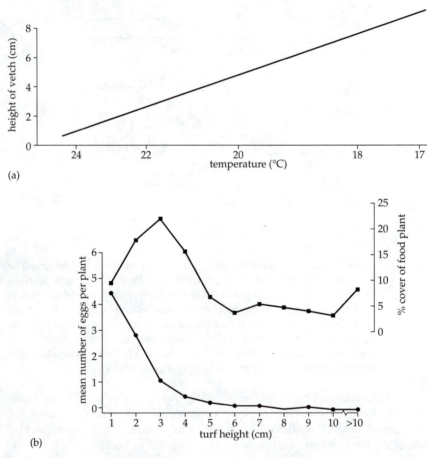

(a)

(b)

Figure 3.15 (a) Ground temperature below horseshoe vetch of different heights; (b) distribution of eggs of the adonis blue butterfly in turf of different heights. Most eggs are laid in the shortest turf, even though the food plant is most abundant when the turf is 3 cm high. (From Thomas and Lewington 1991; Thomas 1991, based on data from Thomas 1983.)

Microclimate

Models have no alternative but to use coarse measurements of temperature that are obtainable from weather stations. However, these measurements are not directly relevant to most animals. What matters is microclimate, the climate in the animals' immediate environment.

For caterpillars, for example, it is the temperature and humidity in their few millimetres of living space that matters, and it can be very different from the macroclimate of which humans, as larger organisms, are aware. Figure 3.15(a) shows how marked the differences can be: a difference in ground-surface temperature of 7°C between exposed short turf and taller vegetation. Such microclimatic differences must make a big difference to insects for which growth rate – and the chance of reaching adulthood and reproducing – depends on temperature.

Adonis blue butterflies make use of different habitats according to local climate. In England the species lays eggs in turf 2.5 cm high or less, on steep south-facing slopes, and even then in warm hollows such as the footprints of livestock (Figure 3.15(b)). However, the butterflies are not found in similar habitats 1000 km south in central France. Instead they are found in meadows of tall grass and caterpillars feed low down in the vegetation. The reason is their need for a precise microclimate, which is found in different parts of the habitat in different parts of its geographical range. Other grassland insects are equally choosy about the height of the turf, even if the plant species composition is the same. In Britain, adonis blue butterflies prefer it to be 0.5–2.5 cm high, chalkhill blues 2–6 cm, common blues 4–10 cm and small coppers up to 20 cm – but all can be found together on the same hillside at the same time of year if the habitat is sufficiently diverse.

The concept of microclimate is important in the consideration of just about any species in any environment. Even a bare and virtually flat two-dimensional habitat such as Arctic tundra has steep vertical temperature gradients extending down into the soil and determined by the warmth of the sun above and the cold of the permafrost below; soil insects such as collembolans are mobile enough to find a suitable thermal environment somewhere on the temperature continuum. In the same way, willow flea beetle distribution within vegetation depends on small-scale changes in humidity (Bach 1993). The choice of tree cavities in which birds such as prothonotary warblers nest can depend on the internal temperature of the cavities in the summer: cavities in open, sunny sites become too hot (Blem and Blem 1994). Ground-nesting birds select nest sites with different degrees of shelter from the wind and shade from the sun. Buntings breeding in the summer prefer sites where exposure to the wind and shade from shrubs and tall grasses keep them cool. Longspurs and larks nesting earlier in the season prefer more exposed sites protected from the wind and exposed to the sun (With and Webb 1993).

Whether for different sides of a tree trunk, depths or a pond, surfaces of a leaf or aspects of a hillside, differences are significant enough to affect the body temperature and physiology of animals. More interestingly, the micro-climatic heterogeneity of the environment allows animals to adapt to new conditions by using different parts of the environment.

Dispersal of animals

Distributions can change only as quickly as animals can move across the landscape. It is important, then, to understand the factors that influence dispersal.

Birds, bats and flying insects avoid the complexities of terrestrial habitats and can move long distances rapidly. Many of the smallest species form aerial plankton high in the air. One report of insects up to 4.6 km above Louisiana describes a catch of 29 000 insects from 216 families, 824 genera and at least 700 species! Not all are winged. Young caterpillars and many small spiders spin silk threads which are caught by the wind and drawn upwards. Distances moved depend on whether the insects are flying or borne by the air currents. Movements of aphids range from 1 km to 1000 km or more, and aphids are deposited at the rate of about 1 aphid/m^2/h on a summer day in England.

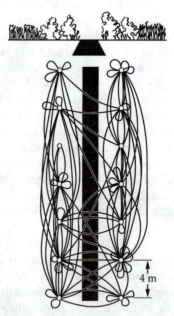

Figure 3.16   Movement patterns of ground beetles beside a tarred road. Beetles were trapped in pitfall traps, individually marked and released. Each line indicates the movement of a marked beetle which was trapped again. Only a small proportion of movements are across the road, probably because the roads resemble an arid, abiotic environment which the beetles would normally avoid. (From Mader *et al.* 1990.)

Dispersal occurs in the same way in the oceans, where larger animals swim and the smallest are carried as plankton in ocean currents. Aerial or marine plankton cannot be selective about their final destination, but dispersal is so wide that adequate numbers of many species reach a variety of new locations, some of them suitable.

On the land surface dispersal is more complicated. Non-flying animals usually require more or less continuous areas of suitable habitat along which to disperse. Microclimate, food, shelter and protection from enemies must be adequate. Habitats often exist in a mosaic across the landscape and animals must cross the gaps between suitable habitats or make use of corridors of suitable habitat. Corridors could be natural (e.g. a river bank) or a result of human activities (e.g. a hedge or roadside verge). Gaps in the corridors could hinder the spread of a species, or prevent it completely. For small, non-flying invertebrates, gaps as narrow as a footpath could hinder their spread. Railway lines and country lanes are significant barriers to larger insects, although a few individuals cross occasionally (Figure 3.16). Flying insects and birds can avoid some of these barriers, although a gap of 2 or 3 km of agricultural land is enough to prevent chalk downland butterflies from colonizing another hillside. Eventually it could happen by chance, but it could take 50 years.

Features of the biology of each species determine how readily animals can cross gaps of unsuitable habitat. Larger terrestrial animals often move further than smaller animals, one reason being simply that their strides are longer. Another is that the distance across a surface differs according to animal size and surface smoothness. Small animals closely follow the ups and downs of a surface; large animals do not notice the ups and downs and treat the same surface as if it were smooth.

Humans are an important influence on the speed at which distributions change. For plant parasitic nematodes the natural spread without human interference would be slow (Thomas 1981). It has been estimated that one species spread from a hedge into a woodland at an average speed of 30 cm/yr over a 75-year period. Another moved at 15 m/yr through a citrus orchard and 21 cm/month in experiments. Perhaps they could move further if accidentally carried by birds or mammals, but human actions such as the mass movement of plant material or soil and adherence to farm machinery increase the speed tremendously (Boag 1985). Cars and trains are other important influences. Human actions take animals outside their natural range at the present time, but the animals do not persist if conditions are not suitable. However, if conditions change, these species could become established.

The distribution of suitable environments for animals will certainly change with the global climate. Whether or not plants and animals can disperse across the landscape of the present day will determine how – and whether – species and communities will persist. To conserve rare species that are not able to disperse rapidly enough across the landscape, positive action might have to be taken (see Chapter 7).

General responses of animals to climate change

The rest of this chapter considers four possible general responses of any species to climate change: change in distribution, tolerance, evolution and extinction. The way that particular species could respond depends on the characteristics of the animal. Features that matter include mobility, size, reproductive strategy, abundance and distribution. We will examine each of the four possible responses in turn and consider which are most likely, and how aspects of animal biology might allow us to make predictions for the future.

Changes in distribution

If temperature and other aspects of climate influence distribution, a change in temperature or climate should lead to a change in distribution. There is evidence for this for many different animal taxa. Two very different groups highlighting a more general pattern are nematode worms and foxes.

Data from a European survey of plant parasitic nematodes show a close association between July soil temperature and the distribution of several pest nematodes (Figure 3.17). Temperature changes are likely to increase the northward distribution of nematodes across Europe as well as increasing their population sizes and the severity of infestation of crop plants. The scale of new pest problems will also depend on soil type, soil moisture and the crops that are present.

Public demand for the pelts of foxes led to their commercial exploitation and the records of fur traders give a good indication of changes in fox distribution and abundance. One study used counts of pelts in fur trappers' bags to show the invasion of Baffin Island, Canada, by red foxes over the last 100 years and the spread northwards of some 1500 km (Figure 3.18). The best explanation is the increase in summer temperature. There was a time lag of 10–20 years because it takes this long for the warmer summer to influence productivity and prey numbers available to the foxes.

For species such as these it is not enough to plot new climate data on a map and assume that distributions will change to fit the new pattern. This is because many species are not found in all the situations in which they could occur, because they are limited by competition and predation by other organisms. Instead they are found in a fraction of situations. In ecological jargon, their 'realized niche' (i.e. the actual place of an organism in an ecosystem) is different from their 'fundamental niche' (its place under ideal conditions without interacting species). The influence of interactions with other organisms through competition, herbivory, predation and mutualism is considered in Chapter 4.

The rate at which species distribution can change is highly variable. Data suggest that birds, some flying insects and larger mammals will move quickly enough to keep pace with rapid changes in climate zones and in the

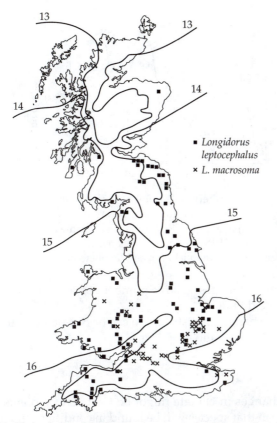

Figure 3.17 The relationship between nematode distribution in Britain and mean July soil temperature (°C). Climate change will extend the distribution northwards, with implications for agriculture. For example, a 1.5°C rise in temperature would allow *Longidorus macrosoma*, a vector of raspberry ringspot virus, to become established in northern Britain. (From Boag *et al.* 1991.)

distribution of food plants and habitats. Less clear is the ability of smaller, ground-living animals with poorer dispersal ability to cross an increasingly fragmented habitat. This is a major concern. One complication is the fact that dispersal can often depend on exceptional long-distance movements by a few individuals rather than on short-distance movements of more typical individuals – knowing the movement patterns of 'typical' individuals may cause the change in distribution that is possible to be underestimated.

Another common assumption is that suitable climate conditions will move smoothly and continuously across the landscape. If suitable conditions move in jumps or disappear completely, even for a short time, extinction is more likely than dispersal.

We have to conclude that only species that can disperse rapidly and have a range determined directly by climatic factors will change their distribution

Figure 3.18 Changes in the northernmost point of red foxes on Baffin Island and in the mean summer temperature. Temperature data are from the nearest weather station in Toronto. Red foxes first became established on Baffin Island in around 1918. Although foxes reached the island before that, a population did not establish. (From Macpherson 1964.)

to closely match climate changes. A large number of species fall into this category, but many more do not.

These examples of changes in distribution can be compared with those for plant species (see Chapters 2 and 4).

Tolerance of change

Even quite major changes in climate might be tolerated by plants and animals. This could mean that species will be found in conditions in which they are not normally found at present. One reason for this is that other species (herbivores, predators, pathogens, competitors etc.) currently interact with them to prevent establishment or survival. If conditions change the interacting species might no longer be present, perhaps because changes have made the interacting species locally extinct or because the plant or animal has spread to a new location where the interacting species does not occur.

Because of the unpredictability of dispersal (see above) and different environmental conditions, there is no certainty that present-day interactions will be restored. An alternative possibility is that different interacting species will already be present or will arrive. Whatever the scenario, interactions among species are likely to change. Interactions are considered in more detail in Chapter 4.

Smaller animals could adapt to environmental changes by modifying their behaviour. We have already mentioned caterpillars of the adonis blue butterfly which use different microhabitats in different parts of their geographical distribution (see page 81). Changes in the use of different aspects or altitudes could be enough to allow them to persist, but if this is to happen the environment must be heterogeneous on a scale that is meaningful to the animal. A flat grassy plain has many different microclimates that can be exploited by insects, but offers fewer possibilities to larger mammals. On the other hand, a landscape of hills and valleys could give many opportunities even to larger animals.

Evolution

Could species evolve quickly enough to allow them to persist in a changed environment? Evolution is the only possibility for species that cannot respond by changing their range or by tolerating new conditions.

Climate change could lead to evolution at different scales. One is the evolution of distinct new species. Another is change in gene frequencies or chromosomes within a species. These will be considered separately.

Evolution of new species of marine animals: a case study

Studies using fossils of marine organisms such as foraminiferans and ostracods have given a good understanding of the relationship between evolution and climate change over the last 20 million years (Cronin and Schneider 1990). Cores of marine sediment obtained by deep-sea drilling are so little disturbed that each sample from a core spans only 1000–10 000 years. Evidence from the cores indicates climate at the time sediment was deposited. For example, the level of ^{18}O isotope from deep-water foraminiferans indicates the global ice volume (see Chapter 1); and sea surface temperatures are estimated based on the distributions of temperature-sensitive planktonic foraminiferans. The precision is now good enough to be able to date the appearance and disappearance of many different species in precise locations. For example, it is clear that a deep-sea foraminiferan *Globorotalia truncatulinoides* first appeared about 2.4 million years ago in the southwest Pacific, but did not reach the north Pacific and Atlantic until 1.9 million years ago. Data are so precise that the first appearance could indicate the time and place of the evolution of new species.

Speciation can happen in different ways. One mechanism is 'cladogenesis' (i.e. lineage splitting). This is where a new species evolves from an ancestral species when a population of the ancestral species becomes isolated in some way. An example is the evolution of a new species of diatom *Rhizosolenia praebergonii* from *R. bergonii*. Microfossils of the diatom show a change in size during speciation 3.1–2.7 million years ago (Figure 3.19). The ^{18}O record indicates a major change in climate at the same time. It is likely that the speciation was initiated by the climate change and that, somehow, the ancestral and descendant populations were separated by some sort of temperature barrier. Another example is the planktonic foraminiferan *Globorotalia pliozea*, which arose from *G. conomiozea* around 5 million years ago. The separation took just 10 000 years, and the morphology of *G. pliozea* did not change in any perceptible way for the next 700 000 years. The cause was the isolation of a population of the ancestral species by a sudden

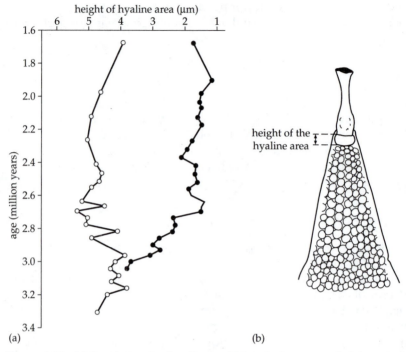

Figure 3.19 (a) Speciation in the diatom *Rhizosolenia* as recorded by microfossils. The two species are the ancestral *R. bergonii* (○) and the descendant *R. praebergonii* (●). One character that was measured was the height of the hyaline area, a part of the valve, (b). This was chosen not because it has any particular significance in itself but because there is a good microfossil record. Other parts of the organism are less well preserved or less easily found. (From Sorhannus *et al.* 1988.)

strengthening of a temperate–tropical climatic boundary crossing the south-west Pacific.

Another mechanism for speciation is 'anagenesis' (i.e. phyletic evolution). This is more or less gradual evolution of morphology over a long period. For example, *Globorotalia conoidea* evolved gradually over 8 million years to produce *G. inflata*. During this time the climate was cooling and the water column was less stable than before. Changes in the morphology of *Globorotalia* included loss of the keel and a more rounded edge to the shell. These changes could maintain buoyancy and prevent sinking. Another rapid change in the seas was a dramatic change in salinity in the Mediterranean 5.5 million years ago. *Globorotalia tumida* showed several changes in morphology, some gradual, some rapid, which could also have been related to buoyancy.

These examples show that new species can evolve as a result of climate change, but how common is this? Marine sediment data show that it is much more usual for species to respond to climate change by changing their geographical distribution, showing no evolutionary change at all in their mor-phology. One calculation estimated that for 18 well-studied genera of ostracod, only 35 new species evolved in the western North Atlantic during 46 glacial–interglacial cycles during the last 2.5 million years. Each cycle caused sea-level changes of up to 100 m and rapid, massive disruption to continental shelf habitats. There must also have been barriers formed between populations, giving a chance for geographic isolation. The amount of speciation, then, is surprisingly low. At the same time, though, distribu-tions of many species changed by 5–6° latitudinally. Even so, there is phenotypic variation that parallels climate change. *Globorotalia truncatuli-noides* has two forms: one, with right-handed coils, is found in warmer waters; the other, with left-handed coils, is in cooler waters; and the propor-tion of each varies depending on climate. A possible reason for this change is that control of the direction of coiling is linked to some other characteris-tic, possibly quite unrelated, that has an adaptive value depending on water temperature. Another close correlation with climate change is the shell size of *Globigerina bulloides*. In warmer periods it is larger and in cooler periods smaller (Figure 3.20).

Studies of foraminiferans answer questions that have not yet been asked for most other groups and which are impossible to answer for many. But questions remain. One thing that is still unclear is why, during climate change, some species evolve and others do not. For foraminiferans, likely important factors are the physiological responses of different species to tem-perature, salinity and the chemistry of the ocean.

Microevolution – and a little genetics

Microevolution is evolution on a small scale. Rather than the appearance of new, distinct species, it is a change in gene frequencies, or in chromosome number or structure due to mutation or recombination during meiosis. It can happen quickly. One example of microevolution is the acquisition of the abil-ity of weeds and insect pests to resist herbicides and pesticides. The weeds and insects are the same species that they were before, but changes in gene frequencies, mutation or recombination have occurred that change their abil-ity to respond to an external factor.

One study of published papers covering 121 animal and plant species found that 26 of them showed evidence of natural selection influenced by climate in one way or another. However, even though it is common, trying to predict possible directions of microevolution that could be brought about by climate change is extremely complicated. After all, most evolutionary the-ory considers single characters or genes, but adaptation to environmental change is likely to need changes in many different characters at the same time.

One approach is to examine genetic polymorphism (the existence of dif-ferent alleles at a single gene locus). A possibility is to look at different forms

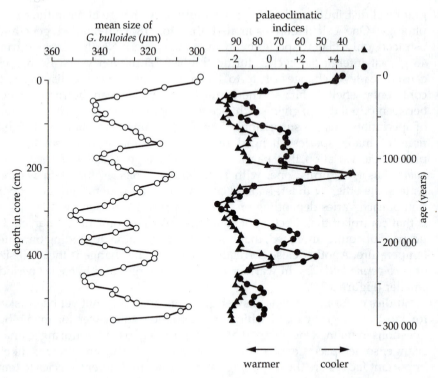

Figure 3.20 Variation in size of *Globigerina bulloides* over 300 000 years in relation to climate. Two indicators of climate are used: a palaeoclimatic index based on abundance data for planktonic foraminifera (●) and the percentage of left-hand coiled *Neogloboquadrina pachyderma* (▲). The percentage of *N. pachyderma* with a left-handed rather than right-handed coil is known to be closely related to water temperature. (From Malmgren and Kennett 1978.)

of the same enzyme which function best in particular conditions (see page 64). It would then be possible to see what climatic factors affect which forms are selected. Evidence from many different species shows that temperature stress has a significant impact on polymorphisms at many loci. A change in climate could affect the probability of different morphs being selected, leading to rapid genetic change.

Another approach is to expose animals to stress and examine the selection that takes place over several generations: tolerance to stress, the extent to which tolerance is inherited by offspring, and correlated responses such as tolerance to other stresses. This method has illustrated selection to tolerate climatic stress for the fruit fly *Drosophila melanogaster* and other animals. Work with *Drosophila* species is discussed in more detail on page 98.

There is clear evidence from the field that selective pressures alter as climate changes. Changes in temperature will have direct effects on

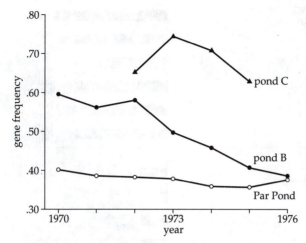

Figure 3.21   Gene frequencies of a thermally stable form of the enzyme malate dehydrogenase in artificial lakes with different thermal histories. Pond C
received hot water at >50°C from an adjacent nuclear reactor for 16
years before the study began and continued to receive hot water
throughout the study. Pond B received hot water for 11 years but this
stopped 6 years before the study began. Par Pond has always been at
ambient temperature. (From Smith *et al.* 1983.)

physiology, but these are hard to spot. One interesting study was on largemouth bass subjected to stress from new hot water outflows from a nuclear
industrial plant. Smith *et al.* (1983) detected an increase of 3.8% per year in
the gene frequency of a thermally stable form of the enzyme malate dehydrogenase. This change occurred over only 15 years, and when the stress
was removed the gene frequency reverted to the natural frequency within 10
years (Figure 3.21).

Responses to changes in resources used by the animal are easier to investigate. *Geospiza fortis*, one of Darwin's finches in the Galápagos Islands, feeds
on seeds of many sizes. When seeds are available in large numbers the finches prefer small, soft seeds. In dry years when seeds are scarce, large, hard
seeds must be eaten and the direction of selection is in favour of birds with
large bills (Figure 3.22). Thus it is possible to picture changes in seed availability driving the direction of microevolution (Gibbs and Grant 1987).

Most traits can be inherited, and so evolution will occur as a result of climate change. However, it is not clear how much variation is available on
which selection could act. There is more variation in some traits than others.
This is shown in another study of Darwin's finches (Grant and Grant 1987).
Exceptionally heavy rains in the Galápagos Islands in 1982–83, with rainfall
20 times greater and lasting 8 months instead of the normal 2–4 months, led
to luxuriant plant growth and enormous production of seeds. In normal
years there is strong selection for length of the breeding period, location of
breeding and the number of younger birds that breed. In the exceptional

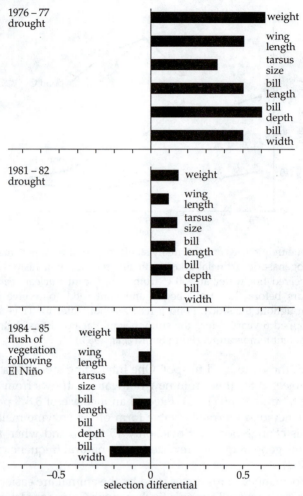

Figure 3.22 Selection differential for characters of *Geospiza fortis*, one of Darwin's finches, in different environmental conditions. In years of drought and poor food supply, larger body size is favoured because only birds with large bills can crack open large, hard seeds. In years when food is abundant, small soft seeds dominate and small adult size is favoured. Selection differential is a way of indicating the effects of natural selection. Here it is calculated by measuring the size of the character before and after selection. A negative value means a decrease in size. The scale on this illustration is in standard deviation units. (From Gibbs and Grant 1987.)

weather conditions some of the environmental constraints on breeding were relaxed. Changes in breeding included:

• The breeding season lasted 7–8 months, twice the usual length.
• New breeding birds established their territories in places not normally used.

• Many 1-year-old birds bred, when normally they do not.

Other characteristics did not change. These included clutch size and maturation rate. The changes are interesting because they show what variation exists in breeding behaviour – which characteristics are flexible and which are not. We need to know this to anticipate the responses of animals to climate change.

It is possible that there is little variation for physiological factors that determine abundance and distribution. However, it is clear there is greater genetic variation in species of less stable environments.

Do populations at the edge of their range differ from populations at its centre? The few data that exist suggest that edge populations often have low fitness, except in the particular conditions in which they are found. One explanation could be that edge populations have less genetic variance for characteristics that determine the distribution limit because the favoured alleles have become fixed. Another explanation could be a genetic trade-off between fitness in favourable and in edge environments: because populations at the centre of the range retain characteristics needed to survive in favourable conditions, there cannot be an increase in characteristics useful for more stressful edge conditions.

Strong selection could lead to rapid change for a number of generations, but then a virtual halt after which no further change is possible. In laboratory experiments this often happens after only 10–20 generations. There are several possible reasons:

• Some genes have additive effects. This means that they each contribute to the phenotype. Selection could use up all the additive genetic variation for the selected character so that there is no variability remaining for further response.
• Often a single gene affects more than one character. This is called pleiotropism. One character could be advantageous in new environmental conditions but other characters controlled by the same gene might be disadvantageous. These disadvantageous changes could limit how far selection for advantageous characters could go.
• In small isolated populations there can be loss of variation by genetic drift (i.e. random changes in gene frequency due to factors other than natural selection).

Larger populations are more likely than small isolated populations to contain alleles that do not have disadvantageous pleiotropic effects. This means they are likely to show a greater response change before the virtual halt. Thus species in smaller populations – the rare species that conservationists want to conserve – are less likely to be able to adapt to climate change.

Even if there is a halt to change after 10–20 generations, further change is possible by genetic recombination or mutation. There is evidence that rates of recombination and mutation increase in a stressful environment, but only if selection for a major mutation is very strong will disadvantageous pleiotropic effects be overcome.

For populations spread across an area as large as a continent, selective pressures are likely to vary in different parts of the distribution. In a continental population compared to a small, closed population:

• There is more genetic variation in the population as a whole.
• There is more chance of other species invading and outcompeting a species before it can adapt.
• Species can change their range or their behaviour so that they do not need to evolve.
• Changes due to selection are likely to be in different directions in different places. If they are not separated, populations adapted in different ways will meet each other, breed and dilute local adaptations.
• Inflow of genes from dispersing large populations slows down adaptation in small populations because changes are diluted.

The truth is that we do not know what effect microevolution has in allowing a population to persist in new conditions, and it is an important area of current research (Holt 1990). Significant factors we know very little about include:

• how the relationship between different characters will change in different physical environments;
• how much genetic variation exists for key traits determining distribution and abundance;
• how stresses on a few species affect other species within the community.

However, we do know that it can occur rapidly enough to keep up with predicted rates of climate change – in only a few years for largemouth bass and Galápagos finches (page 91).

Extinction

If a species cannot tolerate changes in climate, change its distribution or evolve, it will become extinct. Changes in the abiotic environment could cause extinction within a few generations. Changes in interactions with other species, for example competition, could cause eventual extinction after many generations.

There are two main processes that cause extinction:

• when on average the birth rate does not match the death rate, due perhaps to change in habitat, predation, disease or, in small populations, inbreeding depression (i.e. loss of vigour due to inbreeding);
• when a chance event occurs, whether it is a natural catastrophe or natural variability in birth and death rates (the more variable, the greater the chance of extinction);

Both processes could be brought about by climate change.

Some species are at greater risk of extinction than others, but which are most vulnerable? No simple predictions can be made from a knowledge of life histories and an added complication is that rare species can adapt to the state of being rare. All that can be said is that rarer species are usually at greater risk. There are different ways in which an organism can be rare: because of small geographic range, because of restricted habitat or because of low population density. Species with larger geographic ranges tend to be found at higher population densities across their range; species with smaller ranges tend to occur at lower densities. It is not clear why there is this positive correlation, but it has important implications:

• Reducing its range could lead to a reduction in population density in areas where a species remains.

• Reducing the population density could lead to a reduction in range size.

Range size, population density and the interaction between the two are the main criteria used by the International Union for the Conservation of Nature and Natural Resources (IUCN) to categorize the risk of extinction. Changes in temperature and other aspects of climate are likely to affect the range size and the population density of many species, and thus affect their risk of extinction. How extinction affects other species and whole communities is discussed in Chapter 4.

The generalization about range size and population density has particular relevance for species in isolated populations, whether on islands in an ocean, on mountain tops above a sea of tropical forest, or in nature reserves in an agricultural landscape. Implications for conservation are considered in Chapter 7.

Responses to climate change over the last million years

Which of the four general responses is most likely? Palaeobiological studies show some interesting patterns, at least about changes in the past. However, care must be taken in extrapolating these to the present and the future.

Whole sets of insects are preserved in deposits in bogs, marshes, lake sediments and archaeological sites, and these show very clearly what was present at particular times in the past. There have been frequent, rapid and intense climate changes. For example, changes in the presence and absence of carabid ground beetles have indicated a rise in temperature of at least 1.7°C per century around 10000 years ago, and 2.6°C around 13000 years ago. How have insects responded? Studies of preserved assemblages of insects by Coope (1994) give some clues for the last million years.

The first possibility is that insects tracked changes in the environment. As the climate gradually changed, the distribution of the insects changed so that they remained in conditions to which they were adapted. Thus *Aphodius holdereri*, the most common dung beetle in Britain 40000–20000 years ago, is no longer present in Britain but occurs at an altitude of 3000–5000 m in the

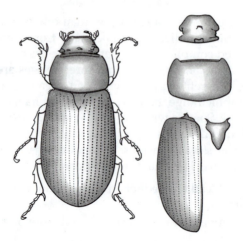

Figure 3.23 Modern *Aphodius holdereri* from the Himalayas and fossil remains of *A. holdereri* from Dorchester-on-Thames, England. Although fragments of the fossil beetle are found, there is no doubt that the two are the same species. (From Coope 1973.)

mountains of Tibet and northwest China (Figure 3.23). There are many similar examples. Two extremes are shown in Figure 3.24.

The second possibility is that the beetles tolerated changes in their environment. This could happen if there were a change in the balance of interacting species, such as competitors, predators and pathogens, but it is extremely difficult to test. We can do no more than guess at the effects of the absence of particular species in communities without detailed laboratory and field work, and even then present-day studies do not necessarily reflect the past. All we can say is that beetles could remain present in an area even if climate changes, without having to adapt in any way. Climate could change but beetle assemblages might not.

Another way beetles might tolerate change is by changing the way they use the environment. It is even harder to guess at the changes that could occur if there are subtle responses to microclimate. Indeed, the fact that insects change use of habitat to maintain a particular microclimate even if climate changes means that beetle distribution might not be as good a reflection of climate as many believe.

The third possible response to climate change is to evolve to cope with

Figure 3.24 The fossil distribution in Britain and present-day distribution in Europe of two beetles. One of these species is currently restricted to the high Arctic. The other is distributed in central and southern Europe and is extremely rare in southeast England, yet both species were once widespread in Britain. (a) *Diacheila arctica*, 16 000 years ago during a cold period in Britain. (b) *Bembidion octomaculatum*; 13 000–12 500 years ago during a warm period in Britain. (From Coope 1994.)

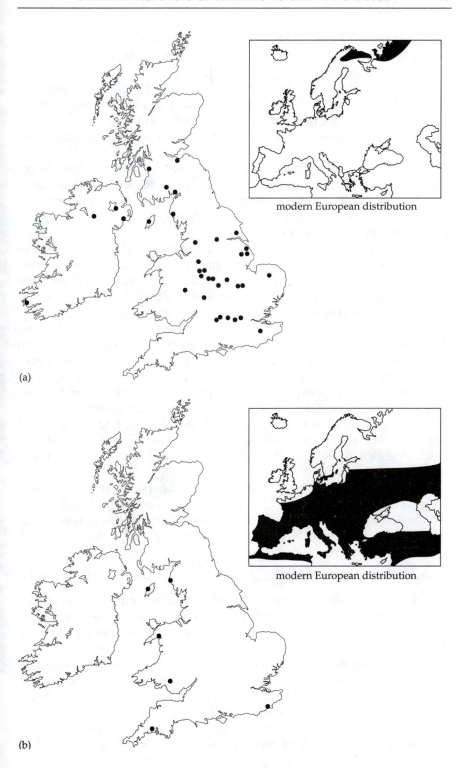

modern European distribution

(a)

modern European distribution

(b)

new conditions. However, there is little evidence of major evolutionary change in the last million years. Sibling species of beetle that can only be separated now by examination of their genitalia were separated by the same characteristics hundreds of thousands of years ago. A present-day entomologist could comfortably put names to ancient specimens. Furthermore, an ecologist could deduce the habitats at different times in the past by knowing the insect species present and seeing where such assemblages are found today.

The final possibility is that ancient species became extinct as a result of climate change. However, for beetles found in 730 000-year-old deposits in Britain, there is little if any evidence of this. The great majority of insect species from the recent past (the last million years) still occur, unchanged in any way but in different places.

The fossil record for vertebrates is less complete and there are gaps in space and time, but it is clear that movements have been just as dramatic: 120 000–110 000 years ago hippopotamus occurred in Britain and France (but not central Europe, where it was cooler) and spotted hyaena, lion and rhinoceros were associated with mixed oak forests in Britain; 70 000 years ago these species were replaced by others characteristic of cold conditions, including mammoths, horses, lemmings, musk oxen and polar bears. Such spectacular changes in distribution continue to occur. The Greenland caribou, a species of the tundra and taiga, was present in Virginia, USA, 13 500 years ago. Ice sheets started to retreat rapidly about 10 500 years ago and shrews and voles characteristic of the cold steppe disappeared from Texas. Gradual warming led to the present-day mammal fauna from around 1000 years ago. All mammals in North America had to be south of the ice sheets, which extended to 40°N in the North American midwest around 18 000 years ago (Gauthreaux 1980).

Note that many of these mammals are the same species that occur today, but in very different locations. Extinctions have occurred, perhaps due in part to climate change but for large mammals influenced much more significantly by the activities of humans.

Experimental studies: response to climate change by Australian Drosophila

Historical evidence on distribution changes, evolution and extinction is complemented by present-day research that allows processes to be examined in much finer detail. The group on which most work has been done, by Parsons (1989) and others, is the fruit fly *Drosophila*.

Drosophila flies are a good indicator of the quality of the environment. In Australia many different species are present in many forest types, ranging from humid tropical to cool temperate. They are so widespread because the larvae feed on rotting plant material and the fungi found on it. Some species are widespread and others are very restricted. Rainforest species, for example, have only low levels of the enzyme alcohol dehydrogenase and so cannot cope with substrates high in ethanol. This means they are limited to a restricted geographical distribution and a narrow range of food resources. A result is that the assemblage of *Drosophila* species at any site can be used to define the habitat type. Furthermore, the genetics of *Drosophila* species are the best understood of any animal. Thus it is possible to consider genetics and ecology together to help understand ways in which *Drosophila* – and other animals – could adapt to climate change.

How readily do *Drosophila* respond to the stress of increased temperature or greater desiccation? Field and laboratory work has shown that tropical rainforest species of *Drosophila* can be significantly affected by a temperature increase of 2°C. This level of increase would be enough to cause extinctions. However, there is variation among *Drosophila* species and among populations of the same species in tolerance of heat and cold. This suggests that it should be possible to carry out laboratory experiments in which researchers select for high temperature tolerance by the flies. In the experiments flies are exposed to the high temperature that produces a mortality of, say, 50%. The survivors parent the next generation, and generation by generation the temperature is increased. The small number of experiments using this approach on *Drosophila* and other insects show that it is actually very difficult to breed for tolerance of extreme temperature. It is easier to breed for tolerance to cold, and possible to breed for tolerance to both extremes. If it is slow and difficult in the laboratory it will be even more difficult in the wild, where many other selection pressures are operating at the same time.

Why is it difficult to have rapid genetic adaptation to higher temperatures? The problem is that metabolic processes are well tuned to the 'normal' temperature. If temperature moves too far away from this, organisms become less fit because many different metabolic processes operate less efficiently. Animals as diverse as otters and crabs can respond to stress by using extra energy for body maintenance and diverting it from growth and reproduction. Observations show that the metabolic rate of otters almost doubles after exposure to crude-oil pollution, and the maintenance cost of crab larvae doubles when they are exposed to copper and cadmium pollution.

Animals can increase their tolerance of stress by reducing their metabolic rate. Desert mammals and desert ants, for example, have a lower metabolic rate than expected when compared to similar animals in less stressful environments. The consequences of lower metabolic rate could include less movement and earlier reproduction. Even behaviours such as mate-calling by frogs and web-building in spiders are energetically expensive: the rate of O_2 consumption by grey tree frogs is proportional to the rate of calling and can be 30% higher than maximum O_2 consumption when the frogs move (Pough 1989). And web building by the spider *Agelena limbata* uses 9 to 19 times the energy used for daily maintenance (Tanaka 1989). These energetically expensive behaviours could be modified or lost completely. The animals will survive, but at a cost to growth and reproduction. If animals adapt to high stresses by reducing metabolic rate, several different stresses at the same time (e.g desiccation, pollution, high temperature) would be too much for them to endure.

However, *Drosophila* are better able to adapt to desiccation. They respond rapidly by reducing metabolic rate and this adaptation has high heritability (in other words, it is readily passed to the next generation). Reduced activity and fecundity are a result. The same flies that are adapted to the desiccation are also tolerant of other stresses, such as starvation or toxic levels of ethanol, because reducing metabolic rate is an effective general response that is successful in many different situations. Perhaps there is an underlying molecular mechanism for stress tolerance in common.

Some genotypes and species are regarded as especially 'stress tolerant' for certain stresses, and tolerance has been linked to particular genes. *Drosophila melanogaster*, for example, is well known for the metallothionein gene (*Mtn*), which allows larvae to tolerate high levels of cadmium and copper if the gene is duplicated many times on the chromosome. Some populations of *Drosophila* have many copies of *Mtn*, and these larvae tolerate the heavy metals. Other populations have fewer copies and are less tolerant. It is possible that tolerance of desiccation might be controlled just as simply. Tolerance of temperature change will certainly be much more complicated.

These studies of *Drosophila* are leading the field in combining approaches from ecology and quantitative genetics. They suggest that stress-tolerant species may persist during climate change where stress-sensitive species cannot. This has important implications for conservation and is discussed in Chapter 7.

Whether *Drosophila* species are a good model for other animals is not known but at present they are the only model we have.

Words of caution

Temperature is one of several factors that will change as part of climate change. Others must be considered at the same time as temperature if changes in animal abundances and distributions are to be explained. The complexity is shown by studies on black-throated blue warblers in the neotropics (Rodenhouse 1992). This bird breeds in hardwood forests. Warmer temperatures will increase abundance of invertebrates taken as food and will lengthen the breeding season. However, an increase in rainfall will increase egg and nestling mortality, reducing the number of fledglings. If rainfall increases by 20%, the numbers of birds fledging could decrease by 26%. If rainfall increases by 10%, the effects of temperature and rainfall will more or less balance out. If rainfall decreases by 10%, fledging could increase by 25%. Some parts of the range of this warbler will have higher rainfall, others lower, so the effects of climate change in different regions will vary. It is not wise to try to generalize!

This chapter has used many different illustrations of ways in which climate change might affect animals. Some of the examples look convincing. One reason the results seem so clear is that most studies consider only a single factor at any one time, sometimes because researchers have not bothered to consider other factors or because on rare occasions they have been lucky enough to work in a situation when only one factor changes. However, if we are to understand the effects of global environment change in the natural world, we need to consider all the different factors at the same time. The amount of information required could only be obtained if a large team worked in a coordinated way on a 'model' animal that is representative of 'typical' species, whatever they are. One danger is that the species chosen would not be 'typical'. A more serious problem is that it is difficult to persuade researchers to work together in such a coordinated way.

References

Bacci G (1965) *Sex determination*, Pergamon Press, Oxford

Bach CE (1993) Effects of microclimate and plant characteristics on the distribution of a willow flea beetle, *Altica subplicata*. *American Midland Naturalist* **130**, 193–208

Berthold P (1993) *Bird migration. A general survey*, Oxford University Press, Oxford

Berthold P, Mohr G, Querner U (1990) Steuerung und potentielle Evolutionsgeschwindigkeit des obligaten Teilzieherverhaltens: Ergebnisse eines Zweiweg – Selektionsexperiments mit der Mönchsgrasmücke (*Sylvia atricapilla*). *Journal of Ornithology* **131**, 33–45

Blem CR, Blem LB (1994) Composition and microclimate of prothonotary warbler nests. *The Auk* **111**(1), 197–200

Boag B (1985) Localised spread of virus vector nematodes adhering to farm machinery. *Nematologica* **31**, 234–5

Boag B, Crawford JW, Neilson R (1991) The effect of potential climatic changes on the geographical distribution of the plant-parasitic nematodes *Xiphinema* and *Longidorus* in Europe. *Nematologica* **37**, 312–23

Caughley G, Grice D, Barker R, Brown B (1988) The edge of the range. *Journal of Animal Ecology* **57**, 771–85

Clarke A (1987) The adaptation of aquatic animals to low temperatures. In *The effects of low temperatures on biological systems*, eds BWW Grout and GJ Morris. Edward Arnold, London, pp. 315–48

Collett CW, Ross JA, Levine KB (1992) Nicotine, RSP, and carbon dioxide levels in bars and night clubs. *Environment International* **18**(4), 347–52

Coope GR (1973) Tibetan species of dung beetle from Late Pleistocene deposits in England. *Nature* **245**, 335–6

Coope GR (1994) The response of insect faunas to glacial–interglacial climatic fluctuations. *Philosophical Transactions of the Royal Society of London B* **344**, 19–26

Cossins AR, Raynard RS (1987) Adaptive responses of animal cell membranes to temperature. In *Temperature and animal cells. Symposia of the Society for Experimental Biology* 41, eds. K Bowler and BJ Fuller pp 95–111

Cronin TM, Schneider CE (1990) Climatic influences on species. Evidence from the fossil record. *Trends in Ecology and Evolution* 5(9), 275–9

Darden TR (1972) Respiratory adaptations of a fossorial mammal, the pocket gopher (*Thomomys bottae*). *Journal of Comparative Physiology* 78, 121–37

Dusenbery DB (1989) A simple animal can use a complex stimulus pattern to find a location: nematode thermotaxis in soil. *Biological Cybernetics* 60, 431–7

Eckmann R, Pusch M (1989) The influence of temperature on the growth of young coregonids (*Coregonus lavaretus L.*) in a large prealpine lake. *Rapport et procès-verbaux des réunions. Conseil permanent internationalpour l'exploration de la mer* 191, 201–8

Eiras AE, Jepson PC (1991) Host location by *Aedes aegypti* (Diptera: Culicidae): A wind tunnel study of chemical cues. *Bulletin of Entomological Research* 81(2), 151–60

Garcia-Barros E (1988) Delayed ovarian maturation in the butterfly *Hipparchia semele* as a possible response to summer drought. *Ecological Entomology* 13, 391–8

Gatter W (1992) Timing and patterns of visible autumn migration: Can effects of global warming be detected? *Journal für Ornithologie* 133(4), 427–36

Gauthreaux SA Jr. (1980) Long term and short term climate changes. In *Animal migration, orientation and navigation*, ed. SA Gauthreaux. Academic Press, New York

Gibbs HL, Grant PR (1987) Oscillating selection on Darwin's finches. *Nature* 327, 511–13

Gilbert N (1980) Comparative dynamics of a single-host aphid. I. The evidence. *Journal of Animal Ecology* 49, 351–69

Grant PR, Grant BR (1987) The extraordinary El Niño event of 1982–83: effects on Darwin's finches on Isla Genovesa, Galápagos. *Oikos* 49, 55-66

Harrington R, Bale JS, Tachell GM (in press) Aphids in a changing climate. In *Insects in a changing environment*, eds. R Harrington and NE Stork. Proceedings of the 17th Symposium of the Royal Entomological Society, Rothhamsted Experimental Station, Harpenden, 8–10 September 1993. Academic Press, London

Hersteinsson P, Macdonald DW (1992) Interspecific competition and the geographical distribution of red and Arctic foxes *Vulpes vulpes* and *Alopex lagopus*. *Oikos* 64, 505–15

Hoffmann AA, Blows MW (1994) Species borders: ecological and evolutionary perspectives. *Trends in Ecology and Evolution* 9(6), 223–7

Holt RD (1990) The microevolutionary consequences of climate change. *Trends in Ecology and Evolution* 5(9), 311–15

Howarth FG, Stone FD (1990) Elevated carbon dioxide levels in Bayliss Cave, Australia: implications for the evolution of obligate cave species. *Pacific Science* **44**, 207–18

Johnston AM, Jukes MGM (1966) The respiratory response of the decerebrate domestic hen to inhaled carbon dioxide–air mixture. *Journal of Physiology* **184**, 38P–39P

Kobayashi F, Yamane A, Ikeda T (1984) The Japanese pine sawyer beetle as the vector of pine wilt disease. *Annual Review of Entomology* **29**, 115–35

Lawton JH (in press) The response of insect populations to environmental change. In *Insects in a changing environment*, eds. R Harrington and NE Stork. Proceedings of the 17th Symposium of the Royal Entomological Society, Rothhamsted Experimental Station, Harpenden, 8–10 September 1993. Academic Press, London

Lindenmayer DB, Nix HA, McMahon JP, Hutchinson MF, Tanton MT (1991) The conservation of Leadbeater's possum, *Gymnobelideus leadbeateri* (McCoy): a case study of the use of bioclimatic modelling. *Journal of Biogeography* **18**, 371–83

Logan JA, Wollkind DG, Hoyt SC, Tanigoshi LK (1976) An analytic model for description of temperature dependent rate phenomena in arthropods. *Environmental Entomology* **6**, 1133–40

Macpherson AH (1964) A northward range extension of the red fox in the eastern Canadian arctic. *Journal of Mammalogy* **45**, 138–40

Mader HJ, Schell C, Kornacker P (1990) Linear barriers to arthropod movements in the landscape. *Biological Conservation* **54**, 209–22

Malmgren BA, Kennett JP (1978) Test size variation in *Globigerina bulloides* in response to Quaternary palaeoceanographic changes. *Nature* **275**, 123–4

Menusan H Jr (1935) Effects of constant light, temperature and humidity on the rate and total amount of oviposition of the bean weevil, *Bruchus obtectus* Say. *Journal of Economic Entomology* **28**, 448–53

Nicolas G, Sillans D (1989) Immediate and latent effects of carbon dioxide on insects. *Annual Review of Entomology* **34**, 97–116

Parsons PA (1989) Environmental stresses and conservation of natural populations. *Annual Review of Ecology and Systematics* **20**, 29–49

Pough FH (1989) Organismal performance and Darwinian fitness: approaches and interpretations. *Physiological Zoology* **62**(2), 199–236

Repasky RR (1991) Temperature and the northern distributions of wintering birds. *Ecology* **72**(6), 2274–85

Rodenhouse NI (1992) Potential effects of climate change on a neotropical migrant landbird. *Conservation Biology* **6**(2), 263–72

Schmidt-Nielsen K (1979) *Animal physiology: adaption and environment*, Cambridge University Press, Cambridge

Seeley TD (1974) Atmospheric carbon dioxide regulation in the honey-bee (*Apis mellifera*) colonies. *Journal of Insect Physiology* **20**, 2301–5

Seiler J (1920) Geschlechtschromosomenuntersuchungen an Psychiden. I. Experimentelle Beeinflussung der Geschlechtsbestimmenden Reifeteilungen bei *Talaeporia tubulosa*. *Archiv für Zellforschung* **15**, 249–68

Smith DH, Goldenberg DP, King J (1984) Use of temperature sensitive mutants to dissect pathways of protein folding and subunit interaction. In *The protein folding problem*, ed DB Wetlaufer. Westview Press, Colorado, pp 115–43

Smith MH, Smith MW, Scott SL, Liu EH, Jones JC (1983) Rapid evolution in a post-thermal environment. *Copeia* 1983, 193–7

Sorhannus U, Fenster EJ, Burckle LH, Hoffman A (1988) Cladogenetic and anagenetic changes in the morphology of *Rhizosolenia praebergonii* Mukhina. *Historical Biology* **1**, 185–205

Tanaka K (1989) Energetic cost of web construction and its effect on web relocation in the web-building spider *Agelena limbata*. *Oecologia* **81**, 459–64

Thomas JA (1983) The ecology and conservation of *Lysandra bellargus* (Lepidoptera: Lycaenidae) in Britain. *Journal of Applied Ecology* **20**, 59–83

Thomas JA (1991) Rare species conservation: case studies of European butterflies. In *The scientific management of temperate communities for conservation*, eds. IF Spellerberg, FB Goldsmith and MG Morris. Blackwell Scientific Publications, Oxford

Thomas J, Lewington R (1991) *The butterflies of Britain and Ireland*. Dorling Kindersley, London

Thomas PR (1981) Migration of *Longidorus elongatus*, *Xiphinema diversicaudatum* and *Dytylenchus dipsaci* in soil. *Nematologia Mediterranea* **9**, 75-81

Warnes ML, Finlayson LH (1985) Responses of the stable fly, *Stomoxys calcitrans* (L.) (Diptera: Muscidae), to carbon dioxide and other host odours. I. Activation. *Bulletin of Entomological Research* **75**, 519–27

Westerberg H (1984) The orientation of fish and the vertical stratification at fine- and micro-structure scales. In *Mechanisms of migration in fishes*, eds. JD McCleave, GP Arnold, JJ Dodson and WH Neill. Plenum Press, New York and London

With KA, Webb DR (1993) Microclimate of ground nests: the relative importance of radiative cover and wind breaks for three grassland species. *The Condor* **95**, 401–13

Further reading

Briggs DEG, Crowther PR (1990) *Palaeobiology. A synthesis*, Blackwell Scientific Publications, Oxford

Research on GEC has shown the value of studies in palaeobiology. This book gives wide-ranging and comprehensive coverage of the major fields of palaeobiology, highlighting studies of changes in the past that shed light on an understanding of changes in the present.

Davenport J (1992) *Animal life at low temperature*, Chapman & Hall, London.

A fascinating and lucid account of all manner of ways in which animals cope with the cold and very cold.

Harrington R, Stork NE (in press) *Insects in a changing environment.* Proceedings of the 17th Symposium of the Royal Entomological Society, Rothhamsted Experimental Station, Harpenden 8–10 September 1993. Academic Press, London

Last J, Gudotti TL (1990) Implications for human health of global ecological changes. *Public Health Reviews* **18**, 49–68

Leaf A (1989) Potential health effects of global climatic change and environmental changes. *New England Journal of Medicine* **321**(23), 1577–83

4 Species interactions and communities

Introduction

A community is a collection of species that are found together in space and time. Each of the species in a community is represented by a number of individuals, forming a population which will have properties such as birth rate, death rate and density. A community can be defined at different scales, for example the northern coniferous forest or the species in a small pond. A community is not just a collection of independent species: many of the species will interact through processes such as competition, predation and parasitism. An important aspect of all communities is that they change with time. Changes may occur as a result of seasonal changes in the environment or over longer periods in response to environmental changes and as a consequence of species interactions.

Past climate change, such as that experienced since the last glacial maximum, has altered the composition of plant communities, but two factors make the current human-made environmental changes different from those that occurred in the past. First, the rate of warming predicted as a consequence of the greenhouse effect is much faster than before. The temperature change between the end of the last glacial maximum 18 000 years ago and today is about 5°C. It is predicted that greenhouse warming will increase global temperature by 3°C in the next century. Secondly, the changes in temperature will be accompanied by a rapid increase in the concentration of CO_2, which also has a profound effect on plant performance. Therefore, the reaction of modern communities to global environmental change (GEC) may be different from that which has been catalogued in response to past climate changes. Nevertheless, the broad pattern of past responses provides us with a valuable picture of the interaction between climate and community composition.

Predicting future changes in communities is very difficult given the complexity of the interactions that can occur. Some insight into the magnitude of possible changes in community composition is essential to judge how much GEC will disrupt the communities with which we are familiar. This has an important input into how the conservation of communities is achieved, or whether it is achievable at all.

In this chapter the possible impacts of both CO_2 and temperature on communities will be discussed, starting at the level of the interactions between species and then considering the whole community response. There are several different approaches to the problem of predicting and understanding the response of communities to GEC. Controlled experiments where temperature and CO_2 concentration are altered and the effect on species performance is assessed is one method. This approach has the advantage that some understanding of the mechanisms by which community changes may occur can be achieved. But what happens to a community as a whole must also take into account the processes of extinctions within the community and the invasion of species from adjacent locations. Also disturbances such as fire and drought can have a particularly strong effect, as such events can clear an old community away and allow a new one to establish.

Effects of GEC on plant assemblages

As discussed in Chapter 2, both temperature and the concentration of CO_2 have profound effects on plant performance. Furthermore, there is great variation in the response of different species to both these environmental factors. Therefore, if the environment changes, in any given community some species will do better than others and as a result competitive balances will shift. It can be inferred from this that the effects of GEC on natural communities, although difficult to predict, are likely to be disruptive. Some of the pathways by which communities may be affected are illustrated in Figure 4.1. However, for a long time it may be difficult to sift out the direct impact of GEC, as even under relatively uniform environmental conditions most communities are in a state of constant change, although in some this may be very slow.

This section will focus on the impact of CO_2 concentration on plant interactions, and will be largely based on information from studies conducted in controlled-environment facilities. Such facilities range from plant growth rooms, where temperature, light and CO_2 concentration are tightly controlled, to field-based chambers where the light and temperature track those of the field environment but the atmosphere can be enriched in CO_2. Results from such studies need to be treated with some caution, as the precise environmental conditions in such facilities are never the same as those in the real world.

It is important to remember that even in the absence of dramatic climatic change the concentration of CO_2 will continue to increase and will affect

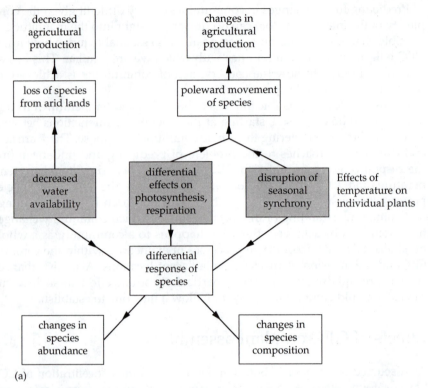

(a)

Figure 4.1   Pathways by which temperature and changes in atmospheric CO_2 concentration could affect plant communities. (a) Effects of temperature; (b) effects of high CO_2.

plant communities worldwide. There is more evidence for the effect of temperature on whole communities, and this will be covered later in this chapter.

Elevated CO_2 may have a direct fertilizing effect by supplying more CO_2 to the site of carboxylation which can increase plant growth (see Chapter 2). However, high CO_2 can also stimulate growth by increasing nitrogen use efficiency, water use efficiency and light use efficiency. Changes in these efficiencies will increase growth, particularly in the situations where carbon, nitrogen, water and light are limiting. Species responses in each of these areas will be different, and this could cause changes at the community level (Figure 4.1).

Because of the nature of the C_4 photosynthetic pathway, C_4 species benefit much less from elevated CO_2 than C_3 species (see Chapter 2). This raises an important question: are C_4 species at a competitive disadvantage in elevated CO_2? In the experiment illustrated in Figure 4.2, two annual species, one a C_3 and one a C_4, were grown together under competitive conditions and the surviving biomass was measured (Bazzaz and Carlson 1984). It

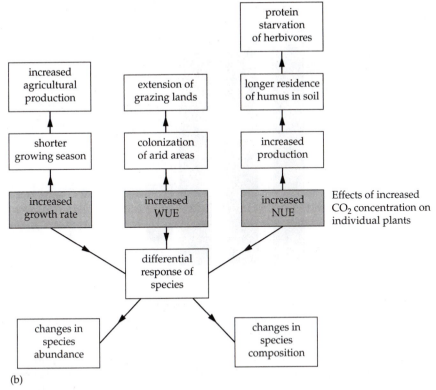

(b)

Figure 4.1 *Continued.*

showed clearly that the C_4 species loses out to the C_3 species as CO_2 concentration rises. It is interesting to note that the effect is more extreme under wetter conditions. This is probably because C_4 species are inherently more efficient in the use of water, and under wet conditions have less of an initial advantage at a lower CO_2 concentration.

This simple experiment confirms the idea that CO_2 concentration can substantially affect competitive interactions between species, but it gives little insight into the mechanism by which the differences in performance are attained.

The principal resources for which plants compete during growth are light, water and nutrients. An individual which grows slightly faster than those surrounding it will extend further, both above and below ground, and by doing so will be able to draw resources from a larger volume. This prevents its neighbours from gaining access to these resources and ensures that the faster-growing individual remains dominant. Thus quite small differences in growth rate can be amplified in a competitive situation. But, in different physical environments, different resources may be limiting. In the under-

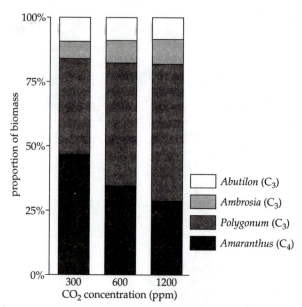

Figure 4.2   The effect of an increase in the concentration of atmospheric CO_2 on the relative performance of C_3 and C_4 species grown in competition. (From Bazzaz and Carlson 1984.)

storey of a tropical rain forest light is a commodity in short supply, and the growth of plants is often suppressed by this. If a gap appears in the canopy when a tree falls there is a sudden increase in the amount of light hitting the forest floor. This stimulates the germination of seeds and the rapid growth of a number of species. The growth of several such species was compared under normal and twice normal CO_2 concentrations (Reekie and Bazzaz 1989). All the plants were C_3, and when grown individually it was found that most grew only slightly faster in elevated CO_2. There was also no evidence of a particular species benefiting more from the elevated CO_2 conditions. However, when grown in competition there was a difference in the relative success of the species in elevated CO_2 when compared with normal CO_2. At 350 ppm CO_2 one species of the genus *Senna* showed very rapid stem growth and dominated the canopy. However, at higher CO_2 concentrations the stem growth of several other species was stimulated more than that of *Senna*, and these did relatively better in competition (Figure 4.3). Thus in this case it is not the absolute differences in growth that are important but the degree to which CO_2 affects allocation patterns. This is because the major determinant of success here is the ability to extend and overtop competitors.

The ability to compete for light by overtopping competitors may be of paramount importance in an opening in a tropical rain forest, but it may be of little importance in a nutrient-poor grassland. In any given environment relative success will depend on a specific set of interactions. Whether CO_2 affects relative success depends on its impact on these dominant interac-

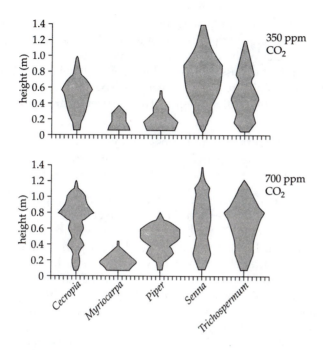

Figure 4.3   The effect of an increase in the concentration of CO_2 on the distribution of leaf area in a growing rainforest tree seedling canopy. This may have an important impact on which species succeed in recolonizing gaps in the rain forest. The width of the profile represents the leaf area at the height in the canopy indicated on the axis. (From Reekie and Bazzaz 1989.)

tions. Therefore, the impact of CO_2 on different communities is inherently difficult to predict.

Species that grow in the same area are not necessarily in competition. Nevertheless, changes in relative performance may change the composition of the community in the long term by favouring one species over another. If a particular species benefits more from environmental change it will set more seed or produce more vegetative propagules. White oak and yellow poplar are both important components of the eastern deciduous forests in North America. Oak has a fixed growth pattern where the buds that grow into leaves develop in the previous year. In contrast, poplar can elongate and initiate leaves during the growing season. It was therefore predicted that poplar would have a greater response to high CO_2 because of greater leaf initiation (Norby and O'Neill 1991). In an experiment which compared the response of these two species to elevated CO_2 it was found unexpectedly that oak increased leaf production by as much as 31%, but poplar by only 22%. It might be that the relative abundance of oak will increase in these forests. This example also emphasizes that it is difficult to predict the impact of elevated CO_2 on communities, as there may be no general physiological rules applying to species with different inherent characteristics.

If groups of species with known characteristics were to respond differently to CO_2 it might be possible to deduce some general patterns in the response of communities to CO_2. Herbaceous species have been classified according to their ecological strategies. Three extreme strategies have been identified:

• species which can tolerate stress ('stress tolerators');
• species which can compete successfully ('competitors');
• species which can effectively colonize disturbed sites ('ruderals').

Few species fall neatly into one these three categories and species with intermediate characteristics can be identified. The effect of CO_2 concentration on growth was examined in 27 herbaceous species with different ecological strategies (Hunt et al. 1991). The ratio of yield at 350 ppm to that at 540 ppm CO_2 was calculated after about 8 weeks. Growth of species in the 'competitor' category was stimulated most, with a ratio of 1.55 suggesting increased growth in elevated CO_2. The average ratio for stress tolerators and ruderals was 1.0. In general the effect of CO_2 decreased the further away species were from the competitor strategy. This argues that CO_2 has the greatest effect in situations where competition between species is an important factor controlling plant community structure.

Reproductive success must be an important influence on community composition. The concentration of CO_2 can affect the timing of flowering, the proportion of resources allocated to seed production, and seed quality. An example is a study which looked at a community composed of annual species growing on disturbed ground in Texas (Bazzaz 1990). When grown in elevated CO_2 two species showed earlier flowering, one later, and one unchanged. Early flowering is important as drought can abruptly end the growing season of this community. These changes could alter the composition of the community by favouring the earlier-flowering species in years with an early drought.

If CO_2 affects demographic parameters strongly, the effects on plant population dynamics may be far-reaching and difficult to predict. The subtlety of the effects of elevated CO_2 are illustrated by a study on an annual plant *Abutilon theophrasti* (Bazzaz et al. 1992). Under natural conditions this plant can occur in almost pure stands with very high plant density. In this species seed production is highest at intermediate plant density: isolated plants do not perform well and nor do tightly packed plants. This can lead to unstable population oscillations as a result of the following sequence of events:

1. If a lot of seed are produced one year the density of the offspring is very high and a small but variable number of seeds are produced in the following year.

2. This will result in a low or moderate density of plants. Therefore, seed production in the third year may be either large or small.

High CO_2 increased growth so that there was more severe competition between plants, and seed production was suppressed at a lower plant density. Also, when there was a low plant density elevated CO_2 increased the probability of flowering and more seeds were produced. This combination of factors would increase the likelihood of the population exhibiting wide fluctuations in numbers.

There are surprisingly few examples where a natural community has been exposed to the combined effects of CO_2 and temperature. Two well documented studies have been performed over a period of several years. One was based on the estuarine marsh of Chesapeake Bay in the United States (Arp et al. 1993). Small chambers were placed over patches of the community in the field and fed with air containing either ambient or twice ambient CO_2 concentrations. The community was composed principally of two species, a C_3 plant Scirpus olneyi and a C_4 grass Spartina patens. The C_4 was not affected by CO_2 enrichment but there was a strong effect on the C_3. For Scirpus, biomass increased, shoot density increased and ageing of the shoots was delayed. In addition, it was found that after 4 years there was no down-regulation of photosynthesis in Scirpus plants exposed to elevated CO_2. The community is therefore likely to become increasingly dominated by the C_3 species as CO_2 concentrations rise.

A similar experiment was carried out on Arctic tundra vegetation (this is one of the areas of the world likely to experience the most dramatic climate change; see Chapter 2). Small controlled-environment glasshouses were placed in the field on the Alaskan tundra and the effects of the combination of a doubling of CO_2 concentration and a 4°C temperature rise were evaluated (Tissue and Oechel 1987). There was no significant effect on overall production, and within 3 weeks of the start of the growing season the rate of photosynthesis in the elevated CO_2 treatment had fallen to compensate for the increased CO_2 concentration.

Thus the effects on these two communities were found to be very different. Alaskan tundra is a nutrient-poor system, and the rate of decomposition and nutrient release is slow in the cool soil where there is always ice a metre or two below the surface. Plant growth is largely dependent on the supply of nutrients, which limits the effect of elevated CO_2. In contrast, nutrient supply is plentiful in the Chesapeake Bay community, which allows CO_2 enrichment to have a strong effect.

There are in most communities many complex interactions that regulate the species composition. For example, in a grassland community the success of species will depend on the mechanisms of clonal reproduction, investment in seed production and the probability of seedling establishment. High CO_2 can have an impact on all of these. Some species may be able to photosynthesize more and therefore put more resources into clonal growth. Some might be able to produce more seed and therefore increase the probability of establishment from seed. Seedling survival may also be affected. High CO_2 will assist species to retain water during the onset of drought, and this may favour some species more than others. In such a community different species develop at different times, reaching a peak of biomass at different points in the growing season. If a species is able to develop slightly earlier due to the effect of CO_2 or temperature bringing forward its phenology, then it may preempt resources and the composition of the community will be radically altered by a seemingly small difference in performance. All this illustrates that in a single community CO_2 concentration can have myriad effects. Which will be the most important in disturbing the community is very difficult to predict, but it is highly likely that the community will experience some sort of disturbance.

Plant–animal interactions

Effects of elevated CO_2 on plant–herbivore interactions

Chapter 2 explains how elevated CO_2 can stimulate carbon assimilation, nitrogen dilution and different patterns of carbon allocation in plants, and increase plant growth. How could these changes affect animals that feed on the plants?

Additional carbohydrate in the leaves has several possible effects. If the carbohydrate is in the form of starch, an essential source of energy for animals, the leaves become more digestible to herbivores. This means that a greater proportion of the food that is consumed can be digested and utilized. If the extra carbohydrate is a structural compound such as cellulose or hemicellulose, the leaves are less digestible. Current evidence suggests that the first possibility is much more common than the second.

Whatever the extra carbohydrate, it could significantly dilute the concentration of nitrogen. Nitrogen, rather than carbon, is the factor that limits the performance of herbivores, and also decomposers such as bacteria, fungi and detritivores. This has been illustrated many times for all kinds of plant-feeding animals, from isopods to mammals and birds (Mattson 1980). Plants grown in elevated CO_2 have a lower concentration of nitrogen and many insect herbivores are forced to consume 20–80% more plant material in order to take in sufficient nitrogen. This compensation allows them to maintain growth rate and overall performance. The results of Lindroth et al.'s (1993) study on three species of deciduous trees and two species of caterpillar shown in Figure 4.4 are typical.

One effect of extra structural carbohydrates is an increase in leaf toughness: experiments have shown that the leaves of quaking aspen and red oak are 10-20% tougher when the trees are grown in high CO_2. Toughness affects how easily small herbivores can consume the leaves. Generalists able to feed on a wide range of plants tend to be larger than specialists, and a likely reason is that their large body size allows them to feed on a greater diversity of plants, including the tougher ones. A good illustration of this is a species of

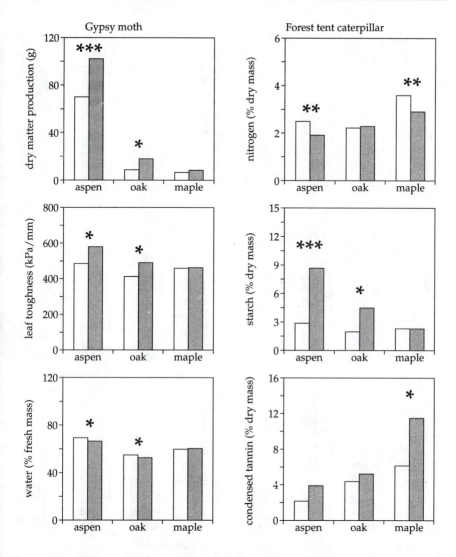

Figure 4.4   Changes in plant quality for three tree species grown in present-day (385 ppm; open bars) and elevated CO_2 (642 ppm; shaded bars) environments and growth responses of forest tent caterpillars and gypsy moth caterpillars. The data show that different species of tree and of caterpillar have unique responses, and that it is unwise to try to generalize.

One-year-old trees – quaking aspen, red oak and sugar maple – were grown in controlled environment rooms for 60 days. Feeding trials with caterpillars were carried out after 50 days using one set of trees. A second set of trees was harvested at 60 days and analysed for physical and chemical characteristics likely to affect herbivore growth. It was predicted that aspen would be affected most by elevated CO_2 and maple

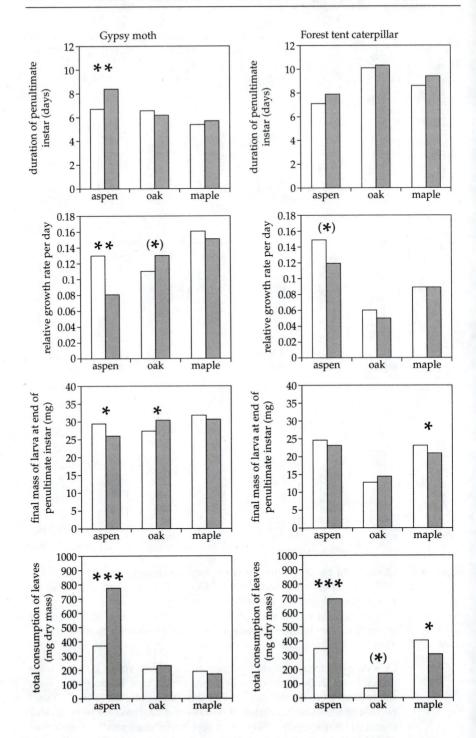

affected least, because aspen is fastest growing and maple is slowest. This was indeed the case for dry matter production, but the magnitude and direction of effects on biomass allocation and on metabolites in leaves depended on tree species. Aspen had the largest change in storage carbon compounds (starch) and maple had the largest change in defensive carbon compounds (tannins).

The effects on caterpillars depended on leaf chemistry. Even though consumption rates of aspen grown in high CO_2 increased dramatically, caterpillar growth rates declined. The two species of caterpillars had different responses to changes in oak and in maple.

Statistically significant differences between results for present day and elevated CO_2 are indicated by stars: *** = $P<0.001$, ** = $P<0.01$, * = $P<0.05$, (*) = $P<0.1$. Remember that a result that is significant at $P=0.05$ would occur by chance in 5% of experiments even if there is no difference in real life. Here we display the results of 24 different tests, so we should expect at least one of the 'significant' results not to be repeated if the tests were carried out again. Because it is a matter of pure chance, we cannot say which. (From Lindroth et al. 1993.)

skipper butterfly in Japan. It has three generations per year. In the spring and early summer generations, newly hatched caterpillars feed on soft tender leaves. However, tender leaves are not available later in the year so the late summer generation is forced to feed on the much tougher leaves of grasses. Eggs (and therefore newly hatched caterpillars) of the late summer generation are twice as large as those in spring and early summer, most likely because the caterpillars need larger mouthparts to cope with the tougher plant material. If leaves become tougher as a result of elevated CO_2, some species and especially smaller individuals, could be significantly affected.

Changes in the water content of the foliage occur when plants are grown in high CO_2, but some studies show higher water concentrations and some show lower. Insect growth rates are lower when water content is low. However, metabolic water produced as a byproduct of the digestion of starch could partly compensate for this. Certainly for grasshoppers, metabolic water could have a significant effect in maintaining growth rate (Johnson and Lincoln 1991).

Often just as important to feeding insects are allelochemicals. These are chemicals produced by one organism that are toxic or inhibitory to another. Many, like tannins in maples, flavonoids in sagebrush and terpenes in peppermint, are based on carbon. In theory, plants in a high-CO_2 environment should be able to allocate more carbon to produce more of these allelochemicals. In practice increases have not been demonstrated, and in some experiments the amounts of allelochemicals actually decrease when CO_2 concentrations are higher. Even so, plants may still be better defended because the amount of allelochemical per unit of nitrogen could be greater.

Other allelochemicals, such as pyridine alkaloids in tobacco, are based on nitrogen. The only study so far published for any nitrogen-based allelochemicals suggests that their levels are lower for plants in a high CO_2 concentration. This is not surprising, because the concentration of nitrogen in the plant is diluted. The result could be a poorer defence against herbivores.

Even though some insect herbivores seem to be able to adjust feeding behaviour to maintain their growth rate, they could still have a decreased fitness. One possibility is that insects that feed for longer each day or grow more slowly could be exposed to predators and parasitoids for longer. Another possibility is that slower-growing insects may not be able to complete their growth within a short summer season, and so cannot survive the onset of winter. Another possibility is that the final adult size is smaller: this matters because size is closely correlated with fecundity in females and the size of the male's spermatophore (the sac containing sperm and other materials produced by glands in the reproductive tract of male insects and transferred to females).

Present-day studies are investigating whether or not these patterns have a significance in natural communities. Some important questions still to be answered include the following:

- Nearly all experiments have used plants and insects from environments at normal CO_2 levels which are exposed to elevated CO_2 for only the short duration of the experiment. But are the results the same if experiments use elevated CO_2 for many generations of plants and of insects?
- In experiments, insects feeding on plants in high-CO_2 environments created in open-top chambers are present in smaller numbers than outside. Will this lower population density be found more generally?
- What effects are there on animals such as predators and parasitoids at other trophic levels and on the ecosystem? Effects will depend on how the population dynamics of the insects are affected.
- Does elevated CO_2 affect the choice by insects of plant species or particular parts of these plants?
- How do changing feeding patterns by herbivores affect the flow of energy and of nutrients?

In contrast with the detailed work on leaf-chewing insects, interactions between plants and other herbivores, such as sap-sucking insects and grazing mammals, have hardly been studied.

Effects of climate

Changes in climate can increase the stress on plants, especially at the edges of their distribution. One cause of stress is drought. A decline in soil moisture could cause desiccation of food plants, early leaf loss and the death of seedlings. On the other hand, water-stressed plants are likely to be warmer because they are less cooled by transpiration; the body temperature of insects on these plants could be 2–4°C (in one study 10–15°C!) warmer, enough to increase growth rate significantly. Also plant defences might

Plate 1

Plate 2

Plate 3

Plates 1 – 3 Before logging, the amount of carbon stored per unit area of land in tropical forest is very high. Plate 1 shows undisturbed primary forest in the background, in comparison to disturbed forest containing pioneer species in the foreground. After logging (Plate 2), the carbon density falls and there will be a net release of CO_2 into the atmosphere. However, as the forest recovers from logging the carbon stored slowly increases. Plate 3 shows forest approximately five years after logging. These examples are from Southeast Sabah in the 438 km^2 Danum Valley Conservation Area, Malaysia. (Courtesy of Dr M. C. Press, Department of Plant and Animal Sciences, University of Sheffield.)

Plate 4 Mist netting allows birds to be trapped, marked by uniquely colour-coded rings and released. Daily, seasonal and lifetime movement patterns of individuals can be detected if locations of ringed birds are subsequently recorded. (Courtesy of Chris W. Dee.)

Plate 5 (Opposite, top) Inside the 'Ecotron' at the NERC Centre for Population Biology, Imperial College, University of London. This is a laboratory facility in which simple artificial ecosystems can be used to test ecological ideas that are difficult to study in the field (Lawton *et al.* 1993, Kareiva 1994). Simple communities contain up to 40 species of plants and invertebrate animals, together with soil microorganisms in four trophic levels. Care must be taken when choosing the species to be used. Plant species chosen have a short generation time, do not require vernalization and reproduce by self-pollination (avoiding the need for pollinators in the Ecotron). Animals include earthworms, snails, leaf-mining flies (the chewing herbivore), aphids (the sucking herbivore), and parasitic wasps. Published studies include the effects of biodiversity on community function (Naeem *et al.* 1994). The facility is now being used to investigate the impacts of GEC on communities, with replicated experiments under different levels of CO_2 and temperature for present-day and future conditions. (Courtesy of Central Office of Information/NERC Centre for Population Biology, Imperial College, London.)

Plate 5

Plate 6(a)

Plate 6(b)

Plate 6 Bleaching of coral. Plate 6(a) shows a healthy coral whilst Plate 6(b) shows a severely bleached example of *Montastraea* from the Anse Chastanet reef in St Lucia. (Courtesy of Dr Lynne Barratt, Hunting Aquatic Resources, University of York.)

Present day CO$_2$ 2 x CO$_2$

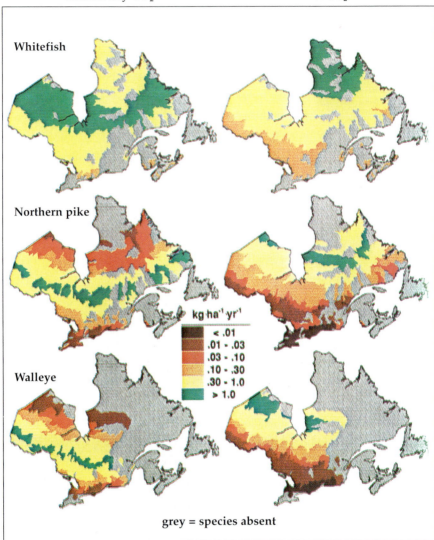

Plate 7 Predicted river fish yields in eastern Canada for current and doubled CO$_2$ scenarios. The model was created using maps of current species distribution, maps of mean annual air temperature and temperature increases predicted by the GISS model. Estimates of yield are based on the biology of the fish and on the availability of suitable rivers and lakes in different parts of the region. (After Minns and Moore 1992.)

become less effective and increase susceptibility to herbivores (Mattson and Haack 1987).

If the flowering period is shorter, the availability of nectar for nectar-feeding insects would be reduced and in drier environments nectar could become more viscous. This could affect the feeding rate (Pivnick and McNeil 1985). For many butterflies, nectar intake affects the number of eggs that are laid. So, even if extra generations are triggered by early springs and warmer summers, they might fail.

As a result of climate changes the whole assemblage of herbivores feeding on any plant is likely to change as herbivores are influenced in positive or negative ways by changes in temperature and humidity and become more or less abundant. GEC could affect herbivore–predator or herbivore–parasitoid interactions. Changes in these and in the quality of the food plant could be enough to release potential pests from the influence of their natural enemies and to cause outbreaks (i.e. explosive increases in abundance). Unusual pest damage and behaviour might be a good early indicator of climate change, especially as detailed monitoring of pests is already carried out.

We have already shown that climate change can cause changes in phenology (timings through the year) for plants (see Chapter 2) and animals phenology (see Chapter 3). For animals, synchronizing with seasonal changes in the quality and availability of their food plants can be critical.

Many caterpillars hatch from their eggs at precisely the time of bud burst. Timing must be precise because they can feed on new leaves which are soft and have not built up large amounts of allelochemicals. In some years bud burst is earlier than others, and newly hatched caterpillars cope with this by active dispersal on wind currents from tree to tree and by accepting many different tree species, or by resisting starvation for a considerable time. Newly hatched obscure wainscot caterpillars that weigh only 0.17 mg can survive for 6 days without food and can move as rapidly as 268 cm/h (Reavey 1992).

However, GEC could affect the synchrony between bud burst and insect emergence if plants and insects use different cues to trigger these events. Dewar and Watt (1992) examined the phenologies of sitka spruce and winter moths in Scotland. Bud burst of the tree is closely linked to winter chilling and temperature, and for sitka spruce is not likely to change by more than a few days in a warmer climate. Hatching of caterpillars is closely linked to temperature and is likely to occur up to 3 weeks earlier. Thus bud burst and the appearance of insects could be separated by several weeks. Even if some caterpillars hatch late and are able to feed on the earliest buds, the effect on the moths would be severe. We do not know whether or not the gradual change in climate will allow the moths to evolve to maintain synchrony with the plant, but in some insects different populations have different phenologies depending on their food plant.

Something is also known about possible effects of climate change on larger herbivores. A 4-year study of rabbits in eastern England by Bell and Webb

(1991) showed close links between weather conditions and reproductive characteristics. Two cooler years were followed by two warmer years, which had significantly higher minimum ground temperatures, more hours of sunshine and less snowfall. Some of the major differences in reproductive characteristics are listed in Table 4.1.

It is likely that climate changes do not affect the rabbits directly: instead, they are likely to influence the quality and quantity of food available. One chemical particularly common in young growing seedlings is DIMBOA (2,4-dihydroxy-7-methoxy-2H-1,4-benzoxazin-3(4H)-one). When plants are damaged by a herbivore this is rapidly converted to 6-MBOA. When animals eat 6-MBOA, it is a reliable cue that the plant growing season has begun at the end of a cold winter or a summer drought. However much the environment fluctuates from year to year, 6-MBOA can indicate the best time to produce young.

Table 4.1   Effects of weather on timing of reproduction of rabbits in eastern England. (After Bell and Webb 1991.)

	1987	1988	1989	1990
Weather conditions months in which snow cover recorded	3	3	0	0
months with mean minimum ground temperature < 0 °C	6	5	3	3
Male testes largest*	May	April	January	February
First female oestrus*	February	February	January	January
Period over which young emerge	4.5 months	4.5 months	5.5 months	5.5 months
First appearance of young above ground	April	April	February	February
Number of young per female	7.2	6.1	10.1	9.1

* These two characteristics can easily be assessed by trapping and examining the rabbits, then releasing them. Measurements of the testis allow an estimate of testis weight to be made. Whether a female is in oestrus can be assessed from the appearance of the external genitalia.

Responses of plants to herbivory

Plants influence herbivores, but how do they respond to herbivory? When plants lose leaf area they compensate for lost leaves by growing more of them. They also maintain their reproductive output. Both of these are at the expense of root growth. If plants are grown in high CO_2, they might be better able to compensate for herbivore damage because they grow in an environment with more carbon and potentially better water relations. But in experiments on plantain *Plantago lanceolata*, plants grown in elevated CO_2 (700 ppm) responded to herbivory in the same way as plants grown at ambient CO_2 concentrations. Under both conditions, shoot weight and reproductive weight were not affected by the removal or leaves (the experimenters' version of 'herbivory') because the plant replaced them with new growth. In both environments plants compensated by reduced root growth, but with a greater proportional reduction in root growth in high CO_2 (Fajer *et al.* 1991).

Thus, at least in this study, plants in high CO_2 seem no more able to compensate for herbivore damage. In fact, the impact of herbivory on individuals that are eaten might be worse because the differences between damaged and undamaged plants will be proportionally greater in high CO_2. One reason is that damaged plants will lose more potential growth than undamaged plants. Another is that damaged plants will have very much smaller root systems than undamaged plants, and will be at a competitive disadvantage.

Interactions of plants and animals with pathogens

Growth rate and allocation of resources in plants and animals influences their vulnerability to pathogens. Physiological changes due to elevated CO_2 will surely have a significant effect on plant responses to microorganisms that include mechanical barriers to infection, secondary compounds such as phenolics and tannins, and compensatory growth of injured tissue. However, the effects of the changing carbon–nitrogen ratio on pathogens have not so far been studied.

Stresses reduce the vigour and resistance of trees and make them more vulnerable to disease. Lack of water, for example, increases the susceptibility of loblolly pines to *Fomes annosus* root rot and the susceptibility of Highland bentgrass to *Pythium* blight. For other diseases, wet conditions increase susceptibility because plant surfaces must be wet for many hours if spores are to germinate. Pathogenic organisms themselves are likely to be affected in a positive way in some places and a negative way in other places by changes in temperature and moisture, and this complicates the picture.

Predictions can more easily be made for the effects of temperature change on interactions between plants and pathogens. The cottonwood leaf rust is a fungus that has the potential to become a major disease of cottonwood (a type of poplar important in paper manufacture in the southern United States). At present it overwinters at low latitudes, where the mean low temperature in winter is >4°C. It can also overwinter at higher latitudes by using larches as winter hosts, from which it spreads to warmer regions in the growing season. Higher winter temperatures could allow the rust to spread north into the main cottonwood areas (Fosberg 1989).

Interactions between mutualists

Mutualism is an interaction from which both species benefit. Mutualists include plants and their pollinators, herbivores and gut bacteria, termites and fungi that break down cellulose, and plants and mycorrhizas (symbiotic fungi which assist plants in the uptake of phosphorus from the soil).

Pollinators often have very specific relationship with particular plant species. If the plant is affected by environmental change, its pollinators are too. One possible effect of elevated CO_2 is a change in the composition of plant secretions, such as nectar used by pollinators or root exudates used by mutualistic mycorrhizal fungi. Carbon concentrations are likely to be higher and nitrogen concentrations possibly lower, with positive effects on some mutualists and negative effects on others, depending on whether the pollinator benefits more from carbon or from nitrogen.

Specificity of interactions

Interactions among mutualists are often extremely specific. Interactions between herbivore and host or between predator and prey can also be very specific. One highly specific predator–prey interaction is the Everglades kite, which feeds only on the apple snail *Pomacea caliginosa*. But as well as specialists there are many generalists. These include caterpillars that feed on the leaves of any deciduous tree or bees that pollinate whatever flowers are available, or goats that eat just about anything. Figure 4.5 shows that the proportion of specialists and generalists varies for different sorts of interactions. The advantages and disadvantages of each are the subject of a continuing debate.

This is important because, at times of change, species that have close interactions with one or a few other species are the most likely to be significantly affected. On the other hand, ecosystems in which the many components interact with each other will be more stable than ones in which there are fewer interactions. Put in the language of food webs, a food web with more links per species is usually more resilient than one with fewer linkages. Pests and pathogens are often very specific to particular hosts. Indeed, one reason why many are particularly prominent as pests or pathogens in the first place is that they have few interactions with other organisms to keep them in check. We might therefore expect the early effects of GEC to be particularly noticeable for these sorts of species.

The strength of interactions can be affected by climate. For example, the rate of predation by ladybirds on aphids increases geometrically as temperature rises, because the proportion of ladybirds that are foraging and ladybird walking speed both increase (Kingsolver 1989). Arboreal lizards fly longer distances in cooler temperatures, which perhaps protects them from predators that are active when lizards are not (Rand 1964). The flatworm *Planaria gonocephala* is excluded by its competitor *P. montenigrina* at <13–14°C but can occur at higher temperatures which *P. montenigrina* cannot survive (Beauchamp and Ullyott 1932). However, when more than two species interact the situation becomes extremely complicated very quickly, as impacts on any one species affect several others. In a detailed computer study of several food webs in which all interactions between all species were well known, one or more species were added or removed and the direction and scale of changes in interactions and abundance were analysed. The effects on the different species in the food web varied enormously and were impossible to

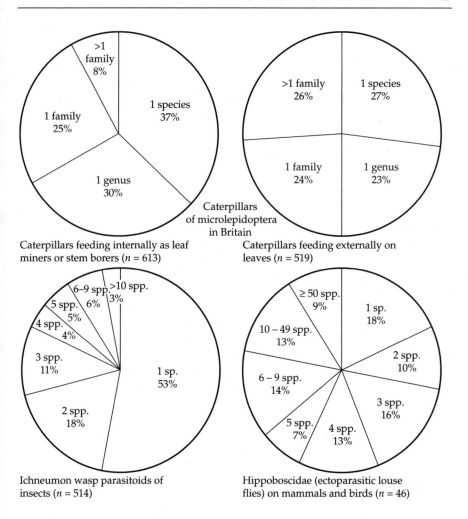

Figure 4.5   Host ranges of plant feeders, parasitoids and ectoparasites. Each seg-
ment represents a different level of feeding specificity ranging from
highly specialist (feeding on just one host species) to very generalist.
(From data in Gaston *et al.* 1992 and Price 1980.)

predict (Yodzis 1988). Predicting the effects of GEC on interactions within
any complex food web will be equally difficult.

Predicting the effect of GEC on communities

It is very difficult to predict the future response of whole communities to rising CO_2 concentrations, mostly because there is no recent precedent for the
changes in CO_2 concentration that are taking place. In contrast, there is a lot

of evidence for the effect of temperature on communities. This is obtained from the current distribution of communities in relation to temperature and the effect of past changes in temperature on communities which can be reconstructed from fossil evidence. Each species has a range of environmental conditions to which it is suited, and this dictates where it can be found in the world. Chapters 2 and 3 discussed some of the direct effects of temperature on plants and animals, and showed that different species have different ranges over which they can grow and temperature extremes which they can survive.

Predicting the disruption of communities: forest model simulations

Predicting large-scale changes in vegetation over a long timescale is difficult and computer models can be of help. Such models have been developed to look at how forests develop. They use information on climate, the response of individual trees to climate, the interactions between forest and soil, and other relationships, to predict the composition of the forest and how this changes with time. One simulation of hardwood forest growth in the eastern USA considered the effect of the predicted temperature changes caused by a doubling of CO_2. The outcome depended strongly on the soil type. On a clay soil, spruce was lost and the remaining trees were faster growing (Figure 4.6). There was good water retention in the soil, increased rates of organic matter decomposition resulted in more nutrients becoming available to the trees, and warmer temperature directly promoted growth. But on a sandy soil the forest was replaced by stunted oak/pine forest of about 25% of the biomass of the original. This was largely due to drying of the soil.

Trees account for about 70% of terrestrial biomass, so whether they act as a net carbon sink or source is of great importance in determining future changes in the concentration of CO_2 in the atmosphere. In another modelling study the growth of forests at sites throughout the eastern USA was simulated and the effect of future climate change monitored. Most deciduous trees showed slower growth and there was often a dieback of the dominant trees. Overall there was a reduction in carbon stored in trees in the southern two-thirds of the region, but an increase further north where the higher temperature enhanced growth. Over the whole area there was a net fall in carbon storage of 10%.

Predicting future shifts of natural vegetation

We showed in Chapters 2 and 3 that individual species show well defined distribution limits more or less related to temperature. The same is true for communities. The distribution of particular vegetation types – and associated animals – is closely related to climate (Figure 4.7). If climate changes, so may the distributions of the different vegetation types.

How can information on the current distribution of vegetation types be used to predict how it could alter in response to future climate change? The

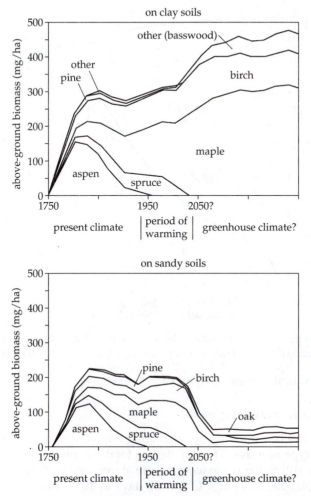

Figure 4.6   Forest growth can be predicted by using computer models that relate climate to tree performance. Climate change is likely to alter the species composition of forests and influence the carbon density of these communities. This figure shows predictions of the species composition and biomass of Minnesota forests under the climatic conditions predicted to occur if there is a doubling of the CO_2 concentration. (After Pastor and Post 1988.)

output from global circulation models (GCMs) gives information on the temperature and precipitation that might be expected in the future. If current temperature and precipitation can be related to vegetation type, then the future distribution of vegetation could be predicted from the information provided by GCMs. One approach has been to assume that the distribution of a particular vegetation type is controlled by three principal factors:

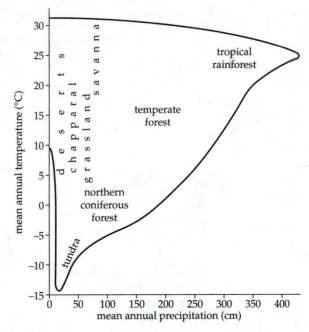

Figure 4.7   The type of vegetation that grows at a particular location is strongly influenced by temperature and precipitation. (After Whittaker 1975.)

• low temperature limit for the survival of the vegetation;
• need for water;
• temperature requirement for growth.

The last of these can be estimated by calculating the number of day degrees each vegetation type requires. The day degree total for the growing season is calculated by multiplying mean temperature above zero by the number of days. For example, 100 days at 5°C and 50 days at 10°C both give a day degree total of 500. Vegetation in the Arctic tundra needs less than 1000 day degrees per year, but tropical rain forest requires in excess of 5000 day degrees per year to survive.

Using this method there is a good overall agreement between the observed distribution of the major vegetation types and the distribution predicted for current conditions using current climate data and knowledge of day degree requirements. This technique was then applied to climate predictions made by a climate model. There was a poleward shift of vegetation types. The Arctic tundra shrank by 4° of latitude and chill resistant vegetation moved polewards by 10° (Figure 4.8). There are also considerable changes in the distribution of forest, continuous vegetation and sparse vegetation types, mostly based on the predicted rainfall changes.

However, these predictions assume that the vegetation is able to reach a distribution in equilibrium with climate instantaneously. Predicting the rate

hemlock

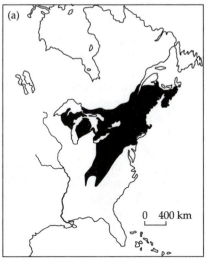

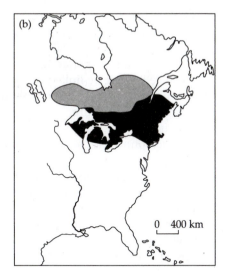

beech

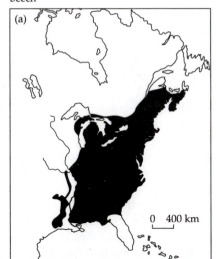

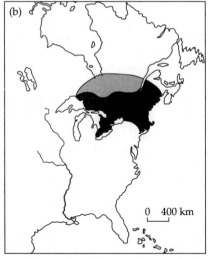

Figure 4.8   Vegetation types may shift polewards in reaction to global warming. (a) The present range; (b) range in 2090 with the climate change predicted in a 2×CO$_2$ scenario. The black area represents the predicted occupied range assuming a generous rate of dispersal of 100 km/century. The grey area is the potential range as yet unoccupied. (From Zabinski and Davis 1989.)

at which vegetation will change is difficult because the processes involved are very complex. These include rates of dispersion of species, competitive interactions at newly colonized sites and the effect of climate on performance. Some insight into these can be gained from looking at historical examples of changes in community structure. Red spruce has been replaced mainly by deciduous American beech as the forests of the northeastern USA have warmed over the last 180 years. These results indicate that replacement takes place over a long period of the order of 100–180 years. This is not surprising, since it must be linked to the lifespan of the trees: replacement can only take place after the death of a mature tree. In contrast, birch was able to spread rapidly into tundra vegetation during a warm period between 1920 and 1950 in Sweden. These studies looked at changes in the altitudinal limit of birch and found that significant movement can occur in a decade. This contrasts with the previous example because the principal limit to birch extent is not competition with tundra plants but its ability to survive the extreme climate. Maps made for the Hudson Bay Company in 1772 at the end of the Little Ice Age show that the northern tree limit in Canada has moved northward by as much as 120–220 km since then.

The way in which vegetation distribution has responded to warming since the last ice age is another source of information. The distribution of vegetation in the past can be reconstructed from fossil evidence. Pollen grains, which are relatively resistant to decay, can be preserved in certain conditions such as lake sediments. Pollen of different types of plants can be distinguished, so an outline of the plants that occurred in the neighbourhood of the deposition site may be reconstructed. Changes in the vegetation over time are revealed by analysing pollen from different depths in the sediment. Using this method the large-scale changes in the location of vegetation types have been followed.

Figure 4.9 shows that there were large shifts in vegetation as the ice sheet retreated from North America: 18 000 years ago the ice sheet edge was just north of central USA and from there it gradually retreated, although this was not a uniform retreat as there were cooler periods when the ice started to advance again. The rate at which different species moved can be estimated from this information. Most tree species moved at 200–250 m/yr, although some moved at up to 400 m/yr. This is much slower than the rate at which temperature conditions are likely to move over the next century: a 3°C increase would move climate zones by about 250 km, ten times faster than trees moved in the past. If the rate of movement of vegetation zones is similar to those observed in the past there will be a long period of readjustment before communities stabilize.

Dispersal of species and the assembly of communities

With such a coarse approach, maps such as those in Figures 4.8 and 4.9 give the impression that whole communities of plants and animals might move across the landscape as intact units that have existed with more or less the same species and the same interactions for a considerable time. Yet there is little historical evidence that this is the case. One suggestion is that whole

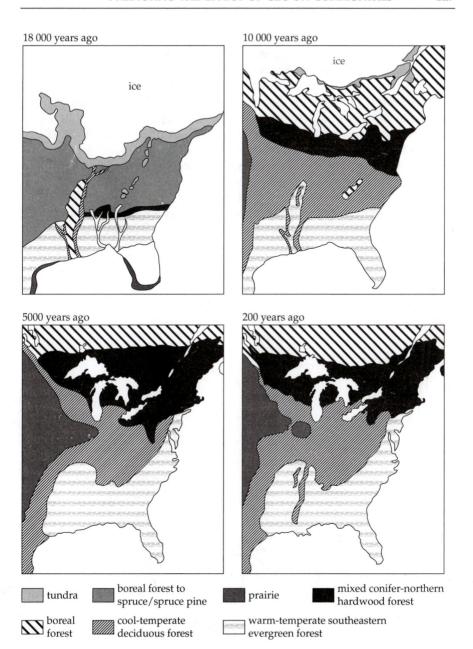

Figure 4.9   Changes in the distribution of vegetation in eastern North America following global warming since the end of the last ice age. (After Delcourt and Delcourt 1981.)

communities were restricted during adverse conditions in the past to refuges where conditions remained suitable, and that they moved out from these when conditions improved. Suggested refuges include parts of the tropics and Florida and north Mexico. However, there are few palaeobiological data to substantiate this theory. Instead, it appears that individual species respond to changes in different ways and at different rates. The result is that future communities are unlikely to be the same as those with which we are familiar. In this section we consider the evidence for this more closely.

One way of looking at this question is to discover whether the same community will arise if the component species colonize a site in a different order. In controlled experiments using aquatic microecosystems the same set of colonizers were introduced in different orders. It was found that the sequence of colonization profoundly affected the community structure that emerged (Figure 4.10).

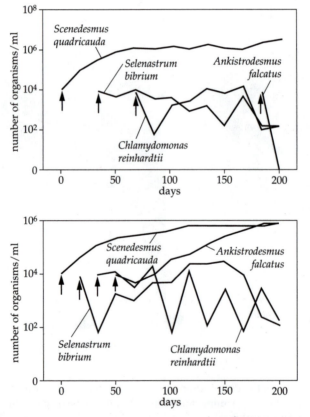

Figure 4.10 The order in which organisms colonize a site affects the community structure that eventually emerges. In this experiment in freshwater microcosms the same species were released at different times, as indicated by the arrows. (Redrawn from Drake 1985.)

Such experiments are a long way from the complexity of the real situation, however. Some clues can be gained from the past. Quite well defined vegetation types followed the retreat of the ice (see Figure 4.9) but these communities were not single entities that moved as a unit. Evidence indicates that individual species moved at different rates. Each community, although a recognizable type, had different components depending on how the community assembled. The assembly process would have depended on the past vegetation at the site, the timing of the arrival of new species and the concurrent changes in climatic conditions. In fact, it can be argued that most communities are transitory associations of species constantly responding to climate change. Some communities which were widespread in the past no longer occur.

The last period of rapid climate change was a period of warming and increased seasonality at the end of the last glaciation, between 12 000 and 10 000 years ago. As far as we know, there were no extinctions of plants and insects: species simply changed in distribution and abundance as they tracked changes in climate. However, there were changes in the ways species fitted together in communities. Communities before climate change had different dominant species, productivity, phenology and habitat architecture than communities after the change. Boreal spruce forests covered much of the midwest of North America 12 000 years ago, and broadly similar boreal spruce forests cover much of Canada today, yet the earlier forests were more open, contained patches of hardwood trees and had a much greater range of food resources and habitats for grazing and browsing animals.

The extinction of the 'megafauna' (species with adult body weight >44 kg, mostly mammals but also some birds and reptiles) in this period happened at exactly the same time as major changes in vegetation detected by pollen analysis. At this time, 33 of 45 North American species, 46 of 58 South American, 19 of 22 Australian and 7 of 49 African species became extinct. Availability of food is certainly a major influence on animal abundance and distribution, and vegetation changes could have contributed to the extinctions of herbivores and the carnivores that preyed on them. The sudden spread of human hunters at about the same time could have had a major impact too, but not sufficient in itself to explain the extinctions of smaller mammals, birds and reptiles at that time.

There are many other examples of past assemblages of plants and animals that are not normally found together in the present. Three rodent species that were found together in one North American locality 23 200 years ago have spectacularly different present-day distributions (Figure 4.11). In the same way, animal assemblages in the Great Plains of North America dating from 10 000 years ago contained species found today only at high altitude or high latitudes, alongside species found in more temperate conditions. The presence of high-altitude and high-latitude species suggests that there were cool summers, and the temperate species that there were mild winters without extremes of cold. These conditions were created by the presence of ice sheets

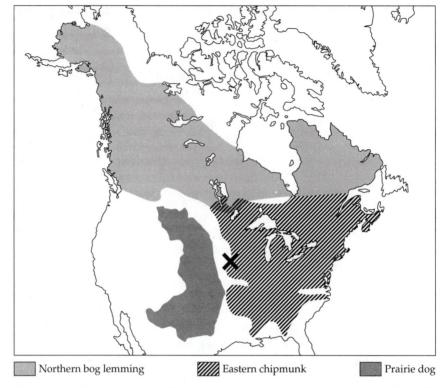

| Northern bog lemming | Eastern chipmunk | Prairie dog |

Figure 4.11 Present-day distributions of three rodents that were found together 23 200 years ago at the site marked by the cross. (From Graham 1986, 1988.)

close by. The same set of environmental conditions does not occur today (Wright 1984).

The study of sediments in Lake Windermere, England, allowed pollen and beetle records for around 13 000 years ago to be compared side by side. Pioneer herbs and shrubs dominated at that time, but birch trees and juniper trees were present too. However, comparing the beetle assemblage with present-day assemblages suggested that there should have been a woodland habitat. This is another example of a plant and animal assemblage that does not occur today. The likely reason that no modern-day analogue of the plant or insect assemblages occurs is that the physical conditions (e.g. unleached soils, thin surface layer of organic matter) are now rarely found.

These assemblages of species are ones that present-day biologists would not expect, but calling them 'disharmonious faunas', as some do, gives the wrong impression. Species assemblages are simply characteristic of whatever climatic conditions occurred at that time and the conditions of the recent historical past. They are no less harmonious just because they do not occur in the present.

What is clear is that climate change will be very rapid and communities will not be able to reach stable equilibrium for a long time after change has occurred. Achieving this will be further hindered by human and natural obstacles to species movement. Current evidence indicates that the speed at which plant species can disperse is slow compared to the rate of climate change, and so the environment will be dominated by regenerating ecosystems of early successional species, the only species adapted to moving long distances quickly. Even though they might be more mobile than many plants, animals may be limited by the distribution of particular plants on which they feed or which they pollinate. Like plants, only some animals are adapted to move long distances quickly and to thrive in disturbed environments, and they are often omnivorous or generalist species with a low mortality rate, large body size or short generation times, a low level of population fluctuations and high carrying capacity. This suggests that the process of rapid invasion of new species will not involve large numbers of species. Nevertheless, those species that can invade quickly are likely to have a considerable impact.

There is a strong relationship between temperature and diversity, with plant family diversity increasing by 8% for every 10°C rise in minimum temperature. So, increased temperature should increase diversity at equilibrium. But during transition from the current state to a new equilibrium the situation is unpredictable. Diversity could increase as new invaders coexist with the present vegetation, and then fall to a new equilibrium state, or it could fall if the extinction rate is faster than invasions.

Effects of extinctions on communities

Initially processes which lead to the disruption of existing communities will be of greater significance than invasions. Disruptions due to GEC could cause species to be lost. Even if it is a local loss rather than global extinction the local consequences could be severe. In a changing climate it is uncertain how readily individuals of the same species might recolonize and which new species might appear.

Does the disappearance of some species from ecosystems affect the way that ecosystems work? This is the subject of considerable debate at present. For a variety of environments, including tundra, tropical forests and coral reefs, it is clear that diversity of species can affect productivity if diversity decreases dramatically. However, the diversity of most natural ecosystems is well above this point, so they can sustain some losses without productivity falling. Temperate forests in eastern Asia have 876 woody plant species, in North America 158 species and in Europe 106 species, but their productivities are identical and so when diversity is this high there is no effect. However, studies on small, self-contained communities (for example, see Plate 5) give higher productivity as the number of species increases because there is a more diverse plant architecture to capture light. Also, more species allows a community to recover more rapidly from stresses such as drought. But these patterns are seen only when the number of plant species is as low as 10 or less, a diversity that is exceeded in even the most disturbed community.

But are some species crucial? Two hypotheses have been proposed. The 'rivet popper' hypothesis suggests that each species has a small but significant role, like a rivet in an aeroplane; if a few are lost there is no problem, but if many are lost the structure of the ecosystem (and the plane) collapses. This contrasts with the 'redundancy' hypothesis in which only a few key species are needed and the rest are like passengers (Baskin 1994). Although the rivet hypothesis is more generally supported by recent studies, it is clear that one or a few species can determine the structure of a whole ecosystem. One example of such a 'keystone species' are the geese that migrate to the Arctic to graze on salt marshes each summer. Their grazing maintains a high productivity for the salt marsh because the plants continually replace the leaf biomass that the geese remove. In the same way, feeding by moose on birch and aspen allows spruce and balsam fir to thrive, and hence this one animal affects the productivity, the soil, and even the frequency of fires in the whole ecosystem. If a keystone species is affected by outside factors such as GEC, the whole ecosystem could change. For example, the number of snow geese reaching Arctic salt marshes each summer has increased because of the increased availability of grains in their winter feeding grounds further south. The numbers now exceed the carrying capacity (i.e. the maximum number of individuals that can be supported indefinitely) of the salt marshes, and large areas of the ecosystem are being destroyed by overgrazing.

Mutualists are keystone species if the loss of one affects the success of many others. Possibilities are the loss of a mutualist from an ecosystem because of GEC, or its absence from new sites because it is unable to move across the landscape. If one partner is absent, the other might ultimately also disappear. If the mutualists include important seed dispersers or pollinators, there could be a collapse in species diversity that encompasses not just the mutualists but also specific herbivores, predators and parasitoids.

If the rivet hypothesis is correct, most extinctions are not likely to have a major impact on communities or ecosystems. They are more likely to affect rare species in restricted habitats that have specific interactions with species that have already disappeared. For example, the extinct species could have been a food plant, or a host of a parasitoid.

One important impact on communities will be an increase in the probability of catastrophes as a consequence of climate change. An increase in wildfire frequency is likely as drier conditions are caused by warmer summers. Warmer summers will also increase the probability of drought, during which plants will die. Pest and disease epidemics could increase as higher temperatures allow the invasion of new pests. Increased plant stress as a result of a warmer climate will increase susceptibility to pest damage. In the Arctic higher temperatures could stimulate soil erosion by melting the permafrost to a deeper level below the binding region of plant roots. Such events are inevitably unpredictable, but an increased frequency of catastrophes is highly likely and therefore sudden and extreme changes in the composition of communities are also likely. Conserving valuable communities may therefore be a particularly difficult problem. We consider this in more detail in Chapter 7.

The plant–soil interface

The effect of GEC on the interaction between plants and soil may hold the key to the fate of many communities. Soil processes can be directly affected by environmental change and indirectly by changes in the vegetation above the soil (Whitford 1992), but generally they are more sensitive to the vegetation above. This affects soil moisture by withdrawing water from the soil via transpiration and temperature by altering the amount of radiation reaching the soil surface. The quality and quantity of plant litter produced is of even greater importance, as it has a direct impact on the activity of soil-dwelling organisms. Decomposition is the breakdown of organic material into soil organic matter. Mineralization is the breakdown of this and mineral soil to release molecules that can be taken up by plants. Both are mediated by the soil biota, a complex community consisting of bacteria and fungi, grazers feeding on these and predators feeding on the grazers.

The direct effect of increased temperature is likely to be greatest in cool climates, where temperature severely limits the soil processes. Increased temperature will increase nutrient cycling and in many places decrease soil moisture. The reaction of Arctic vegetation to global warming is intimately linked to the effects of increased temperature on soil processes. Arctic soils are usually nutrient poor as the rates of decomposition and mineralization in the soil are slow because of the low soil temperature. Therefore the rate of plant growth is more limited by nutrient availability than by any other factor. Higher rates of nutrient release, particularly nitrogen and phosphorus, are likely as the soil warms. These will in turn stimulate plant growth and drawdown of CO_2 from the atmosphere. But at the same time CO_2 efflux from the ecosystem will be stimulated by the higher rates of decomposition.

The activity of decomposer organisms is strongly affected by the quality of the plant material on which they feed. As the nitrogen content decreases so does the rate of decomposition. Plant material grown in elevated CO_2, particularly leaves, is usually found to have increased carbon/nitrogen and carbon/phosphorus ratios (see Chapter 2). The result is that rates of decomposition of plant material grown in elevated CO_2 are likely to be lower than at present because of the dilution of nitrogen and phosphorus (Figure 4.12). There has been speculation that decomposition may also be slowed because high CO_2 grown plants could allocate more carbon to structural compounds that are resistant to decomposition. However, there is no evidence from the data illustrated that this is true.

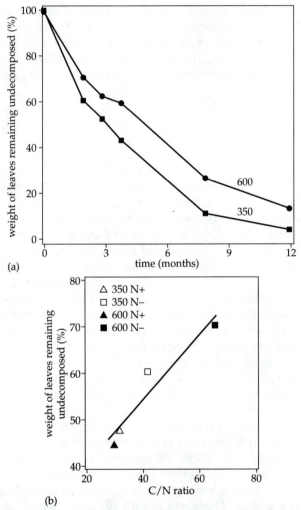

(a)

(b)

Figure 4.12 (a) Decomposition of birch leaf litter from trees grown in elevated (600 ppm) CO_2 was markedly slower than that from trees grown in normal (350 ppm) CO_2. (b) This change in decomposition rate is linked to the nitrogen content of the tissue. The graph shows the relationship between the nitrogen content and rate of decomposition for birch leaf litter grown in 350 ppm and 600 ppm CO_2 and at two nitrogen addition rates. (Data courtesy of P. Inneson, Institute of Terrestrial Ecology.)

Whatever the reason, the retarding of decomposition can be a very significant effect. In one experiment the time taken for the decomposition of 50% of birch leaf litter was extended from 3 to 4.5 months. If the rate of decomposition is slowed, the rate of release of minerals back into the soil will also be slowed. In addition, the composition of the plant litter will favour organisms such as fungi which can grow on energy-rich, nutrient-poor media:

fungi are good at scavenging the available nutrients, thereby reducing their availability to plants. In many situations the rate of plant growth is limited by the supply of minerals, and where this is the case a slowing in the rate of decomposition will slow plant growth. This may be a feedback mechanism which will regulate the enhancement of growth caused by CO_2 increase.

The increase in the supply of carbohydrate that results from growing plants in elevated CO_2 may help support plant symbionts such as nitrogen-fixing bacteria and mycorrhizas. It has been established that elevated CO_2 can increase symbiotic nitrogen fixation, and there have also been observations of increased mycorrhizal infection. Furthermore, plants with a plentiful carbohydrate supply can show increased root exudation of carbon compounds into the soil – up to 5% of fixed carbon can be lost by this route. The root exudates of plants are a rich food source on which soil microbes can grow and an increased microbial population should encourage decomposition and mineralization. Such changes would alter the productivity of plant communities by releasing them to some extent from nitrogen or phosphorus limitation. It may also change competitive interactions by favouring species with strong symbiotic relationships more than others.

The fact that environmental change can act to decrease or increase the cycling of minerals makes it difficult to predict the net effect. Most likely the impact of environmental change on the complex interactions between soil and the vegetation above will depend to a great extent on the circumstances of the individual community.

Communities and global feedbacks

Whether or not plants act as a negative feedback controlling the rise in the concentration of CO_2 in the atmosphere depends on whether the global biomass increases. Net primary production will probably increase, but if this is simply accompanied by a similar increase in respiration and decomposition there will be no net storage of carbon. To an extent, whether increased production acts as a sink depends on how plants partition and utilize the extra carbon. If it is in longer-lived components such as wood there will be a net increase in biomass. Also, if the nature of the biomass changes so that it decomposes less rapidly (for example if it contains more lignin and phenolics) this will lock up more carbon in the litter. Increased water use efficiency and nitrogen use efficiency could lead to greater production in places where these factors are limiting, and so increase biomass.

The reaction of individual communities to GEC may be important as a positive or negative feedback altering the concentration of greenhouse gases in the atmosphere. The response of forests and the Arctic may be particularly important, as large amounts of carbon are held in these communities. Increased storage of carbon in forests may occur as a result of increasing temperature in northern forests, and also as a consequence of CO_2 fertilization. Tropical deforestation releases about 1.6 Gtonnes of carbon into the atmosphere, but there is great uncertainty about how much carbon might accumulate in more temperate regions. One estimate is 1–2 Gtonnes/year, another is 2–3.4 Gtonnes/year, but the removal of trees in forestry and the decay of cut forest returns carbon at an unknown rate which could largely counteract this.

A reduction in the biomass of forests is predicted in many mid-temperate regions as increased temperatures reduce soil moisture availability. For example, the forests of the northwestern USA are some of the highest carbon density ecosystems in the world. The effect of soil moisture is evident in the region as there are marked differences in the composition of communities with different moisture regimes. The predicted climate change for this area is an increase in temperature of 2–5°C, with little change in rainfall. This will lead to a substantial increase in evapotranspiration. It was calculated for one site that there would be a 32% increase in potential evapotranspiration for a 2.5°C increase, and a 64% increase for a 5°C increase (Franklin *et al.* 1992). As a result there would be 3 months in the summer when evapotranspiration exceeded precipitation, instead of 1 month as at present. Using current vegetation zonation as a guide, this would cause large shifts in the location of different vegetation types, with overall forest cover decreasing and giving way to savannah and grassland-type habitats in some areas. But mature stands will only change gradually, as mature trees can survive long periods in a marginal climate. Also the stands will buffer the climate change, especially the climate experienced by regenerating seedlings. Of particular importance may be an increase in wildfire frequency as the moisture regime becomes drier.

Most of the carbon fixed in the Arctic tundra communities goes below ground to roots, rhizomes and other structures. As the roots and rhizomes die they decompose slowly in the cool soil and accumulate as peat. It is estimated that about 25% of the carbon fixed each year builds up like this, resulting in the accumulation of large amounts of organic material over many centuries. The soils of cool regions may account for more than 25% of the world's soil carbon. Accelerated decomposition of this during global warming could be a strong positive feedback. Recent measurements on the tussock tundra of north-shore Alaska indicate that this area has indeed changed from a CO_2 sink to a CO_2 source in response to climatic warming in the region (Oechel *et al.* 1993). This is thought to be due to an increase in the depth to which the surface layers thaw, increased drainage and greater soil aeration. Arctic soils are also an important global source of methane and, if they remain waterlogged, methane production would increase by 45–65% for a 4°C increase in soil temperature. However, drying of the soils could counteract this.

In a series of experiments, W. D. Billings and co-workers removed soil blocks from the Arctic tundra of north-shore Alaska and placed them in controlled environment units where the conditions could be altered to simulate global warming (see, for example, Billings *et al.* 1984). They were also able to investigate the direct effect of a doubling of the CO_2 concentration on the rate of carbon fixation by these monoliths. They concluded that warming would cause a net release of CO_2 into the atmosphere. Increased soil decomposition outweighed the increase in plant productivity that resulted from a longer growing season and warmer temperatures. Although elevated CO_2 slightly stimulated photosynthesis the increase was not great, probably as a consequence of nutrient limitation of plant productivity.

The response of Arctic communities to global warming is likely to be dramatic, not only because they will experience the greatest temperature change but also because they are exquisitely sensitive to temperature. This is not surprising, as the adaptations that enable organisms to survive the cool temperatures also make them highly temperature sensitive. This has consequences not only for the conservation of the plants and animals that inhabit these regions but also for the balance of the global carbon cycle.

Conclusion

Changes in both CO_2 and climate will disturb the equilibrium between plant species, between plants and animals and between animal species in many communities. Communities will be forced into a period of change, which in the short term may result in a loss in diversity as the distribution of species readjusts to reflect the new environmental conditions. The populations of species within the community will alter to reflect the differential impact on performance. Future compositions of communities will differ from the present day, but the many different processes involved make it nonsense to speculate on the forms that new communities will take. This picture of a constantly changing landscape has profound implications for our perception of our natural surroundings and their management.

References

Arp WJ, Drake BG, Pockman WT, Curtis PS, Whigham DF (1993) Interactions between C_3 and C_4 saltmarsh plant species during four years of exposure to elevated atmospheric CO_2. *Vegetatio* **104/105**, 133–43
Baskin Y (1994) Ecologists dare to ask: how much does biodiversity matter? *Science* **264**, 202–3
Bazzaz FA (1990) The response of natural ecosystems to the rising CO_2 levels. *Annual Review of Ecology and Systematics* **21**, 167–96
Bazzaz, FA, Carlson RW (1984) The response of plants to elevated CO_2 I. Competition among an assemblage of annuals at two levels of soil moisture. *Oecologia* (Berlin) **62**, 196–8

Bazzaz FA, Ackerly DD, Woodward FI, Rochefort L (1992) CO_2 enrichment and dependence of reproduction on density in an annual plant and a simulation of its population dynamics. *Journal of Ecology* **80**, 643–51

Beauchamp RSA, Ullyott P (1932) Competitive relationships between certain species of fresh-water triclads. *Journal of Ecology* **20**, 200–8

Bell DJ, Webb NJ (1991) Effects of climate on reproduction in the European wild rabbit (*Oryctolagus cuniculus*). *Journal of Zoology* **224**, 639–48

Billings WD, Peterson KM, Luken JO, Mortensen DA (1984) Interaction of increasing atmospheric carbon dioxide and soil nitrogen on the carbon balance of tundra microcosms. *Oecologia* **65**, 26–9

Delcourt PA, Delcourt HR (1981) Vegetation maps for eastern North America: 40 000 BP to the present. In *Geobotany II*, ed. RC Romans. Plenum Press, New York

Dewar RC, Watt AD (1992) Predicted changes in the synchrony of larval emergence and budburst under climatic warming. *Oecologia* **89**, 557–9

Drake JA (1985) *Some theoretical and empirical explorations of structure in food webs*. DPhil Thesis, Purdue University, USA

Fajer ED, Bowers MD, Bazzaz FA (1991) Performance and allocation patterns of the perennial herb *Plantago lanceolata*, in response to simulated herbivory and elevated CO_2 environments. *Oecologia* **87**, 37–42

Fosberg MA (1989) Forest productivity and health in a changing atmospheric environment. In *Climate and geo-sciences. A challenge for science and society in the 21st century*, (eds) A Berger, S Schneider and JC Duplessy. NATO ASI series. Series C: Mathematical and Physical Sciences **285**. Kluwer, Dordrecht, pp.681–8

Franklin JF, Swanson FJ, Harmon ME, Perry DA, Spies TA, Dale VH, McKee A, Ferrel WK, Means JE, Gregory SV, Lattin JD, Schowalter TD, Larsen D (1992) Effects of global climatic change on forests in northwestern North America. In *Global warming and biodiversity*, eds RL Peters and TE Lovejoy. Yale University Press, New Haven, pp.105–23

Gaston KJ, Reavey D, Valladares GR (1992) Intimacy and fidelity: internal and external feeding by the British microlepidoptera. *Ecological Entomology* **17**, 86–8

Graham RW (1986) Response of mammalian communities to environmental changes during the late Quaternary. In *Community ecology*, eds J Diamond and TJ Case. Harper & Row, New York, pp.300–13

Graham RW (1988) The role of climatic change in the design of biological reserves: the paleoecological perspective for conservation biology. *Conservation Biology* **2**, 391–4

Hunt R, Hand DW, Hannah MA, Neal AM (1991) Response to CO_2 enrichment in 27 herbaceous species. *Functional Ecology* **5**, 410–521

Johnson RH, Lincoln DE (1991) Sagebrush carbon allocation patterns and grasshopper nutrition: the influence of carbon dioxide enrichment and soil mineral limitation. *Oecologia* **87**, 127–34

Kareiva P (1994) Diversity begets productivity. *Nature* **368**, 686–7

Kingsolver JG (1989) Weather and the population dynamics of insects: integrating physiological and population ecology. *Physiological Zoology* **62**, 314–34

Lawton JH, Naeem S, Woodfin RM, Brown VK, Gange A *et al.* (1993) The Ecotron – a controlled environment facility for the investigation of population and ecosystem processes. *Philosophical Transactions of the Royal Society of London* **B 341**, 181–94

Lindroth RL, Kinney KK, Platz CL (1993) Responses of deciduous trees to elevated atmospheric CO_2: productivity, phytochemistry, and insect performance. *Ecology* **74**, 763–77

Mattson WJ Jr (1980) Herbivory in relation to plant nitrogen content. *Annual Review of Ecology and Systematics* **11**, 119–61

Mattson WJ, Haack RA (1987) The role of drought stress in provoking outbreaks of phytophagous insects. In *Insect outbreaks*, eds P Barbosa and JC Schultz. Academic Press, San Diego, pp.365–407

Naeem S, Thompson LJ, Lawler SP, Lawton JH, Woodfin RM (1994) Declining biodiversity can alter the performance of ecosystems. *Nature* **368**, 734–7

Norby RJ, O'Neill EG (1991) Leaf area compensation and nutrient interactions in CO_2-enriched seedlings of yellow-poplar (*Liriodendron tulipifera* L.). *New Phytologist* **117**, 515–28

Oechel WC, Hastings SJ, Vourlitis G, Jenkins M, Riechers G, Grulke N (1993) Recent change of Arctic tundra ecosystems from a net carbon dioxide sink to a source. *Nature* **361**, 520–3

Pastor J, Post WM (1988) Response of northern forests to CO_2-induced climate change. *Nature* **334**, 55–8

Pivnick KA, McNeil JN (1985) Effects of nectar concentration on butterfly feeding: measured feeding rates for *Thymelicus lineola* (Lepidoptera: Hesperiidae) and a general feeding model for adult Lepidoptera. *Oecologia* **66**, 226–37

Price PW (1980) *Evolutionary biology of parasites*, Princeton University Press, Princeton

Rand AS (1964) Inverse relationship between temperature and shyness in the lizard *Anolis lineatopus*. *Ecology* **45**, 863–4

Reavey D (1992) Egg size, first instar behaviour and the ecology of Lepidoptera. *Journal of Zoology* **227**, 277–97

Reekie EG, Bazzaz FA (1989) Competition and patterns of resource use among seedlings of five tropical trees grown at ambient and elevated CO_2. *Oecologia* (Berlin) **79**, 212–22

Tissue DT, Oechel WC (1987). Response of *Eriophorum vaginatum* to elevated CO_2 and temperature in the Alaskan tussock tundra. *Ecology* **68**, 401–10

Whitford WG (1992) Effects of climate change on soil biotic communities and soil processes. In *Global warming and biodiversity*, eds RL Peters and TE Lovejoy. Yale University Press, New Haven, pp.105–23

Whittaker RH (1975) *Communities and ecosystems,* 2nd edn. Macmillan, London

Wright HE Jr (1984) Sensitivity and response times of natural systems to climatic change. *Quaternary Science Reviews* **3**, 91–131

Yodzis P (1988) The indeterminacy of ecological interactions as perceived through perturbation experiments. *Ecology* **69**, 508–15

Zabinski C, Davis MB (1989) Hard times ahead for Great Lakes forests: A climate threshold model predicts responses to CO_2-induced climate change. In *Potential Effects of global climate change on the United States,* eds JB Smith and D Tirpak. US Environmental Protection Agency, Washington DC, Appendix D

Further reading

Cook GC (1992) Effect of global warming on the distribution of parasitic and other infectious diseases: a review. *Journal of the Royal Society of Medicine,* **85**, 688–91

Changes in vector ecology and greater human susceptibility will affect the incidence of parasitic and viral diseases of humans. One possibility is that multiple sclerosis could decrease.

Gates DM (1993) *Climate change and its biological consequences,* Sinauer, Sunderland, Massachusetts

Particularly good on the response of vegetation to past climate change and the impact of future environmental change on forests.

Lincoln DE, Fajer ED, Johnson RH (1993) Plant–insect herbivore interactions in elevated CO_2 environments. *Trends in Ecology and Evolution* **8**, 64–8

A good review showing that different species of plants and animals respond to elevated CO_2 in different ways and that it is difficult to generalize.

Peters RL, Lovejoy TE (1992) *Global warming and biodiversity,* Yale University Press, New Haven

A collection of articles including general concepts, diversity changes in response to past climate changes and prediction for future impacts in different regions.

5 The impact of GEC on agriculture

Introduction

Even in countries where there is a substantial food surplus supplies can rapidly decline after a poor harvest. This is a consequence of the limited ability to stockpile food and is usually dealt with by buying supplies from other countries where the harvest was better. Some scenarios about the consequences of GEC conjure up a picture of global climatic disturbance resulting in widespread harvest deficiencies and subsequent devastating famine in countries unable to purchase food (Gribbin and Kelly 1989). Others argue that crop production will be substantially increased as a direct consequence of CO_2 fertilization, and that temperature increases will actually release constraints on food production in many regions which currently experience cool summers. There has also been considerable speculation about the consequences of changes in regional climates, for example the possible drying of central North America, the warming of northern Europe and an increase in the intensity of the Asian monsoon. Changes in climate will also affect agricultural pests and diseases, altering their geographical range and influencing the virulence and timing of outbreaks. Unless climatic change is extreme it is likely that there will be regions that win and regions that lose as a consequence of GEC.

The impact of GEC on agriculture can be considered at three levels, which will form the three parts of this chapter. On the level of individual crop response, changes in temperature, precipitation and CO_2 concentration can have direct effects on crop performance by reasonably well characterized mechanisms. On a regional scale, predicting changes in the yield potential of crops needs to take into consideration the blend of environmental changes that occur in each region. Only sketchy predictions of these can be made using the output from computer models. Nevertheless, these predictions can be used, together with the known effect of environment on crop performance, to outline the possible consequences of GEC at the regional level. The final part of this chapter will consider to what extent agricultural practices can adapt to GEC and the implications for food security.

Crop responses to environmental change

In this section the mechanisms by which crop yield may be affected will be covered, although more detailed explanations of the effect of CO_2 and temperature on plant performance can be found in Chapter 2.

Environmental changes that may increase crop productivity

The direct effect of enriched CO_2 on crop growth

An increase in the concentration of atmospheric CO_2 will stimulate the growth of most crops, particularly where nutrients are not limiting. In many agricultural situations nutrients are added to optimize plant growth and it is likely that under these conditions the maximum increase in performance will be achieved as a result of CO_2 fertilization. Research into crop growth in enriched CO_2 has shown that growth increases by about 1% for every 10 ppm increase in CO_2 concentration (see Chapter 2 for further details). Over the last twenty years the concentration of CO_2 in the atmosphere has increased by almost 30 ppm, therefore crop growth could have increased by 3% in this period. However, the other environmental factors that alter crop performance from year to year mean that it is difficult to detect whether any such stimulation in production has actually occurred. In the future the benefit to agriculture may be greater and more easily verified, as the concentration of CO_2 rises faster.

Many experiments conducted under controlled-environment conditions have used an approximate doubling of atmospheric CO_2 to investigate the eventual impact of CO_2 enrichment. There is considerable variation in the response of different crop species (Figure 5.1). In some there is almost a doubling of growth, whereas in others there is a much smaller increase. At the top end of the range, therefore, some crop species could increase production by as much as 3% for every 10 ppm increase in CO_2 concentration. However, the response of plant growth to enriched CO_2 may not be linear. There is evidence that in some species at least, the greatest stimulation of growth takes place up to a concentration of between 500 and 600 ppm CO_2, with a less sensitive response above this concentration. There is as yet little information on how different cultivars of the same species respond although experiments on a range of wheat varieties have produced different growth responses.

Increases in total growth do not tell the whole story. It is likely that in enriched CO_2 the partitioning of resources to different plant components will alter. If this is in favour of the harvestable component, such as the grain of a cereal crop, then the increase in crop yield could be greater than the

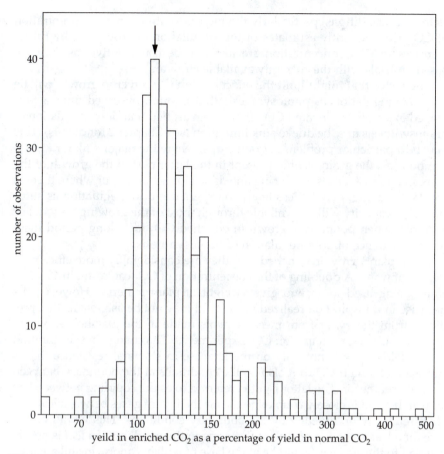

Figure 5.1   This diagram collects together a large number of observations on how growing in enriched atmospheric CO_2 affects crop yield. The most common observation (indicated by the arrow) is that yield is enhanced by 30%, but in many cases the yield increase was higher. It is also interesting to note that in a very few cases there was a decrease in yield. (After Kimball 1982.)

growth increase. Of course this could also work in the opposite direction: an increased allocation to root growth, which has been observed in many experiments, would decrease the harvestable component of a grain crop. In addition to altering the proportion of harvestable material, the changes in allocation pattern can alter the growth rate of the plant, as discussed in Chapter 2. Plant breeding has been particularly successful in the manipulation of crop allocation patterns to maximize the harvestable component. One of the greatest contributions to increased world food production in recent times has been the introduction of fast-maturing short-stemmed varieties of rice. Breeding programmes will continue during a period of GEC and will help to ensure that the cultivars in use take best advantage of changed environmental conditions, particularly the increased atmospheric concentration of CO_2. Consequently estimates of the stimulation of crop yield by future increases in CO_2 concentration are likely to be conservative, as they are based on trials with the currently available cultivars.

One factor that might limit the effect of high CO_2 on crop growth will be the downregulation of photosynthesis that is often observed after a prolonged exposure to elevated CO_2. It has been argued that downregulation of photosynthesis may be due to sink limitation (see Chapter 2 for details). This may be a particular problem in grain crops, where the major sink for carbon compounds, the grain, is only present in the latter part of the growth of the crop. In contrast, crops producing an edible storage organ, or where there is constant grazing, may be less likely to experience downregulation as sufficient sink capacity will be available through most of the growing period. For example, when potato was grown in enriched CO_2 for a long period there was no evidence of downregulation of photosynthesis.

When plants grow in enriched CO_2 they are considerably more efficient in the use of water. A doubling of the concentration of CO_2 can result in 40% less water being used to grow a given weight of plant material. However, the decrease in transpiration realized in the field may not be as great as that predicted from theory, or from measurements made in the glasshouses where plants are often grown in high CO_2 experiments. The change in transpiration in the field depends not only on the increase in stomatal resistance that is stimulated by high CO_2 but also on the conditions at the boundary between the leaf and the air. The latter is often referred to as the coupling between leaf and air. If a leaf is closely coupled to the air the flux of gases between leaf and air is relatively unimpeded by the boundary conditions. This would be the case for a leaf at the top of a plant fluttering in the wind, but if a leaf is poorly coupled to the air, as it would be at the base of a plant canopy in still air, then the reduction in transpiration may not be large, possibly in the region of 10%.

The decrease in water use caused by enriched CO_2 may have little effect if there is either a plentiful water supply (as with a heavily irrigated crop) or during severe drought, when there is much too little water available. However, in many parts of the world crop production is directly water limited for part or most of the growing season. For example, in many parts of the Australian wheat belt yield may be directly related to water availability, especially in years with below average rainfall. An estimate of the impact of the combined effect of direct CO_2 fertilization and improved water use efficiency (WUE) estimated that Australian wheat yields may be increasing by 5–13 kg/ha/yr (Gifford 1979); total yields are about 1.2 tonnes/ha. The impact of improved WUE may be particularly important throughout the semiarid tropics and subtropics, where crop growth is tightly regulated by the availability of water.

Nitrogen use efficiency is also higher in plants grown in enriched CO_2. Improvements in nitrogen productivity are very variable, with very large increases for some species, for example an 80% increase in wheat (see Table

Table 5.1 Percentage change in key aspects of crop performance caused by a doubling of atmospheric CO concentration. Data are mainly means for several experiments from Cure and Acock (1986). Nitrogen productivity is taken from Luo *et al.* (1994). * indicates single results from various research papers

Crop	Yield	Photosynthesis	Transpiration	Nitrogen productivity
Wheat	35	27	-17	80
Barley	70	14	-19	
Rice	15	46	-16	
Cotton	209	13	-18	
Clover	45 *	90 *		9
Pasture grass	43 *	46 *		10
Maize	29	4	-26	
Sorghum		6	-27	

5.1). Markedly increasing crop growth for no extra expenditure on chemicals may be particularly important for subsistence farmers, for whom the cost of fertilizers is a major investment or even beyond their means altogether.

Increased temperature

Low-temperature constraints on crop production

In many parts of the world agricultural productivity is limited by low temperature at a particular location. This may restrict the range of crops that can be used or limit the rate of crop growth. There are two principal ways in which low temperature can reduce crop production. Temperatures near or below zero can severely damage many crop plants. This limits their use to places with a low incidence of frost during the growing season. Crop growth can also be restricted if the length or warmth of the growing season is insufficient. The effect of low temperatures can therefore be very dependent on the crop species. For example, the region where olive trees can be grown is particularly affected by the occurrence of frosts, thus in Europe olives tend to be restricted to the southern Mediterranean and to coastal areas in the northern Mediterranean, where the incidence of frosts is lower. As winter temperatures are likely to rise more than those in the summer, crops that are limited by frost occurrence, such as olives, citrus fruits and grapevines, may be able to be grown much further north in the next century. In contrast, the northern limit to maize depends more on the length and warmth of the growing season, and in particular on the occurrence of cool temperatures in the early part of the growing season. Periods of cool weather during the spring can markedly check maize growth by causing chilling damage, and by a process called photoinhibition when cool temperatures are accompanied by bright days (Baker *et al.* 1994). During such days bright light can damage leaves when photosynthesis is restricted by low temperature.

The net growth of a plant is the difference between the amount of carbon fixed by photosynthesis and the amount lost through respiration. Therefore higher temperature can increase growth if photosynthesis is stimulated more than respiration, but it may also reduce growth if the reverse is true. Figure 5.2 approximates to the response of wheat photosynthesis to temperature. It shows that the rate of photosynthesis is about 75% of the maximum at 10°C, so on average for every 1°C increase in temperature between 10 and 20°C wheat photosynthesis should increase by about 2.5%. However, growth is likely to increase less than this because of respiration. Above 20°C, though, there will be a decrease in photosynthesis at a similar rate and a decrease in growth. So the impact of temperature on net carbon flux will depend on the temperature conditions where the crop is grown: in cooler climates higher temperatures will increase growth by stimulating photosynthesis, but in warmer regions growth will be reduced by higher respiration rates.

There may be some interaction between the direct effect of temperature on crop performance and the effect of enriched CO_2. CO_2 enrichment, by stimulating plant growth, may reduce the length of time for maturation of a crop while at the same time increased temperatures will relieve temperature constraints on the growing season. The impact of GEC on agriculture in currently temperature-limited locations may not therefore be simply predicted by considering the effects of temperature alone.

Environmental changes that may decrease crop productivity

The direct impact of CO_2 and temperature

Enriched CO_2 is likely to have a few direct detrimental effects on agriculture. One of the areas of concern is the possible implications of a reduction in the

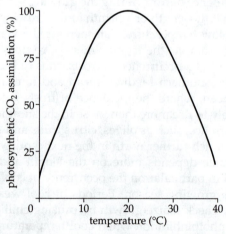

Figure 5.2   The effect of temperature on the rate of photosynthesis in wheat. (After Larcher 1980.)

nitrogen content of plants grown at high CO_2. As discussed in Chapter 2, the amount of plant growth per unit nitrogen tends to increase in enriched CO_2, largely as a consequence of the increased efficiency of photosynthetic carboxylation. The nitrogen content of leaves may also fall as carbohydrate accumulates in leaves as a result of the stimulation of photosynthesis by CO_2 enrichment. This reduced nitrogen content may directly affect the growth of animals that eat the plants, but this is only likely to be of importance where the animals are entirely dependent on grazing and receive no feed supplements. Probably of greater importance, especially to the subsistence farmer, is the possibility of reduced rates of decomposition of this organic matter. This will slow the release of nutrients into the soil and may directly affect crop growth where additional fertilizer is not available.

In warmer countries increased temperatures can reduce crop yield. Higher temperatures usually accelerate the development of a plant, so that it goes through the successive stages in its lifecycle more rapidly. In many crop species there is a particular developmental stage during which the yield component of the crop is produced. In grain crops this is the period between the initiation of the grain and its maturation. More rapid grain maturation results in less time for the grain to grow and hence reduced yield. Thus, although higher temperature may accelerate expansion of the leaf canopy early in the season, later in the season increased temperature accelerates maturation and reduces yield. Which is dominant? Grain yields in the UK are negatively correlated with temperature, with a 6% fall in yield per 1°C (Monteith 1981; Figure 5.3). But climate change predictions are for a greater increase in winter temperature, which could change the balance from that observed in the past if spring temperatures increase more than summer.

Some plants, such as barley and oats which are planted in the autumn, require a cool period during the winter in order to stimulate flowering later

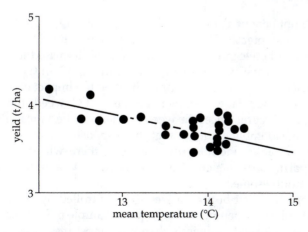

Figure 5.3   The effect of mean temperature (May, June, July) on the yield of wheat in England (1956–1970). (From Monteith 1981.)

in the growing season. This process is called vernalization. If winter temperature increases the vernalization period may be insufficient, causing low flower bud initiation and hence reduced yield. However, using cultivars that require less vernalization, or using completely different crops, would help farmers adapt to this.

Extreme events

Extreme events are the principal cause of the year-to-year variability in agricultural output. An increase in the frequency of extreme events such as droughts, storms and heat waves may be more important than average changes in climate. Although there is little hard evidence that the frequency of such extreme events will increase, there are at least two arguments that favour this conclusion. First, if the average temperature rises the frequency of extreme temperature events will increase at any given location. Heat stress could reduce crop production, especially in particularly hot years and where temperate cereals are grown near to their high-temperature limit. In northern India, where wheat is grown near its southern tolerance limit, one calculation indicated that yield could decrease by 10% if temperature increased by 0.5°C and was not accompanied by any increase in rainfall.

Secondly, the results of some climate modelling work indicate that the intensity of monsoons and tropical cyclones may be increased. Storms can have a devastating impact on agricultural production over the area they affect, causing complete crop loss in some circumstances. However, the results of the climate models are highly uncertain about whether or not there will be any increase in frequency.

Weeds and pests

C_4 species will not benefit as much as C_3 plants from CO_2 enrichment in the atmosphere (see Chapter 2). The change in the competitive interactions that might be expected between C_3 and C_4 plants were discussed in Chapter 4. Fourteen of the 17 worst weeds are C_4 species that grow in C_3 crops. If the competitive balance is tipped in favour of the crop the impact of weed infestations may be lessened. However, there are cases of C_3 weeds that infest C_4 crops, and in such circumstances the weed species may be a greater problem. There is now considerable evidence that the response of plants to enriched CO_2 is highly variable: undoubtedly, therefore, there will be some weed species that particularly benefit from enriched CO_2 and may therefore become more troublesome.

As with crops the distribution of weeds is controlled by climatic conditions, and particularly by temperature. A good example is *Striga hermonthica*, also known as witchweed. This is probably the most troublesome weed in Africa, but does not perform well in areas where the air temperature is below

28°C during the growing season (see Parker and Riches 1993 for further details). This weed affects the principal grain crops, maize, millet and sorghum, and causes crop loss estimated to exceed $500 million/year in Africa. It is particularly a problem of subsistence farmers as it thrives on nutrient-poor soils and often has a devastating effect on yield, in some cases causing complete crop loss. This is because it is a parasitic plant that attaches to the roots of its host to withdraw water, nutrients and carbon compounds. But the seeds of witchweed cannot germinate and locate a suitable host root unless there is a sufficiently high soil temperature. Already nearly 4% of the world agricultural land is under threat from this weed; with increasing temperatures the area at threat would expand into higher latitudes and altitudes.

GEC could increase the impacts of pests and diseases on crops and livestock by increasing their abundance and virulence. However, it is not possible to make sweeping generalizations. Each of the 6000 potential pests listed by the United States Department of Agriculture, for example, must be considered individually.

Growth rate, fecundity and survival of animals are often improved by increased temperature and humidity so long as changes do not take temperature beyond the upper lethal limit for the species. Physiological reasons for these effects are discussed in Chapter 3.

If growth rate is faster, more generations could be fitted into the year. This has been predicted by experimental work on many species of insects and mites, for example the corn earworm in the grain belt of the North America, the frit fly in Finland and the codling moth in New Zealand. The result could be larger pest populations.

In addition, the length of the season of activity might also increase if favourable weather conditions start earlier in the year. An interesting example of possible changes in the way the lifecycle fits into the year is the cabbage root fly, a pest of crucifer crops across Europe (Collier et al. 1991). The number of generations per year ranges from one to three according to weather conditions. A temperature increase of 3°C is likely to bring the fly pupae out of winter diapause about a month earlier, although there would still not be sufficient time to fit another generation into the year. An increase of 5°C would allow time for an extra generation. It is also likely to force aestivation for the time that summer temperatures remain above a critical level, and this will disrupt egg laying patterns. Root fly is controlled by pesticides applied at particular times during the lifecycle. Farmers will have to be sensitive to changes in the root fly lifecycle when deciding on a control strategy.

An earlier start and/or more generations might affect the way in which pests are synchronized with the crop as the degree of synchrony will affect the level of damage. One possibility is that earlier pest emergence could allow the pest to infest the crop when it is in a young, more susceptible stage. On the other hand, a pest may emerge at a time when the crop is less vulnerable, so that damage is reduced. If emergence occurs over a longer period, it could be difficult to time the application of insecticides with precision.

Crop pests will also respond to changes in the quality of their food supply. The higher carbon/nitrogen ratio of plants grown in high CO_2 could mean that plant feeders will need to consume more plant material to obtain the same amount of nitrogen, and so damage to plants could be greater. Alternatively, insects might grow less well on higher–carbon, lower–nitrogen plants, so that their fitness is reduced although they cause the same amount of damage. Outbreaks of many pests are more likely to occur when their food plants are stressed, because plant defence mechanisms operate less effectively and resistance to pests is poorer. Crop plants are more likely to be stressed if droughts become more frequent.

If new crops and new cultivars are introduced in response to GEC, these could be affected by the same or different pests – but they could also affect existing crops by providing new food plants or overwintering at times when none were previously available. For example, areas of grassland recently planted to restrict soil erosion in parts of North America have inadvertently created new hosts for the Russian wheat aphid.

The distribution of many pests is limited by climate. Others are limited by geographical barriers such as oceans or mountain ranges, or by the presence of their food plants. As climate changes pest distributions will also alter. Often it is low winter temperatures that control distribution (see Chapter 3), and so higher winter temperatures due to GEC will allow distribution to be extended to higher latitudes. The Colorado beetle is a serious pest of potatoes across most of Europe, but beetles reaching Britain (either naturally or inadvertently with imported vegetables) cannot survive low winter temperatures. The northern limit of another major pest in Europe, the European corn borer, a caterpillar, is predicted to extend up to 1000 km northwards with GEC (Porter *et al.* 1991). Remember, though, that if temperatures increase above the upper lethal limit the distribution could contract, and that changes in other climatic factors are superimposed on the effect of temperature to complicate the picture.

Other pest insects are migrants and move each year from overwintering sites to infest areas in which they cannot survive winter conditions. One example is the potato leafhopper, a serious pest of many crop species in North America. Overwintering adults can only survive if winters are warm, so overwintering populations are limited to a small area (along the coast of the Gulf of Mexico) from where they migrate northwards in spring each year. Predicted increases in winter temperatures during GEC will expand this area (Figure 5.4), so that the migration will be larger, start earlier and reach further northwards. In the same way, when weather conditions are favourable mass migrations of many species, some of them pests, occur from mainland Europe to Britain. Even if pest species do not permanently extend their range into Britain, migrations might become more frequent with GEC. One pest that is limited solely by temperature is the desert locust. So long as conditions are favourable, populations expand and the range is extended. Between 1986 and 1988, when conditions were perfect, its range increased across Africa and into southern Europe, although this contracted as soon as

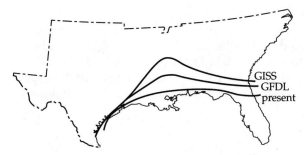

Figure 5.4   Current and predicted northern distribution of overwintering populations of potato leafhopper *Empoasca fabae* in southern USA. The two
predicted distributions come from different computer models, one from
GISS (Goddard Institute for Space Studies), the other from GFDL
(Geophysical Fluid Dynamics Laboratory). (From Stinner *et al.* 1989.)

conditions became cooler. GEC might increase the frequency and length of
these favourable periods.

It is not only crops and pests that are likely to be affected by GEC but natural enemies of the pests too. These natural enemies – their predators,
parasites and pathogens – have an important role in the natural regulation
of pest populations, but whether they exert more or less control after GEC
will depend on the responses of both pest and natural enemy to the new conditions. One possibility is that new pests will appear. These might be species
that are normally maintained at low numbers by their natural enemies, but
which are released from the influence of these enemies by changes in climate. We have no way of predicting in advance which such species these
might be. It is possible only to look back and attempt to explain reasons for
outbreaks by disruption of their enemies.

Diseases of crops and livestock

As with crop pests, vectors of disease are likely to increase their distribution
as a result of GEC. One example is the blood-sucking mosquito *Culicoides imi-
cola*, vector of the virus causing the devastating African Horse Sickness. The
virus requires a continuous cycle between its two hosts, horse and mosquito.
Once infected, the horse acts as a carrier of the virus for around 18 days, and
if it is not passed on within that time the cycle is broken. This means that any
absence of the vector must be shorter than 18 days if the virus is to persist in
a region. In the south of Spain and Portugal the mosquito is present all year
round and African Horse Sickness can persist. Successful overwintering by
the mosquito is only possible in frost-free areas where the mean daily minimum temperature in the coldest month does not drop below 12.5°C. But the
distribution of the mosquito appears to be extending northwards, and with
GEC the area of continuous activity of the vector is likely to increase.

Another livestock pest is the horn fly, a blood-sucking fly that irritates cattle to the extent that weight gain and milk yield are dramatically reduced. The number of flies directly influences the daily weight gain of cattle (Figure 5.5 (a)). Temperature is the main factor determining distribution and period of activity, and models for the United States suggest that the impact of GEC will be considerable (Figure 5.5 (b)). In the southern United States extreme summer

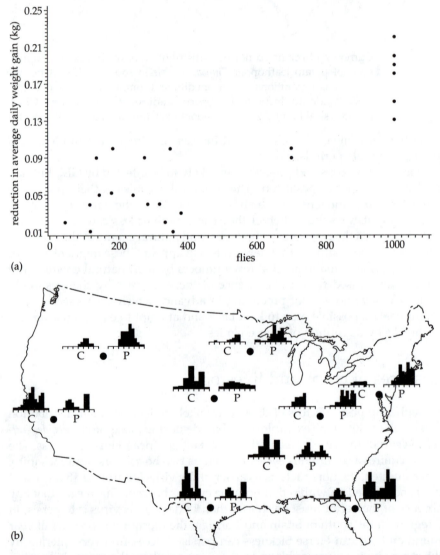

(a)

(b)

Figure 5.5   (a) Effects of horn fly numbers on reduction in daily weight gain of cattle. (b) Current (C) and predicted (P) populations of the horn fly in the United States for the 12 months of the year. (After Schmidtmann and Miller 1989.)

temperatures will reduce populations, because the cattle dung in which the larval stages develop becomes too hot. To the north, conditions will favour an increase both in numbers and in the period of activity. One model predicts increased annual losses to the beef cattle industry of $2 million to $30 million for a study of nine northern states (1989 prices). However, an increase in beef sales of $104 million is predicted for Texas, where horn flies will be suppressed by warmer summers. For the dairy industry of the northeast United States, the present-day losses of 1% per cow in milk production and $80 million per year due simply to the increased numbers of horn fly are likely to increase, although the current practice of rearing cattle in sheds is reducing the fly's impact.

Effect of environmental changes on the soil

Soil moisture is the principal factor affecting crop productivity over large areas of the world, particularly in warmer climates. The amount of water in the soil available to plants depends on the balance between supply and loss of water. It may be supplied by precipitation or by irrigation. Water can be lost from the soil as it drains through or runs over the surface, by direct evaporation from the soil and through the transpiration of the plants. The latter two are often referred to together as evapotranspiration. The rate of evapotranspiration depends principally on temperature, but is also affected by the humidity of the atmosphere. Higher temperatures will increase evapotranspiration and thereby cause more rapid depletion of soil water. This will bring forward the onset of drought stress during a dry period. For example, a 2°C increase in temperature could increase evapotranspiration by as much as 20%.

In the future plants will be growing in a higher concentration of CO_2 which will reduce transpiration significantly but higher temperatures will tend to increase evapotranspiration. Predicting how GEC will affect soil moisture depends on the interaction of three factors:

• the changes in rainfall;
• the extent to which increases in temperature drive faster evapotranspiration;
• how effective elevated CO_2 is at depressing transpiration in the crop.

Soil moisture content also has a strong effect on soil fertility. However, fertility can be affected by a range of other factors, so that predicting the impact of GEC depends on the cocktail of environmental changes occurring at a particular site. Higher soil temperature can increase the rate of nutrient cycling, but a reduction in soil moisture can substantially reduce it. If rainfall increases at a site it may increase leaching of soil nutrients but could also reduce susceptibility to wind erosion, whereas if rainfall drops the opposite applies. One constant effect is that enriched CO_2 will increase the carbon/nitrogen and carbon/phosphoros ratios of the plant litter. This will reduce the rate of decomposition of litter and alter the nutrient recycling schedule (see Chapter 4).

Livestock production

GEC will directly affect livestock production because of effects of temperature, rainfall and humidity on metabolism, nutrition, growth, reproduction
and health (see Chapter 3). All of these contribute to animal 'performance'.
There have been many attempts to relate cattle performance to environmental conditions. One of these for the southern United States relates milk
production to temperature and humidity by the equation

decline in milk production in kg/cow/day =
−1.075 − 1.74(normal production) + 0.0247(normal production)(index of
temperature and humidity)

where

index of temperature and humidity = temperature in °C + 0.36 (dewpoint
temperature in °C) + 41.2

Depending on which computer model is used, milk production in the southern United States could decline by 10–20% (Figure 5.6). At the same time, a
decline in conception rates of up to 35% is predicted. This is important
because it increases the length of the dry period (i.e. the time when the cow
is not producing milk) between calvings, thus reducing production levels.
Heat stress also reduces the percentage of butterfat in milk. It can also reduce
beef production, although if the stress is only of low intensity or for a short

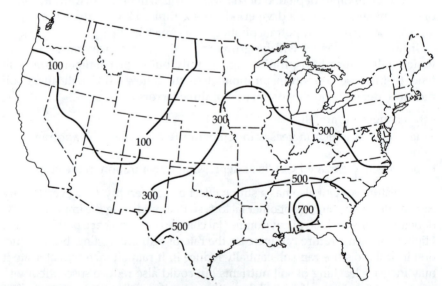

Figure 5.6   Decline in milk production (kg/cow/season) predicted for dairy cattle
that normally produce 23 kg/cow/day in a changed climate due to a
doubling of CO_2. A similar analysis for Europe shows much smaller
declines of <100 kg/cow/season. (After Klinedinst et al. 1993.)

period cattle can compensate for the growth they have missed. The only realistic responses by farmers are to increase the amount of natural or artificial shade and to ensure that sufficient drinking water is always available.

GEC will also affect the suitability of areas for livestock because of changes in pasture production and species composition. For example, every 1°C increase in temperature in Australia is likely to shift the northernmost boundary of sheep production by 167 km further south. Extreme boundaries of cattle production are not likely to be affected, but there could be a reduction in livestock density. Reasons include a change in the dominance of particular pasture plants, such as *Medicago* spp. (important legumes) and native grasses (Russell 1991). Another example is from the United States. In much of the country, most pasture production comes from 'cool season' grasses and mixtures of these grasses with legumes. The main problem is their susceptibility to drought and high temperature, causing very slow growth or dormancy in the summer and reducing carrying capacity for livestock to near zero. However, before these cool season grasses were introduced by European settlers, 'warm season' grasses dominated. Warm season grasses are C_4 plants, whereas most cool season grasses are C_3. Warm season grasses thrive during warm summers. They are less of a risk in a more variable climate and could fill the gap in summer grazing. However, problems with establishing new pastures and with their susceptibility to overgrazing mean that warm season grasses are not as simple a solution as they might seem (Decker *et al.* 1986).

Current livestock breeds are not necessarily adapted to the new combination of temperature and rainfall (Decker *et al.* 1986): each has its own optimum conditions. Cattle in temperate regions are breeds of the species *Bos taurus*. Cattle in tropical regions are breeds of *Bos indicus*, the zebu cattle, characterized by larger surface areas – a hump across the shoulders, a fold of loose skin hanging from the neck and drooping ears – thought to increase heat loss. *B. indicus* is used in Mexico and the very southernmost United States, and crosses between *indicus* and *taurus* are ideal for the southern United States. GEC is likely to shift these breeds further north. The price to pay for better heat tolerance is the decline in productivity (milk yield and weight gain) compared to conventional *B. taurus* breeds.

Regional changes in climate and their impact on agriculture

As outlined in Chapter 1, it is not yet possible to make accurate predictions about the changes that might occur in regional climate, yet it is likely that such changes will have a profound effect on agricultural output, with important social ramifications. One regional change that is quite certain is an above-average warming in the north. Predicting changes in the pattern of precipitation is much more difficult, but as we have seen these will be very important in determining agricultural potential. Globally rainfall is likely to increase, because of the increase in temperature (see Chapter 1 for details), but regionally there may be areas where rainfall decreases or increases. One possible change in a regional climate system is an increase in the intensity of the monsoon. This could bring more rainfall in the monsoon season but also could generate more frequent storms. What can be said is that regional climates will change and some possible scenarios can be explored.

An increase in the temperature in the north temperate regions could affect agriculture by altering the range of crops grown and by increasing productivity. In the northern hemisphere all crop plants have a northern limit beyond which it is not economically feasible to grow them. As we move further north from the equator the selection of crops used changes markedly as a consequence of falling temperature. An increase in temperature will move the northern boundaries for crops further north, altering the range of crops available to farmers. A 1°C increase in temperature may move the northern agricultural boundary 150–200 km further north. An important constraint on the benefit of such a shift is the quality of the soil, so for example, these changes are more likely to be of benefit on the richer soils of Siberia than on the poor ones of the Canadian shield. In cool climates the yield of a crop can be limited by the length of the growing season. Often this is determined by the onset of frosts late in the season. Conditions at the start of the season can also be important, including how long snow lies, whether the soil is frozen or the occurrence of frosts. During the growing season low temperature may limit the rate of growth.

The first step in trying to predict the future distribution limit of a crop is to relate the known current limits to an environmental variable. This will be different for different crops, depending on the factors that influence its distribution. For example, the northern limit to grain maize cultivation corresponds closely to 850 day degrees above a base temperature of 10°C. This is related to the facts that maize is particularly limited by warm summer temperatures and growth may be adversely affected by periods below 10°C. In contrast, the boundary to citrus fruit growing is determined by the number of frost-free days, as these plants are particularly susceptible to frost damage. The shift of growing areas can therefore be estimated by deciding which are the factors that limit production and then using future climate scenarios to evaluate new boundaries.

In Europe the northern limit of maize production would move 300 km north for each 1°C rise in temperature. As a consequence grain maize may be a viable crop throughout the British Isles and much of Scandinavia by the middle of the next century. The possible shifts in the extent of maize and other selected crops are shown in Figure 5.7. A study on the extent of the US corn belt assumed that it was limited to the north by the number of frost-free days and the thermal requirements for maturation, and to the west by soil moisture. It was estimated that there would be a movement of 175 km per 1°C in a northeasterly direction as the climate became drier and warmer.

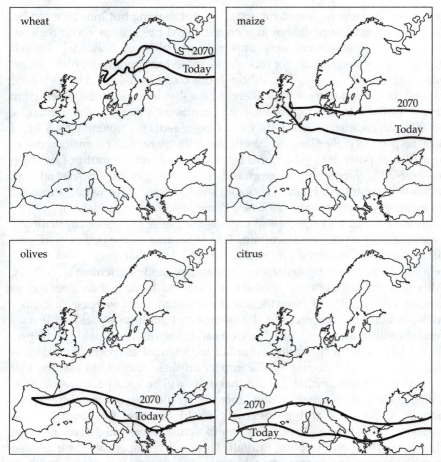

Figure 5.7 Predicted changes in the northern cropping boundary of four selected crops in Europe.

There are likely to be regions that particularly benefit from any temperature rise. Iceland is a country where temperature is a severe constraint on agriculture. As a consequence, much of the agricultural activity is currently based on sheep rearing. It is estimated that Icelandic agricultural output could more than double by the middle of the next century (Parry and Carter 1988). This is based on several changes that would be triggered by warming. The start of the growing season would be brought forward by 50 days, decreasing the requirement for overwintering of stock. On improved pasture production will increase by 66% and on unimproved by 50%. There would be a 50% reduction in the need for bought overwintering feed and overall sheep numbers could increase by as much as 250%. In addition, there could be a switch away from livestock to grain crops.

In the cool regions of the world GEC will increase yield, but the nearer the equator you go the more likely it is that yield will be adversely affected. This is because in these regions temperature is not limiting but moisture can be. Although overall rainfall should increase, GCM predictions about regional precipitation changes are very uncertain and there is only very limited agreement between computer models. Increased temperature will undoubtedly reduce water availability, although this could be balanced by increased rainfall. In Europe there is thus likely to be a shift in agricultural potential in favour of the northern countries, with Scandinavia increasing potential by 10–20% but countries such as Italy and Greece reducing potential by 5% and 36% respectively. Similarly in North America there will be an increase in agricultural potential in the north but a decrease further south of between 5% and 20%, depending on crop and region. In contrast, in Australia an increase in summer rainfall of about 40% is predicted. This would stimulate an increase in yield of over 20% (see Parry 1990 for further details).

In the tropical and subtropical regions the future changes in agricultural potential are particularly uncertain. This is because of the difficulty of predicting rainfall changes coupled with the fact that there is a strong relationship between moisture availability and agricultural output. Although the temperature increase is likely to be less than average, at around 1.5°C, this will nevertheless cause a significant increase in evapotranspiration. In large areas of the tropics and subtropics yield is directly related to the amount of water the crop can transpire. Thus yield can be predicted largely from the ratio of rainfall to potential evapotranspiration. A starting point for considering the impact on these areas is to assume that rainfall will remain unchanged but that there will be a temperature increase. Under these circumstances a 1.5°C increase would increase evapotranspiration by about 10% and productivity could decrease by about 10% in response. In addition to altering temperature there might be regional changes in the distribution of rainfall. This could compensate for increased evapotranspiration in some areas, but might also result in areas where there is a severe reduction in agricultural potential.

Even in cooler climates rainfall can be the principal factor determining yield. In the breadbasket areas of North America and the Ukraine there is a strong relationship between yield and rainfall, but not so strong with temperature. One scenario predicted as a possibility by some of the models is a drying of the North American continental interior accompanied by an increase in temperature. The decreased rainfall coupled with increased evapotranspiration could cost as much as $33 billion in reduced crop production.

Adaptive changes

Most of the predictions about the possible effects of climate change on agriculture assume that there will be no adaptive response by farmers. This is a useful viewpoint to illustrate the magnitude of the effects of climate change. However, in reality farmers will adapt to climate change by altering the crops grown or their methods of cultivation. At any given latitude and water availability a farmer will have a range of crops which will be most likely to succeed. Which are chosen depends on an assessment of the costs and benefits associated with each crop. This must include a consideration of the total yield and likelihood of a success (profit) or failure (loss) in any given year.

One of the most important adaptive changes in cultivation technique will be an increased use of irrigation in areas subjected to a reduction in soil moisture. Estimates for the southern region of the US Great Plains indicate that a 25% increase in irrigation could be needed, whereas a 10% increase would be required in the north. This is expensive but would help maintain production. Other smaller adaptive changes could include altering the timing of planting and harvest, the growing of windbreaks to reduce erosion problems and the application of additional fertilizer to cope with reduced soil fertility.

It should also be remembered that most global environmental changes will be gradual, occurring over many years, so there will be ample opportunity for making adaptive changes. An exception to this is the possible increase in occasional extreme events such as droughts and storms. There is also a certain amount of inertia involved: farmers will tend to continue to use familiar crops until it is clearly more appropriate to change. Exactly when the switch from one crop to another occurs is therefore a threshold process, where there is a sudden switch from one state to another as climate alters.

Genetic resources

Changes in the zonation of vegetation (see Chapter 4) may result in a reduction in biodiversity and genetic diversity within plant species. This is particularly important for many crop species, where much of the genetic diversity is preserved as land races growing wild in the areas from which the crop originated. Genes in these land races may confer tolerance to pests and diseases or help cope with environmental stresses such as drought. Take, for example, maize, which originates from a fairly restricted area of central America. If climate change greatly alters the environmental conditions in this area any surviving wild relatives of maize may be lost. There are reasonably well stocked gene banks for the more important agricultural species where seed samples of large numbers of land races are kept, but these can only hold a sample of all the genes available and, furthermore, they are not so well developed for many tropical crops.

Plant breeders are likely to be able to supply new varieties of major crops that are bred to thrive in new conditions. The network of gene banks stores vast numbers of varieties and genotypes and makes seeds and tubers available to breeders worldwide for use in traditional breeding and micropropagation. Table 5.2 indicates the scale of this genetic resource for plants. However, there are only a few small gene banks for domestic live-

Table 5.2 Numbers of genetically distinct crop varieties, mutants and wild taxa in gene banks for some major crops (from Cohen *et al.* 1991)

Centre	Crop	Number of varieties
Asian Vegetable Research and Development Centre	Tomato	3 814
CIMMYT*	Barley	7 200
	Bread wheat	48 600
	Durum wheat	15 300
	Primitive wheats	4 320
	Triticale	11 700
	Wild relatives	2 700
International Potato Center	Potato (clonal, *in vitro*, seed)	4 500
International Crops Research	Groundnut (peanut)	12 841
Institute for the Semi-Arid Tropics	Pearl millet	21 919
	Sorghum	32 890
	Chickpea	15 995
International Rice Research Institute	Rice	86 000

* International Maize and Wheat Improvement Centre.

stock. This is because, at present, animal material can only be stored as frozen semen or embryos. Storage time is limited and the cost in time and money of using the material in animal breeding programmes is considerable. Not surprisingly, there is much more of a cost to breeding, rearing and evaluating large numbers of cattle for several generations than plots of wheat.

Food security

There is currently a 20% surplus in world food production, but the yearly variation is approximately 10% above and below this. A computer model of the global agricultural system was used to look at the implications of an increase or decrease in agricultural production that might occur as a result of GEC (Liverman 1983). It was assumed that there would be a gradual decrease in yield potential of 20% over a period from 1985 to 2000. This is a much more severe reduction in potential than is likely to occur. Actual world output only decreased by 5–7% as the land area under production, the intensity of production and the area under different crops altered as a consequence of price changes. Therefore there is the capacity to absorb a considerable amount of change in agricultural potential but still maintain agricultural output. Another model assumed that grain production in the USA, Canada and Europe would be most affected, whereas the rest of the world would remain unaffected. It was found that a 20% decrease in production in these areas could be absorbed without a major disturbance to world food supplies, but that there would be a significant price rise of 5–10%, which could affect countries requiring large grain imports. Thus global food security may be only marginally affected by climate change. However, this analysis does not take into account the increasing requirements placed on food production by the rapid expansion of world population.

Regional food security is more likely to be threatened by GEC. This is unlikely to be a gradual process of decreasing yield tracking long-term changes in the climate: it is more likely to be the consequence of the increasing probability of a food crisis. Years in which the harvest is very low can occur as a consequence of a single extreme event, such as a storm, a heat wave or a pest infestation. A sequence of milder events occurring together may also result in a poor growing season. A single poor year is likely to have limited consequences for a region, as there will be sufficient reserves to compensate. However, two or more such seasons in succession can result in severe regional food shortages, and in some cases famine. If the probability of a single poor season doubles, the probability of two in a row will increase fourfold. So, relatively small changes in the probability of crop success in a region can substantially increase the likelihood of a food crisis. This will be especially important for regions with a large number of marginal farmers, who are more at risk from disaster. These people may be surviving on plots only just sufficient to supply their needs, or farming land which is marginal in terms of climate.

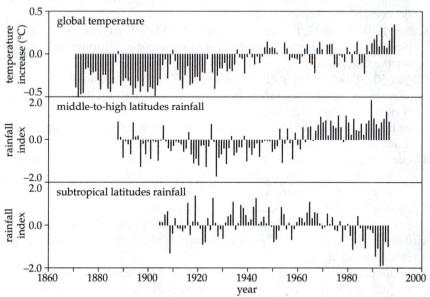

Figure 5.8   Recent changes in global temperature compared to changes in average rainfall at different latitudes. The data are expressed as differences from the 1951–1979 mean. An arbitrary index of rainfall has been used to allow for the variation in rainfall from place to place. (from Gribbin and Kelly 1989.)

Future changes in the environment can act to both increase and decrease agricultural output. Most likely some regions will benefit from the environmental changes, whereas others will be adversely affected. Yet human populations will be unable to migrate to take advantage of such changes because of national interests. This means that almost inevitably some regions will experience food shortages. When looking at a graph of temperature and rainfall in a region, the effects of climatic change may appear small. Yet the occurrence of successive drought years was a major contributor to severe famine in these regions in the 1980s. Most aid agencies involved with coping with these famines will point out that the loss in agricultural output need not have resulted in famine. The famines often occurred in countries troubled by political conflicts, and the relief effort was often hampered by poor access to the affected people. In a world where regional food shortages become more likely, political stability and a well organized relief operation are probably the best hopes for coping with the inevitable problems.

References

Baker NR, Farage PK, Stirling CM, Long SP (1994) Photoinhibition of crop photosynthesis in the field at low temperatures. In *Photoinhibition of photosynthesis from molecular mechanisms to the field*, eds NR Baker and JR Bowyer. BIOS, Oxford, pp.1–24

Cohen JI, Williams JT, Plucknett DL, Shands H (1991) *Ex situ* conservation of plant genetic resources: global development and environmental concerns. *Science* **253**, 866–72

Collier RH, Finch S, Phelps K, Thompson AR (1991) Possible impacs of global warming on cabbage root fly (*Delia radicum*) activity in the UK. *Annals of Applied Biology* **118**, 261–71

Cure JD, Acock B (1986) Crop responses to carbon dioxide doubling: a literature survey. *Agricultural and Forest Meteorology* **38**, 127–45

Decker WL, Jones VK, Achutuni R (1986) *Impact of climate change from increased carbon dioxide on American agriculture.* US Department of Energy Report TR-031, Washington DC

Gifford RM (1979) Growth and yield of CO_2-enriched wheat under water-limited conditions. *Australian Journal of Plant Physiology* **6**, 367–78

Gribbin J, Kelly M (1989) *Winds of change. Living with the greenhouse effect*, Hodder and Stoughton, London

Kimball BA (1982) *Carbon dioxide and agricultural yield. An assemblage and analysis of 430 prior observations.* WCL Report 11. US Water Conservation Laboratory, Phoenix, Arizona

Klinedinst PL, Wilhite DA, Hahn GL, Hubbard KG (1993) The potential effects of climate change on summer season dairy cattle milk production and reproduction. *Climate Change* **23**, 21–36

Larcher W (1980) *Physiological plant ecology*. Berlin, Springer Verlag

Liverman DM (1983) *The use of a simulation model in assessing the impacts of climate change on the world food system*. NCAR Cooperative thesis 77, National Centre for Atmospheric Research, Boulder, Colorado

Luo Y, Field CB and Mooney HA (1994) Predicting responses of photosynthesis and root fraction to elevated [CO_2] interactions among carbon, nitrogen, and growth. *Plant, Cell and Environment* **17**, 1195–1204

Monteith JL (1981) Climate variation and the growth of crops. *Quarterly Journal of the Royal Meteorological Society* **107**, 749–74

Parker C, Riches CR (1993) *Parasitic weeds of the world: biology and control*, CAB International, Wallingford

Parry M (1990) *Climatic change and world agriculture*, Earthscan, London

Parry M, Carter TR (1988) The assessment of the effects of climatic variations on agriculture. In *The impact of climatic variations on agriculture, Vol. 1. Assessments in cool temperate and cold regions*, eds ML Parry, TR Carter, NT Konijn. Kluwer, Dordrecht.

Porter JH, Parry ML, Carter TR (1991) The potential effects of climatic change on agricultural insect pests. *Agricultural and Forest Meteorology* **57**, 221–40

Russell JS (1991) Likely climatic changes and their impact on the northern pastoral industry. *Tropical Grasslands* **25**, 211–18

Schmidtmann ET, Miller JA (1989) Effect of climatic warming on populations of the horn fly, with associated impact on weight gain and milk production in cattle. In *The potential effects of global climatic change on the United States. Appendix C: Agriculture. Volume 2*, eds JB Smith, DA Tirpak. United States Environmental Protection Agency, Washington DC

Stinner BR, Taylor RAJ, Hammond RB, Purrington FF, McCartney DA (1989) Potential effects of climatic change on plant–pest interactions. In *The potential effects of global climatic change on the United States. Appendix C: Agriculture. Volume 2*, eds JB Smith, DA Tirpak. United States Environmental Protection Agency, Washington DC

Further Reading

Hanson JD, Baker BB, Bourdon RM (1993) Comparison of the effects of different climate change scenarios on rangeland livestock production. *Agricultural Systems* **41**, 487–502

Excellent example of a model that includes effects of GEC on plant production and quality and relates them to animal performance.

Parry M (1990) *Climate change and world agriculture*, Earthscan, London

Porter JH, Parry ML, Carter TR (1991) The potential effects of climate change on agricultural insect pests. *Agricultural and Forest Meteorology* **57** 221–40

Considers characteristics that matter for pest insects, and includes a model for spread of the European corn borer.

6 Aquatic ecosystems

Introduction

Water bodies cover 70% of the earth's surface but we have made little mention of aquatic environments until now. One reason is that there are important differences between aquatic and terrestrial environments in the ways that temperature, O_2 and CO_2 concentrations fluctuate. This means that organisms must respond to different forms and degrees of environmental change, and they do this in different ways from terrestrial species. Part of the reason is that there are major differences in the physiology and ecology of aquatic organisms because water is such a different environment from land. The other reason is that there is considerable uncertainty about the possible effects of GEC on aquatic environments because the environments themselves are so poorly understood.

In this chapter we consider first the changes that might be expected during GEC and their consequences for biological productivity. We then examine possible effects on plants, animals and communities. Finally, we consider the implications for the fishing industry and for coastal ecosystems.

Effects of GEC on aquatic environments

It is much more difficult to predict changes in aquatic than in terrestrial environments, especially for large bodies of water. The main problem is that we have a very poor understanding of the relationship between global climate and the oceans. It is clear that each influences the other, but we know little of the main processes that operate, never mind the subtleties.

Oceans, seas and lakes

The following major changes in oceans, seas and lakes are predicted using models of global climate and combining the results with historical evidence about past climate changes.

- Global increase in **air temperature at the water surface** and in **water temperature**, especially during the winter and at higher latitudes (>70°). Ocean warming is likely to lag behind atmospheric and terrestrial warming by about 20 years, longer for the deeper oceans. However, temperature below the surface is not related in a simple way to surface temperature. This is because waters often do not mix completely and there can be a complex stratification (layering of water, caused when warmer water floats on denser, cooler water or less saline water floats on denser, more saline water) of water at different temperatures at different depths. Temperature affects stratification, but other factors such as winds and discharges from rivers influence it too.
- Change in **freeze–thaw cycles**, with snow and ice thawing earlier and freezing later.
- Warmer water will lead to a **decline in dissolved O_2** because the higher temperature will increase the rate of bacterial activity in water and sediment. One model applied to Lake Erie allows for a doubling of atmospheric CO_2 and an increase in monthly temperatures of 3 to 8°C. The model predicts a decline in dissolved O_2 in summer of around 1 mg/l in the upper layers of the lake reducing the O_2 level to around 7–8 mg/l and a decline of 1-2 mg/l in the lower layers reducing the O_2 level to 1–3 mg/l. An increase in the volume of the lake that is anoxic (0 mg/l dissolved O_2) is also predicted (Blumberg and Di Toro 1990).
- **No significant increase in dissolved CO_2.** The chemistry of carbonate in seawater works in such a way that if the concentration of CO_2 in the atmosphere increases by 10% that of seawater would only increase by 1%.
- **Widespread movement of water masses** through the oceans means that climate change in one region could affect conditions in another region after a time lag.
- Changes in **wind direction and intensity** affecting the mixing in water bodies and modifying ocean and coastal currents.
- Changes in **rainfall**, leading to major changes in **regional hydrology**. Predicting these effects is difficult because climate change will affect both vegetation and soils, so that estimates of evapotranspiration are little more than guesswork. A 25% decrease in rainfall could decrease runoff by 80% in dry temperate areas, 60% in wet temperate areas and 70% in wet tropics. In other regions rainfall will increase and flooding will become more severe. Whatever the pattern, the amounts of water entering water bodies from runoff, from rivers and from groundwater are likely to change.
- Changes in **cloud cover**, causing changes in the depth to which light penetrates below the water surface. If nutrient-rich layers are deep down and less light reaches them, productivity could be reduced.

Taking all these factors into account, changes have been predicted for particular regions. One model for the northwest Atlantic is summarized in Table 6.1.

Flowing water

Flowing water behaves in a very different way from standing water. The characteristics that matter to plants and animals include depth, speed of flow, O_2 level, temperature and substrate on the river bottom. Each of these varies much more widely in rivers and streams than in standing water. This variation is found over short distances and over short periods of time.

The biggest impacts of GEC on flowing water will be caused by changes in rainfall patterns. If rainfall is reduced during climate change, effects on rivers and streams could include the following:

• reduced stream flow;
• major changes in seasonal patterns of stream flow but not necessarily in the total annual flow;
• more significant changes in arid areas, where water supply could be less than human demand;
• contraction of lakes and wetlands;
• highly variable precipitation leading to more flash floods. Consequences are increased erosion and transport of sediment;
• changes in water quality, for example more and longer droughts and more fires in a catchment would affect water quality. There would be an increase in SO_4^{2-} and H^+ ions in particular and a consequent reduction in pH. This is the same environmental effect as acid rain.

In areas where rainfall is increased, results will be different again.

Productivity of marine ecosystems and the effect of GEC

Primary productivity is closely linked to temperature and the length of the growing season, but although it is true that higher temperatures often

Table 6.1   Predicted effects of GEC on the North Atlantic off Canada. (After Wright et al. 1986, Frank et al. 1990)

Increase in water temperature
Greater freshwater discharge from rivers
Reduction in salinity close to the shore due to greater freshwater discharge
Sea ice thinner, less widespread, forming later in the year and breaking up earlier
Small decrease in strength and variability of winds
Increase in stratification of the water column leading to less mixing of water through tidal action
Stronger Labrador Current, weaker Gulf Stream, changes in patterns of water movement across ocean shelves and banks

---

increase biological activity (see Chapters 2 and 3), it is not temperature itself that leads to the change in productivity in marine ecosystems. More important is the degree of stratification in the water body. When air temperature is higher, stratification is greater. This is because there is a greater contrast between high temperatures near the surface and low temperatures in deep water, and a result is less mixing. Stratification is present throughout the year in the tropics because the surface temperatures are always high. In temperate regions it is present only during the summer, when surface temperatures are high. It is never found in polar regions because the temperatures at the surface and in deep water are similar.

Stratification has important consequences:

- There is less upward mixing of nutrients.
- Less organic material reaches the ocean bottom because (1) it is in the upper layers for longer so more is recycled, and (2) decomposition is more rapid at the higher temperatures.

The result is that primary production – and the biomass of the seafloor fish community – is reduced.

The contrast is most striking when tropical and temperate marine ecosystems are compared. Temperate oceans are 2–3 times as productive as tropical oceans. Tropical waters have distinct stratification all year round and are dominated by pelagic (upper-layer) fish species. Temperate waters have less stratification and more mixing and are dominated by demersal (seafloor) fish. Within the north Atlantic a temperature difference of several degrees causes a spectacular difference in the proportions of pelagic and demersal fish landed by commercial fishing vessels (Figure 6.1). Global warming will enhance temperate stratification, lowering primary production as there is less upward mixing of nutrients. The data for north Atlantic fish suggest that a change in mean annual bottom temperature from 3°C to 6°C, as predicted in global climate models, will lead to demersal species forming 20% less of the catch. That means fewer cod and more haddock.

Patterns of stratification can also affect the types of phytoplankton that dominate. Mixing of waters and a high input of nutrients lead to dominance by large, fast-growing diatoms (>100 µm). This is often the case in shallow coastal waters. However, away from the coasts stratification is usually greater and there is less turbulence. As a result, diatoms tend to sink below the surface layers to depths at which it is too dark for them to photosynthesize and survive. Smaller dinoflagellates (5–25 µm) can more easily maintain their position and they dominate instead. Why should this matter? One reason is that food chains based on smaller dinoflagellates tend to have one or two more links to reach commercial fish species than larger diatoms. For each link, energy transfer has an efficiency of only 10–20%, so that fish production from coasts where diatoms dominate is likely to be around 100 times greater than production in the oceans, where dinoflagellates are predominant.

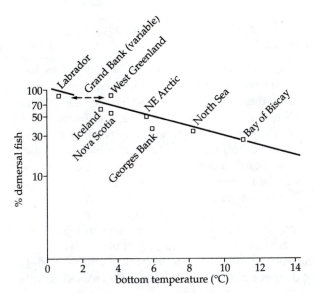

Figure 6.1   Relationship between ocean bottom temperature and the percentage of demersal fish in commercial catches. (From Jones 1982.)

Winds probably have a greater effect than temperature on stratification. During GEC the frequencies and intensities of local winds are likely to change. If winds decrease, stratification will be prolonged, dinoflagellates might become more dominant in shallow waters and fish production could be reduced. However, if winds increase there will be more mixing, larger diatoms will continue to dominate and productivity will increase as nutrients will not be limiting and temperature will be high.

There would be an even greater impact if there were changes to the winds and currents that cause coastal upwelling. At present there are a few areas – off Peru, California, northwest and southwest Africa, Somalia and Arabia – where the prevailing winds push surface waters away from the shore and ocean currents bring in deeper water which is rich in nutrients. These areas of coastal upwelling are easily the most productive in the world, yielding 50% of world fish production from only 0.1% of the ocean area (Table 6.2). Changes to the winds and currents that cause the upwelling could have a dramatic impact.

Table 6.2   Levels of primary productivity in the oceans. (After Ryther 1969)

	% of ocean	Mean productivity g carbon/m^2/yr
Open ocean	90	50
Coastal zone	9.9	100
Upwelling areas	0.1	300

Possible changes in the drawdown of CO_2 into aquatic ecosystems and effects on the global carbon cycle

Marine photosynthesis draws down between 30 and 50 Gtonnes of carbon from the atmosphere each year, but this is approximately balanced by the release of CO_2 into the atmosphere from the oceans (Williamson and Holligan 1992). Only 10–15% of this production is transported to deeper water. The rest is released to the atmosphere by respiration. The marine organic detritus takes several weeks to reach the bottom of the ocean and eventually, after being carried by deep currents for hundreds of years, this carbon reappears at the surface in upwellings. A small amount of the detritus, less than 0.5%, is incorporated in marine sediments.

There has been on average a 0.2–0.3°C increase in sea surface temperature since 1900, but there are marked regional variations in this record. A continued increase in surface temperature could affect phytoplankton productivity near the surface, but the increase in temperature will take 50–100 years to penetrate to the deeper ocean. The net effect of increased stratification and lower primary productivity would be a decrease in the uptake of CO_2 in places like the north Atlantic. Increased production may occur in polar seas currently covered by ice, and in the upwellings at the western continental margins. So, the net effect is uncertain but will probably act as a positive feedback by reducing CO_2 drawdown from the atmosphere.

Of the seven billion tonnes (7 Gtonnes) of carbon that is released into the atmosphere only about half remains there. The rest is absorbed by as yet unknown sinks. It was originally thought that the oceans were the primary missing sink, as large-scale land use changes, particularly tropical deforestation, argue against its being terrestrial, but recent comparisons of the CO_2 budget between the northern and southern hemispheres have revealed that a considerable fraction of the drawdown of CO_2 is in the north. The northern hemisphere is dominated by land not sea, and the most likely sink for CO_2 would be the extensive northern forests reacting to atmospheric CO_2 enrichment. Calculations based on these observations indicate that only 1 Gtonne is absorbed by the oceans and 2 Gtonnes by the northern sink. It is difficult to verify these speculations by direct observation of changes in marine or terrestrial productivity because of the considerable heterogeneity in both environments.

Productivity of streams, rivers and lakes and the effect of GEC

An excellent example of the possible consequences of increased temperature on lakes and lake organisms is provided by a long-term study on the lakes of northwest Ontario in Canada (Schindler *et al.* 1990). Monitoring started in 1970, and since then there has been an increase in air temperature of 2°C in the region. This is comparable to the maximum rates of temperature change expected by global warming, even though this example is more likely to be a consequence of a natural temperature fluctuation than evidence of global warming itself.

The direct effects of increased temperature were predictable. There was a higher water temperature and the ice-free period increased by an average of 23 days. But other important changes in the lake environment were less predictable. One of the most important was a decrease in precipitation, resulting in lower rates of water renewal in the lakes. As a consequence the concentration of nitrogen compounds and many other ions in the lake increased. However, the concentration of phosphorus compounds increased only slowly and then fell abruptly in 1986–1988. The nitrogen/phosphorus ratio changed from 25:1 to 50:1, resulting in increasing phosphorus limitation of primary production. There were more fires on the land around the lakes, and this may also have led to an increase in the input of solutes into the lakes. The fires and the lower inflow of water combined to reduce the amount of organic matter entering the lakes and so the waters became clearer, allowing more light to penetrate. Another consequence of more fires was more mixing of the lake waters as the burnt landscape did not shelter the lake surface as effectively from the wind. The productivity of the lakes increased as a result of the higher temperature and ion concentrations. However, the diversity of organisms present was only slightly increased and the dominant phytoplankton were unchanged. This example emphasizes the diverse and often unpredictable effects of a simple rise in temperature. The complex web of interactions that can occur make prediction of future changes very difficult, especially if human impacts such as fire are also involved.

Much of the nutrient supply for streams and small lakes comes from vegetation on their banks. For streams in deciduous forests, total respiration exceeds primary production. For desert streams with open canopies, low input of leaf litter and lots of sun the reverse is true (Busch and Fisher 1981). Either way, some of the organic matter from vegetation on the banks is respired by aquatic animals and some is transported downstream. Streams and lakes can therefore supply organic matter to other aquatic ecosystems. As temperatures rise primary production increases and so does respiration rate. Depending on the balance, streams and lakes could change from being a source of organic matter to become a sink in which the organic matter is respired. A result could be that less organic matter moves downstream.

GEC could also change the species, biomass and productivity of riverside and lakeside vegetation. The effects of these changes on aquatic communities can be significant. Until the early 1900s many river banks in eastern North America were lined by American chestnut trees. In 1904 chestnut blight disease was accidentally introduced from Asia. It spread and destroyed large numbers of the chestnuts. Oaks and hickory grew up in their place. Leaves falling from trees into water below are a food source for many aquatic invertebrates and leaves from different trees have a different nutritional value. For example, stonefly larvae reared on oak rather than chestnut eat less, grow more slowly and develop into smaller adults (Smock and

MacGregor 1988). One consequence of stonefly larvae and other leaf shredders eating less is that they release smaller amounts of fine particles of organic matter, and so less is available for other invertebrates that feed by collecting it from the water. These changes are certainly subtle, but could matter to populations and communities.

On a broader scale, climate change could combine with other environmental changes to affect the quality of water entering rivers and streams. A study of one catchment in the uplands of Scotland considered three environmental changes simultaneously: deposition of sulphur and nitrogen oxides (acid deposition or 'acid rain'), land use conversion from moorland to forestry, and climate change. If moorland is retained climate change would have little effect on stream water alkalinity (i.e. the capacity to neutralize acid, related mostly to the quantity of bicarbonate HCO_3^- ions). Converting moorland to forestry plantations would reduce the alkalinity by 15–28%, and a further 3–6% if accompanied by climate change. If acid deposition is reduced to the levels envisaged by international agreements, alkalinity would increase by 8–34% (Ferrier *et al.* 1993). Thus climate change plays a part, but it is one of several components which are very rarely considered together. However, climate change could have very visible effects at certain times of year. In summer there would be increased mineralization of sulphur and nitrogen in the soil, causing high concentrations in streams during autumn storms and creating problems of low pH for fish and invertebrates.

Several different influences make it a complex picture, but it is clear that changes in inputs from the terrestrial ecosystem will affect aquatic communities. This will occur not only at the point of entry of inputs but downstream too.

Responses of aquatic organisms to changes in the aquatic environment

Differences between aquatic and terrestrial environments

To see how these changes could affect aquatic organisms, we need to consider first the fundamental differences between aquatic and terrestrial environments and the ways in which aquatic organisms detect and respond to change in their environment.

Changes in CO_2, O_2 and temperature will affect aquatic organisms in very different ways from terrestrial organisms because CO_2 and O_2 are present in different quantities in water from air, and because temperature change will not only have an effect itself but will also alter CO_2 and O_2 levels. Therefore, before considering particular responses to climate change it is essential to see the fundamental ways in which aquatic and terrestrial environments differ.

All the gases present in the air are soluble in water, but the solubilities of different gases in water are different. At 15°C and normal pressure the solubility of CO_2 is around 30 times higher than that of O_2. Because atmospheric air contains 21% O_2 and only 0.035% CO_2, the actual concentration of CO_2 in water is around 23 times less than the concentration of O_2. O_2 and CO_2 diffuse through water at approximately the same rate because their molecules are of roughly similar size, but because of the different solubilities the amount of CO_2 that diffuses is greater.

As temperature increases solubility decreases. For O_2, solubility is halved as temperature increases from 0°C to 30°C (Figure 6.2). Solubility is also decreased by salts dissolved in the water, so that for typical seawater the solubility of O_2 is 20% lower than for fresh water (Figure 6.2).

Change in temperature is determined by heat capacity. The heat capacity of water is greater than of air to the extent that over 3000 times as much energy is required to heat water as the same volume of air. Temperatures change with the season of the year in both aquatic and terrestrial environments, but because of the high heat capacity of water the extent of the changes is much less in seas and oceans than on land (Figure 6.3). Similarly, fluctuations throughout the day are over a vast range in most terrestrial environments but are negligible in seas and lakes.

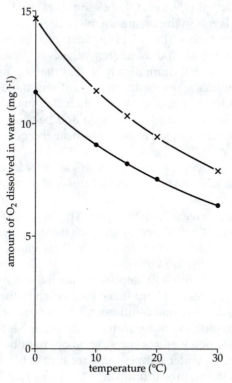

Figure 6.2   Effect of temperature on the amount of dissolved O_2 in fresh water (×) and seawater (•). (Data from Krogh 1941.)

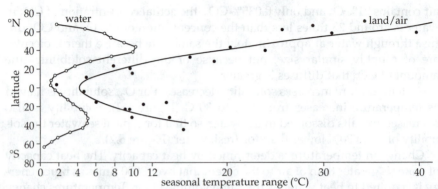

Figure 6.3   Seasonal temperature range for oceanic surface waters (O) and terrestrial air temperature (●). For both oceans and continents the temperature
range is narrow in the tropics and wide at temperate latitudes. The patterns diverge at high latitudes because continental temperatures
plummet to well below freezing, whereas seawater temperatures drop
no further than the freezing point of seawater (After Moore 1972, Times
Books 1985.)

Depth has an important effect on O_2 concentrations and water temperature. At all depths O_2 levels in the oceans are more or less adequate for plant
and animal life. Towards the surface, O_2 is not depleted because it is continually replenished from the air and by photosynthesis of plants. However, at
500–1000 m, O_2 levels can fall dramatically to less than 0.5 ml/l because of
high respiration by animals, no photosynthesis (there is no light) and no
mixing with the O_2-rich water above. Deeper than 1000 m O_2 supply is not a
problem, because so few animals live so deep and because ocean currents
maintain a flow of O_2-rich surface water from near the poles to ocean bottoms all over the world.

The level of CO_2 at all depths is almost always at a low level that does not
affect animals because it is so soluble and because, in seawater, it is highly
buffered.

Water temperature decreases with depth. The temperature of surface
waters in the tropics is usually above 20°C, but it decreases to 5°C at 1000 m
and to a constant 3°C at 3000 m or more. Despite these changes, the temperatures at the different depths are virtually constant for long periods of time.
Different temperatures at different depths create the stratification of the
water body. For ponds, lakes and land-locked seas such as the Black Sea and
the Gulf of California, the situation is different. The same stratification exists,
but it causes deoxygenation in deeper water because there is no mixing with
upper layers and no O_2-rich water is entering on ocean-bottom currents.

Annual fluctuations in water temperature are greatest in temperate latitudes and smallest in the tropics and towards the poles (see Figure 6.3). On
average, the ocean surface temperature range is 2.5 times greater in temperate latitudes than in the tropics, and in coastal waters greater still. The

amount of the sun's radiation reaching the sea surface does not differ to any great extent (30% more for locations between 10°N and 10°S than for locations between 30° and 52° N and S), although it is less seasonal in the tropics. Tidal range is greater in temperate latitudes, giving strong tidal currents that improve oxygenation and the distribution of food.

The O_2, CO_2 and temperature environments of aquatic animals

The concentration of O_2 in fresh water is around 10 mg/l or 0.7% (less at higher temperatures and at higher salinity) compared with 21% in normal air. Clearly, O_2 is less readily available in water. This means that aquatic organisms need to bring more water into contact with respiratory organs. Because water is so much denser than air, the mass of water to be moved is enormous. One calculation suggests that aquatic animals need to move 100 000 times their weight in water to obtain a given amount of O_2 compared to terrestrial animals that need only to move 3.5 times their weight in air to obtain the same amount. This is one reason why ventilation systems for aquatic and terrestrial organisms are so different. Gills that provide a throughflow of water are an efficient way of coping with the volume of water and its enormous mass.

The main stimulus for increased respiration for aquatic animals such as crustaceans and fish is a low level of O_2. This contrasts with terrestrial animals, which respond to high levels of CO_2 (see Chapter 3). There is an important reason for this. As we have already said, the level of CO_2 in water is almost always low because it is so soluble and, in seawater, because seawater is highly buffered. Because CO_2 is so soluble in water, aquatic animals cannot build up high levels of CO_2 and so cannot rely on it to indicate the need for O_2. In these circumstances the only suitable stimulus is a deficit of O_2. The only exceptions are diving mammals and birds, which move below the water surface only temporarily. They normally respond to CO_2 levels in their bodies, but when they are diving they simply ignore indications that CO_2 is building up.

Hypoxic (low O_2) and anoxic (no O_2) conditions are a common problem for aquatic organisms, such as invertebrates in muddy lake bottoms, molluscs sealed within their shells at low tide and fish in rivers that warm up. One response is for animals to rely on anaerobic metabolism when O_2 is in short supply. Others increase the efficiency of respiratory and blood systems to make the most of whatever O_2 is available. A third response to low O_2 is to move in search of more favourable conditions.

Responses to temperature and temperature change are broadly similar to those of terrestrial species. However, the high heat capacity and conductivity of water make it difficult for animals to maintain a different body temperature from their surroundings. The only exceptions are a few large, active fish. All aquatic animals are adapted to the temperature ranges which are typical of the places where they occur: molluscs from the tropics cannot cope with large changes in temperature, but temperate species can (Figure 6.4).

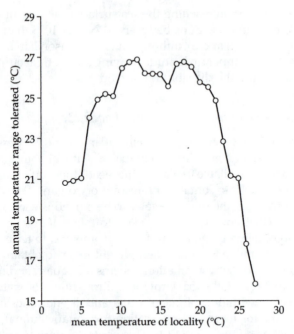

Figure 6.4   Range of temperatures tolerated by communities of American coastal molluscs for localities of different mean temperature. (From Moore 1972.)

Some species show seasonal acclimatization to lower temperatures in cooler seasons. Experiments have shown that environmental temperature affects the O_2 affinity of the blood of fish. When fish from waters of different temperatures are tested at the same temperature, fish acclimatized at higher temperatures have a higher O_2 affinity than those acclimatized at lower temperatures. However, if they are measured in their own environments the O_2 affinities are much closer. (There is still a slightly higher O_2 affinity for fish in warmer environments because of their higher metabolic rate.) Seasonal changes in O_2 affinity depend on characteristics of the red blood cells rather than changes in the properties of the haemoglobin.

As for terrestrial species, temperature matters because growth rate usually increases as temperature rises (see Chapter 3 and Figure 3.6). However, it eventually reaches a maximum and then declines sharply as the lethal upper temperature is approached. The consequence is that many fish species grow faster in the warmer parts of their range. Even so, fish growing in cooler waters can reach a greater final size despite growing much more slowly. A likely reason is that mortality is less because levels of predation are lower.

We showed in Chapter 3 that temperature also affects other aspects of biology. A particularly important factor for fish is size-dependent winter starvation. Only fish of a certain size at the start of winter have sufficient food reserves to survive the winter, a time when feeding can be severely

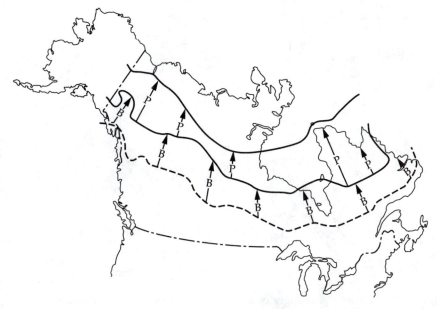

Figure 6.5   Present and predicted northern limits of yellow perch (P) and small-
mouth bass (B) in Canada. The northern limits are determined by the
ability of the fish to resist winter starvation. This model is based on an
air temperature increase of 4°C and no change in food availability. It is
a coincidence that the future northern limit of the bass is close to the current northern limit of the perch. (From Shuter and Post 1990.)

restricted. The problem is that smaller fish have a higher basal metabolic rate
than larger fish, but without any increase in capacity to store energy. The
consequence is that smaller fish are less tolerant of starvation because their
energy reserves are used up more quickly. This is often the overriding factor
that limits the distribution of fish species (Figure 6.5).

Cues used by aquatic animals

Low levels of O_2 cause a behavioural response in aquatic animals, which
move around the environment to select suitable conditions from those available. The animals respond in the same way to unsuitable temperatures, with
scales of movement ranging from a few metres in ponds to seasonal migrations of hundreds of kilometres.

Events such as breeding and migration are nearly always cued by temperature. For spawning the most frequent cue is rising temperature. This is
shown vividly by comparing the dates at which waters warm up after winter with the timing of spawning (Figure 6.6). There is a close correlation:
cold-water species spawn in the summer, temperate species spawn in the
spring and tropical species spawn in the summer. In locations where there is

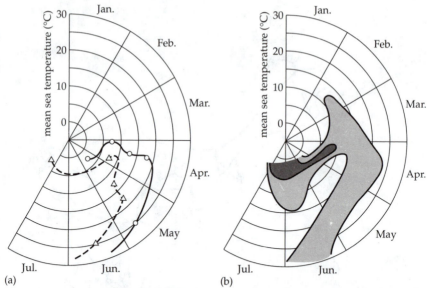

Figure 6.6   Influence of changes of sea temperature on spawning dates of marine invertebrates in the northern hemisphere. In the illustrations data are given for mean sea temperatures, ranging from around 3°C (at the centre of the circles) to around 25°C (at the edge). (a) Dates at which sea temperature rises to 2°C (——) and 4°C (- - -) above the winter minimum. (b) Dates at which species start spawning. The heavier shading indicates spawning by ≥30% of species, the lighter shading by ≥10% of species. Spawning is least synchronized in the tropics. (From Moore 1972.)

a wide seasonal fluctuation in temperature, changes are more striking and animals will respond at more or less the same time. If there is very little variation in temperature, as in the tropics, there will be much less synchrony.

Temperature is the **cue**, but not usually the **reason** why marine animals migrate. This is probably to allow animals to exploit different food resources. Species of tuna, for example, move from the tropics to temperate areas rich in food when water temperatures are warm enough and return to the tropics to spawn.

Possible responses of particular groups

Because of the complexity of the aquatic environment, simple links between local climate and responses of aquatic organisms are going to be rare. Even so, a little is known about the possible responses of a few species.

Invertebrates

Temperature affects invertebrate growth and survival in many different ways, which are not always predictable (see Chapter 3). However, studies on commercially valuable species give some indication of how species could respond (Frank *et al.* 1990). For example, production of American lobster in any year can be related to water temperature in their first winter, and whole generations of a population can be decimated if water temperature falls below a critical minimum. In the same way, abundance of sea scallops can be related to water temperature because higher temperatures give faster larval development and better survival, and because the sea currents at higher temperatures increase the chance of scallops settling close to their parental beds where conditions are good. Green sea urchins, however, can suffer mass mortality on rare occasions when water temperatures rise. This is because they become vulnerable to an amoeboid protist pathogen which causes loss of spines and necrosis. They can resist infection at below 8–12°C but above this temperature they cannot. Mass mortality of green sea urchins can have far-reaching consequences for the whole community because they graze and destroy large areas of seaweed, and their presence or absence determines the whole nature of the ecosystem (Scheibling and Stephenson 1984). Clearly, each species responds to small temperature changes in a characteristic way and it is not sensible to generalize. However, the impact throughout the community of small temperature changes can be considerable, and consistently higher temperatures during GEC are likely to be very significant.

Fish in large water bodies

The presence of a fish species in a habitat and its wider geographical distribution are determined by two main factors. The first is the need to avoid extreme temperatures. Laboratory and field data suggest that many fish occupy a thermal band within ±2.0°C of a preferred temperature, and actively avoid higher or lower temperatures at which their metabolic efficiency is poorer. The second is the need to avoid low concentrations of dissolved O_2. Water quality criteria from the US Environmental Protection Agency state that 'cold water' fish in fresh water require a minimum of 3 mg/l dissolved O_2 for adult fish and 8 mg/l for early life stages.

   Fish actively respond throughout the year to changes in temperature and O_2 profiles of water bodies in order to remain in their preferred environment. In response to temperature, fish will move between warmer shorelines and cooler deeper waters, or into and out of tributaries discharging water at different temperatures from the main water body. In warmer months, concentrations of dissolved O_2 can decrease to critically low levels in large parts of the water body and fish respond by moving to refuges where temperature and O_2 levels remain favourable. If no such refuges are available, there is no alternative but to avoid the volume of water with critically low O_2 levels. This means moving into warmer water at shallower depths, where metabolic inefficiency and crowding can lead to poorer performance, reduced reproductive success and mortality.

Warmer water and lower dissolved O_2 concentrations during GEC will increase the intensity and length of the stressful summer period. The model for Lake Erie suggests that the predicted decrease in dissolved O_2 for shallower waters is not likely to affect fish, but the decrease at greater depths could take dissolved O_2 concentrations to less than the physiologically critical $3 \, \text{mg/l}$.

It is possible to relate abiotic changes to possible impacts on particular fish species. One model predicts the effects of GEC on striped bass. This species occurs off the eastern coast of North America, with a relict population in the north of the Gulf of Mexico (Figure 6.7). For adult fish, the preferred temperature range is 19–23°C; for juveniles it is 24–28°C. A proportion of the fish follow these temperatures in a seasonal migration, moving north as temperatures rise and south as temperatures fall. Others maintain these temperatures by moving into and out of cooler water in estuaries. GEC models suggest that there will be increases in water temperature at all latitudes, and that zones of the preferred temperature will shift northwards by several hundred kilometres. Maturation of the adults is set by day length, but spawning is cued by temperature and the models suggest that spawning will occur 3–4 weeks earlier than at present. In the Gulf of Mexico conditions may become too severe, with water temperatures rising to 30°C, and the population could disappear altogether. However, it might be maintained by cool river waters reaching the Gulf and creating lower-temperature refuges. If this occurs it would not be the result of a natural phenomenon: it would result from human demand for water forcing water companies to make summer discharges from cool, deep reservoirs or underground reserves.

Similar changes in distribution are likely for large lakes. With the thawing of the Great Lakes after the last glaciation, 122 fish species colonized the Lakes from refuges in the Mississippi and the Atlantic. Other species did not colonize but still remain in these refuges. Mandrak (1989) considered 58 of these and concluded that 27 are likely to invade the Great Lakes with climate change. Most of these are small near-shore warm-water omnivores such as minnows and sunfish. The speed at which they colonize will depend on routes of invasion through rivers or canals.

Another species to be affected by warming is whitefish, a dominant species in Lake Constance in Central Europe. Early stages feed in April and May, and prefer the shallows or upper layer of open water where the water is warmest. In these 2 months, and only then, there is a strong correlation of water temperature with growth (Figure 3.6(b)) and survival. In June the larvae move to deeper water at 10–12°C, which is preferred by adults. A GEC model developed by Trippel et al. (1991) suggests that water temperatures will increase in April and May, a critical time for the whitefish, and this will cause a considerable increase in the number of whitefish produced. A mean of 1.5 million per year during 1962–1985 could rise to 2.0 million, 3.7 million or 6.7 million as the temperature of surface water in April rises by 1.5°C,

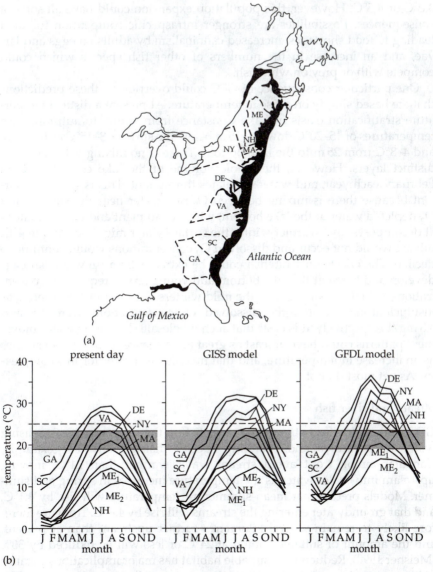

(a)

(b)

Figure 6.7   (a) Coastal distribution of striped bass in eastern North America. (b) Coastal water temperatures at the present day and under two different models for GEC. The shaded area is the preferred temperature for striped bass (19–23°C). The dashed line shows the upper temperature limit for the fish. Data are given for coastal stations in Georgia (GA), South Carolina (SC), Virginia (VA), Delaware (DE), New York state (NY), Massachusetts (MA), New Hampshire (NH) and two sites in Maine (ME). (After Coutant 1990.)

3.0°C or 4.5°C. However, this population expansion could have all sorts of consequences. Possibilities are stronger intraspecific competition for food leading to food shortages, increased cannibalism by adults on eggs and larvae, and an increase in the numbers of other fish species which could compete with or prey on whitefish.

One particular consequence of GEC could override all these predictions that are based simply on a rise in temperature. At present a distinct temperature stratification exists in Lake Constance from spring to autumn, with temperatures of 15–20°C down to 15 m below the surface, 8–15°C at 15–25 m, and 4–8°C from 25 m to the lake bottom. There is no mixing between these distinct layers. However, the whole volume of the lake cools to 4°C in February each year, and water circulates throughout. This is vitally important because there is mixing between O_2-rich water near the surface and O_2-depleted water at the lake bottom, where dead plant and animal material decomposes. In a warmer winter the surface water might not cool to 4°C, mixing would not occur and dissolved O_2 concentrations would continue to decline. The effects on whitefish could be extreme, because whitefish eggs develop and hatch at the lake bottom and young larvae require O_2 concentrations as high as 6–7 mg/l; in the mild winters of 1988 and 1989 there was insufficient mixing and the dissolved O_2 concentrations were 4.5 and 4.3 mg/l respectively. It is clear that such wholesale changes in water movement patterns could have at least as great an influence on many fish species as an increase in temperature, and that models must cater for this complexity. As yet most do not.

Stream and river fish

GEC is likely to affect stream and river fish in the same way by increasing water temperatures and changing species distributions. For example, Canadian brook trout avoid stream water warmer than 24°C, moving upstream into cooler water as the temperature increases in spring and summer. Models predict that mean summer air temperature will rise by 4.1°C, and that groundwater entering the streams will rise by 4.8°C. Trout are therefore likely to remain several kilometres further upstream than at present, and the amount of suitable habitat at 24°C or less will be reduced by 30% (Meisner 1990). Reduction in suitable habitat has major implications because habitat space determines the size of the trout population in the stream. The direction of river flow also matters. Many rivers flow east–west. Fish in these rivers will not have access to the cooler waters available in rivers flowing north–south.

Similar major changes are predicted by studies on implications for the fishing industry. Temperature increases ranging between 2.5 and 7.7°C predicted for eastern Canada will lead to a dramatic redistribution of freshwater fish productivity. Areas that have the highest yields at present will become marginal, and areas at the margin or outside present distributions of species will become optimal. The spectacular scale of the change is illustrated in Plate 7.

Models for streams in the southern United States predict increases in surface water temperature of up to 7°C. However, shading by riverside vegetation could reduce this, and GEC models predict an increase in forest cover that makes this a possibility in some regions. If, on the other hand, vegetation cover were reduced, the increase in water temperature could exceed 7°C. Technology exists that would allow the concentration of dissolved O_2 to be maintained at a desirable level despite an increase in water temperature. This would involve using advanced waste-water treatment to drastically reduce the amounts of high O_2-demanding materials that enter the water, and this equipment would need to be used much more widely than at present. A much simpler alternative is to use tall riverbank vegetation to provide shade for narrower rivers (Cooter and Cooter 1990).

Water temperature is just one of the several factors that influence the numbers of spring Chinook salmon. Important ones are listed in Table 6.3. Any predictions of the effects of GEC on the salmon must incorporate this whole set of factors, not just temperature. Conditions 6000–8000 years ago in the Pacific northwest were 2°C warmer than at present. It has been possible to piece together a picture of other differences at that time. These include:

• stream flow was <70% of its current rate;
• many more streams were dry for part of the year;
• sedimentation was greater and finer sand grains were deposited on stream beds;
• water temperatures were higher;
• the peak springtime flow ended 3–4 weeks earlier.

If this set of conditions recurs, Chatters et al. (1991) predict that the number of adult salmon returning each year to the Yakima River will drop from 9800 to 3900. However, there are many ways to improve the management of rivers to benefit salmon and these could boost numbers enormously, perhaps to 46 000 in present conditions or 24 000 if it is 2°C warmer. Even so,

Table 6.3 Environmental factors affecting Chinook salmon. (After Chatters et al. 1991)

Sedimentation
More sedimentation on the stream floor leads to greater suffocation of eggs and displacement of fry

Water temperature
Higher temperatures increase the incidence and severity of disease for adults returning to breeding sites

Volume and timing of the peak flow of the stream
If the peak flow is earlier and/or shorter, fewer fish are ready to leave the streams, the speed of the migration is slower and predation is greater

---

there are competing demands on the river and a solution for the salmon will not necessarily suit other fish or other uses of the river.

Species with specialized ecological requirements are most immediately at risk as precipitation declines. Fish in desert pools and streams are already endangered. Streams in the Great Plains of the United States can reach 38–40°C and in hotter summers the heat causes the death of some fish. It also has indirect effects on others by forcing them into cooler refuges, which become crowded, inhibiting foraging and increasing disease. Other fish require shallow waters with very precise environmental conditions as a refuge for gametes and a nursery for early life history stages. Even though such habitats will continue to exist, they are likely to be in different places and might not be found by the many fish that have strong homing behaviours. At least 20 fish species which are restricted to the Great Plains are likely to become extinct if water temperatures rise by 3–4°C (Matthews and Zimmerman 1990).

Communities and ecosystems

Changes in the aquatic environment will affect not only the occurrence and numbers of individual species but also whole assemblages of species. The result could be a simple shift of characteristic communities to new locations. The high mobility of marine organisms contrasts with the poor mobility of many terrestrial plant and animal species, and so the distribution of whole communities is likely to change more readily. For example, almost all reef fish disperse widely as planktonic larvae for several weeks, possibly over hundreds of kilometres; where populations establish is not limited by larvae failing to reach a suitable location but depends on factors such as turbidity, nutrient levels, productivity and turbulence, which determine whether they survive and how well they compete (Roberts 1991). Understanding such processes is an aim of current and future work and will give insights into the responses of communities to GEC. For now, we can look at several case studies of particular environments – coral reefs, Atlantic fishing grounds, the Pacific coast of South America, and coastlines – that have attracted the attention of biologists for very different reasons.

Coral reefs

Coral reefs are extremely diverse marine communities found in warm tropical waters where the temperature does not drop below 20°C. The basis of the reefs are coral animals (anthozoans, close relatives of sea anemones) which exist symbiotically with microorganisms such as dinoflagellates, red and green algae, and bacteria. Photosynthesizing microorganisms provide the host with the products of their photosynthesis. The calcium carbonate structures of coral reefs are a side-effect of this photosynthesis.

The modern-day distribution of corals is highly correlated with sea surface temperature. There are diverse coral communities (but not coral reefs) off the Japanese coast at Tateyama close to Tokyo. Studies of fossil and present-day corals have shown that the number of species has decreased from >70 to 34 over the last 5000–6000 years. This is probably due to a decrease in temperature. Studies of this site and others to the south have shown that the distribution limits of many species in these cooler waters change very rapidly, and that there are several itinerant species that move quickly into environments that suddenly become suitable. A rise of 2°C is enough to double species diversity at higher latitudes and would dramatically increase abundance (Veron 1992).

Whereas a rise in temperature could increase coral diversity in cooler latitudes, it could adversely affect corals in warmer water. Corals are 'bleached' when symbiotic microorganisms leave or are expelled from the host coral animals. The loss of the symbionts leaves the coral looking pale or white (Plate 6). Bleached corals are unable to capture food and can survive without feeding effectively for 1–2 months. However, if bleaching continues for long enough the corals die and the whole reef ecosystem is degraded.

Several different hypotheses have been suggested to account for bleaching (Brown and Ogden 1993). One is high temperature. It has been suggested that a rapid increase in the reported incidents of bleaching since the mid 1980s is a consequence of temperature and a sign of GEC. The only global study so far (Goreau and Hayes 1994) has indicated that bleaching occurs at different times in different regions. There was high incidence in 1983 throughout the Pacific, in 1987–1990 in the Caribbean, and in 1991 in the western Pacific. A comparison of patterns with satellite data on average ocean temperatures suggests that bleaching is triggered by regional warming rather than global. Bleaching occurs when the water temperature reaches >1°C higher than the long-term average (Figure 6.8). An interesting obser-

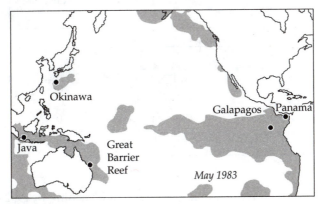

Figure 6.8   Ocean 'hot spots' (shaded) and sites of subsequent coral bleaching (•). Hot spots are regions where the water temperature is >1°C above the long-term average. (From Goreau and Hayes 1994.)

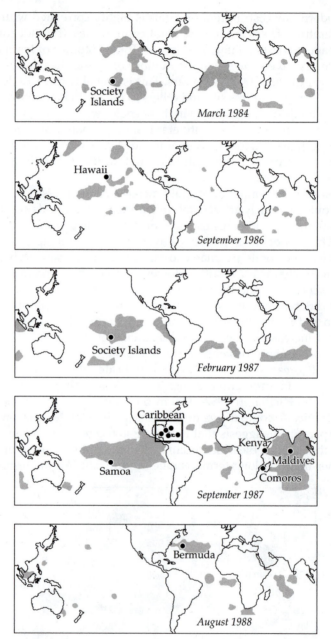

Figure 6.8 *continued.*

vation is the sudden reduction in new cases of bleaching in 1992 – possibly because of the eruption of Mount Pinatubo volcano in the Philippines, which ejected vast amounts of dust into the upper atmosphere and caused a general cooling.

There are problems with the hypothesis that temperature causes bleaching. One is that bleaching is often greatest in deeper waters, even though high temperatures are more likely to be in shallower waters. Another is that there are insufficient long-term data on environmental conditions with which to compare changes in the reefs.

Another suggested impact of GEC is the 'drowning' of reefs, which could take place if the sea level rises much more rapidly than reefs accrete new material. Drowning is unlikely because reef growth can continue as much as 20 m below the water surface, so long as the water is clear. Vertical accretion rates range from <1 mm/yr to >10 mm/yr. One estimate puts the rise in sea level at 6 mm/yr. Even if there were no vertical accretion this rate of sea level rise would submerge reefs by less than 1 m in the next 100 years. A further possibility is that higher CO_2 levels in seawater will increase the solubility of calcium carbonate $(CaCO_3)$ in the water. Many reef organisms are likely to respond directly to the amount of $CaCO_3$ available. Calcification (the process by which reef corals deposit an exoskeleton of calcium carbonate) of reef animals could decrease, so that reefs accrete more slowly. Alternatively, the organisms may construct weaker skeletons, giving a greater risk of physical damage. Perhaps non-calcifying organisms will become more dominant, changing the structure of the community.

Rapid changes and the fishing industry

New research programmes designed by marine biologists to monitor gradual changes in aquatic environments can provide only limited amounts of data because of the vast expense of continuous monitoring. Furthermore, they will take many years to detect any patterns that exist. An alternative approach is to use historical records. Although they might not include all the parameters that biologists would like, data from the fishing industry give useful clues about the directions and scale of changes in recent decades.

There are many documented cases in which climate changes have affected fish catches. Often the first indication of some sort of climate change is the surprise appearance of large, exotic individuals that are conspicuous in a catch. But a few individuals cannot tell us much. However, if the change is prolonged whole populations could move to new localities and some could remain and breed. One particularly well documented change is in the cod fishing industry off west Greenland. Very small numbers of cod were taken there during the second half of the nineteenth century. Annual catches then began to rise from 24 tonnes in 1912 to 247 tonnes in 1917 to 600 tonnes for 1919–1923. Catches then rocketed to up to 100 000 tonnes in the 1930s, up to 300 000 tonnes in the 1950s and 400 000 tonnes in the 1960s as populations increased, the distribution moved northwards and new locations were exploited (Figure 6.9). Tagging experiments since the 1920s showed a connection between cod populations off Greenland and off Iceland until the mid 1940s, with movements of fish in both directions, but since then only a few

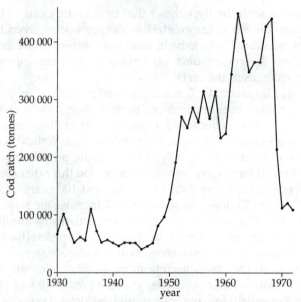

Figure 6.9   Cod catches off West Greenland. (From Cushing and Dickson 1976.)

movements from Greenland to Iceland have been recorded. The spectacular changes in numbers and migration patterns corresponded to a distinctly warm period. One possibility is that during warmer conditions cod spawned further north and east of Iceland, and this was in the path of an ocean current that transported the fish to west Greenland.

Another response to environmental change is in population size. Exceptional weather gives the most striking result. The winter of 1946–7, one of the coldest of the century in northwest Europe, caused large mortality in many North Sea invertebrates and fish. Half of the soles taken by fishing vessels were already dead (700 kg per landing). Other effects were the deaths of intertidal organisms such as barnacles, crabs and bivalves, and the eggs and larvae of fish that spawn close to the shore. Climate in any year affects the food available to fish larvae and affects the number of larvae that mature to join the fish population. Poor conditions in one year are often reflected in the numbers of fish landed several years later. The number of cod taken by the north Atlantic fishing industry, for example, depends on the food available to the same generation when feeding as larvae 7 or 8 years before.

Whole marine communities can change. In the English Channel, the Plymouth herring began to decline in 1925 and the fishing industry based on the herring collapsed completely by 1937. The biomass of macroplankton (organisms of 2–20 cm) decreased to a quarter, but at the same time pilchards began to be recorded in large numbers. A pilchard community then dominated until the late 1960s, when the change was reversed. These changes are likely to be a result of climatic events and the change from one community to another took about 10 years (around three generations).

These illustrations show that there is a lot to learn about the processes taking place in marine environments. Even so, many attempts have been made to create mathematical models of populations of particular species or of whole marine communities. Models are usually based on population dynamics and incorporate factors such as recruitment (the number of individuals entering the population), survival, breeding age and death rate. Modellers assume that the population is at some sort of equilibrium and use the model to predict changes that will occur if a few of the parameters vary. The models can cope with changes to parameters such as growth rate and survival, and give some idea of **directions** of changes even though the **scale** of change remains uncertain.

However, even the best models show 'noise' (scatter of data that is not predicted). Occasionally there are 'anomalies' (unexpected increases or declines in numbers, perhaps because of an unusual combination of favourable conditions or a single devastating event). There can also be 'catastrophes' where fish populations flip from one stable level to another, perhaps because of a major change in the environment. If noise, anomalies and catastrophes increase with GEC, the basic models on which governments and fishing authorities depend for planning sustainable fishing will need major revision. Subtle refinements to try to maintain the status quo are not likely to be enough, even though they would be the most convenient solution (and the most likely response). A much more adaptable approach will be required (Healey 1990).

Seas and oceans provide only 0.8% of human food supplies. Nevertheless, fish and seafood are staple foods in some countries and an important source of protein. If GEC has a significant effect on fisheries, the consequences could be extreme. Undoubtedly the expansion of range and greater abundance of fish stocks could benefit the fishing industry, but changes could also have negative effects. Striped bass, for example, could colonize the Great Lakes and might threaten salmon, which are economically much more valuable. Also, the ways in which humans exploit fish stocks will undoubtedly change in response to GEC, with inevitable effects on natural ecosystems.

El Niño and the Pacific coast of South America

A spectacular short-term change in the ocean environment has been recognized by Pacific fishing peoples for centuries. Rapid, extreme changes in ocean temperature take place in the Pacific Ocean at intervals of around 2–7 years. Unusually warm water appears off the South American coast in a phenomenon called El Niño. The temperature change in 1982–3 reached 14°C above normal in some places, the most extreme in recent years. The change can last months or years before conditions switch rapidly back to normal. The scale and speed of the changes are shown in Figure 6.10.

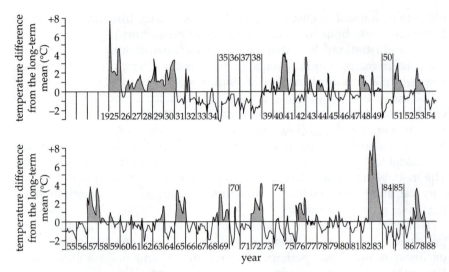

Figure 6.10   Sea surface temperature at Puerto Chicama, Peru, from 1925 to 1988. Temperature differences from the long-term mean are given. The scale of the most spectacular El Niño of the century, in 1982–3, is clear. (From Fahrbach *et al.* 1991.)

El Niño occurs because of a tight coupling between the dynamics of the ocean and of the atmosphere. Normally easterly winds draw warm water away from the South American coast and bring up nutrient-rich cold water in its place. But occasionally the wind speed is reduced. Warm surface waters are no longer drawn away from the coast and coastal upwelling virtually stops. Why does this matter to marine life? When El Niño occurs there is no upwelling of nutrients and the ocean's productivity falls dramatically. Because productivity falls there is a sudden reduction in food resources for animals further up the food chains, including fish and seabirds. The consequences for marine ecosystems of the 1982–3 El Niño included the following:

- Peru's anchovy, sardine and silverside fisheries failed completely because fish were trapped close to shore in the one or two pockets of remaining upwelling, and died, or because they migrated south into less extreme conditions, or because they moved into deeper waters.
- Larger fish moved vast distances to cooler waters. For example, barracuda were found off Oregon and bluefin tuna off British Columbia.
- The whole seabird population of Christmas Island in the Pacific disappeared because of reductions in the numbers of fish and squid and because of higher sea levels. Boobies, cormorants, pelicans and penguins in the Galápagos and Peru abandoned nests and chicks and there was almost complete failure of breeding. Adult mortality was estimated at 85%.
- Seabirds as far away as Oregon had an exceptionally poor breeding season because of reductions in the numbers of fish.

• Breeding success of seals was dramatically reduced because prey were in different places, at greater depth, in poorer condition and in smaller numbers. Mothers spent more time fishing at sea away from their pups. Growth rates of pups fell and in the Galápagos there was almost complete mortality of fur seal pups within months.
• Serious, possibly irreversible, damage occurred to the coral reefs, including bleaching (see page 187).

In contrast, terrestrial organisms benefited from the prolonged wet conditions leading to extensive vegetation growth, fruiting and seeding. Population sizes for many invertebrates increased dramatically. Birds feeding on fruit, seeds and insects reached high numbers. The sudden population increase of finches in the Galápagos (see page 91) was due to weather changes related to El Niño.

El Niño has also had less direct effects. A severe El Niño in 1992–3 forced fish to swim deeper or move northwards into cooler water. As a result, young Californian sealions that cannot fish at depth also moved northwards, and began to feed on coastal fish that are not normally a large part of their diet. This brought them into increasing conflict with California fishermen, who blamed them for dwindling fish stocks and shot increasing numbers.

Although these results are spectacular, El Niño is a frequent event to which marine animals seem able to respond. The speed and the scale of ocean temperature changes and upwelling patterns are very extreme compared to the gradual events predicted for GEC.

Each new El Niño is the subject of a major international research effort and can provide an opportunity to ask and answer basic questions that need to be understood if we are to predict the responses of marine life to GEC. Some of the questions sound simple: How far do marine organisms from different groups move around the oceans? How quickly can they become established at new locations? How tolerant are less mobile organisms of a changing environment? An important question that remains to be answered is whether climate change will alter the frequency of El Niño.

Responses of coastal ecosystems to sea-level changes

The global mean sea level has risen by between 10 and 20 cm over the last 100 years. The uncertainty in this estimate is because mean sea level is very difficult to measure. At any point on the coast the apparent change in sea level depends on true changes in the mean sea level and changes in the height of the coastline, which can sink or rise. For example, the Mississippi Delta is currently experiencing an apparent sea-level rise of 1 cm/year, but this apparent rise has three components. There is a true rise in the mean sea level, but this is augmented by local subsidence of the delta region due to the weight of sediment deposited by the river. However, these two processes are partially counteracted by the accumulation of sediment from the river. So the impact of a rise in the global mean sea level depends very much on local conditions.

The coastal habitats most directly affected by sea-level rise are those in the intertidal zone that already experience some inundation by seawater. The nature of these habitats is strongly dependent on the regular changes in sea level caused by the tides. In most intertidal habitats the communities exhibit a strong zonation related to the amount of time that is spent inundated.

One of the most productive plant communities in the world forms on salt marshes, which occur where coastal areas are protected from wave action. In such places sediment can accumulate and plants tolerant to salt water become established. Many salt marshes support large bird communities and therefore have a high conservation value. Salt marshes can be divided into three zones, the low, middle and high marsh, related to the heights of the neap (the lowest tide on the 14-day cycle), spring (the highest tide on the 14-day cycle) and highest-possible tides (the particularly high tides caused by astronomical events). Two environmental factors change up the salt marsh: the frequency of inundation by salt water and the firmness of the mud. Both influence the type of plants that can survive. On the low marsh there are pioneer species which must be salt tolerant (halophytes) and hold on in the sloppy mud. In the middle marsh the amount of vegetation increases markedly and the plants may spend long periods out of the water. The high marsh is much less saline and can support some non-halophyte or facultative halophyte species. The establishment of plants in these saline habitats encourages the accumulation of sediment, which is brought in on each tide. Potentially accumulation can be very rapid compared to the rate of sea-level rise that is occurring. The mean accretion rate for salt marshes in the Pacific northwest of North America is 3.6 mm/year. This compares to a current sea-level rise of 1.3 mm/year and a predicted sea-level rise of 5.5 mm/year for 2050. As sea level rises many salt marshes should be able to keep pace if sediment is available, and thereby provide a valuable natural barrier to the penetration of salt water further inland.

In order to survive frequent inundation by seawater the plants must be able to cope with the high salt concentration and the direct effects of flooding. Diffusion of oxygen in water is 10000 times slower than in air. Therefore in waterlogged soil the oxygen supply can be rapidly depleted by plant roots and anoxic soil conditions produced. Some species are capable of growing in anoxic soil by employing two strategies:

- diffusion of air into the root via hollow spaces in the centre of the stems and roots (aerenchyma tissue);
- increased use of anaerobic alcoholic fermentation as a source of energy. However, this can lead to starvation as it requires more carbohydrate, and the alcohol produced can be toxic.

If non-halophytic plants are watered with seawater they are unable to transpire and will wilt. In order for water to move into the roots of a plant, and from there to the leaves, there must be a gradient of increasingly negative water potential to drive water flow. In order to produce this water potential gradient, halophytes must maintain a very high solute concentration in their cells, well above that of seawater. Most of this is in the form of sodium and chloride ions. But such high concentrations of these ions in the cytoplasm would inhibit metabolism, and so they are restricted to the cell vacuoles. This would cause dehydration of the cytoplasm, so many salt marsh plants accumulate less damaging (compatible) solutes such as the amino acids, betaine and proline in the cytoplasm. Often salt marsh plants look similar to plants from dry habitats, with thick leaf cuticles or cactus-like shoots to reduce the surface area. This helps limit transpiration, which reduces the amount of salt taken up. The need for such a range of mechanisms to cope with salt water illustrates that the impact of flooding from the sea can be disastrous for normal plants.

Salt marshes are important breeding sites for some birds. Others graze the salt marsh plants. Large numbers feed on the invertebrates that live in and on mud flats below the salt marsh. The number of birds that can exploit mud flats is limited by competition: the more birds there are, the more they interfere with each other and the faster the food is depleted.

Apart from the intertidal zone many coastal areas have large expanses of land close to sea level which can occasionally be flooded by seawater. This is only likely to happen when events combine to cause a particularly high sea level, such as a storm coupled with a particularly high spring tide. If the mean sea level rises, the frequency of such storm surges that flood coastal areas will increase. As the plants in these low-lying areas seldom come into contact with salt water they are severely damaged by flooding with seawater.

Coastal defences are often built to protect such low-lying land from inundation. Salt marsh lies in front of the defences. A sea-level rise of 0.8 m would reduce the area of the salt marsh and reduce the width of each vegetation zone in front of the defences. A rise of 1 m or above would probably lead to the total loss of salt marsh vegetation, except perhaps for patches of pioneer species. The width of mud flats would be reduced, increasing competition among birds feeding in the mud and reducing their numbers. The food available to feeding birds is also likely to be reduced because of changes in the nature of the substrate: cloudier water (bad for phytoplankton and suspension feeders) and a coarser sand low in organic matter. If new sea defences are constructed further inland salt marshes and mud flats could probably be regenerated, but the loss of agricultural land and the expense of habitat creation and management would be high.

Predictions of further increases in sea level vary widely. A conservative estimate is a 1 m rise by the end of the next century, due to thermal expansion of the oceans, and the melting of glaciers and some ice caps. The consequences for humans could be very severe. Possibilities include:

• inundation of large population centres. In 2000, 70% of the world population will live within 60 km of the coast;

- inundation of fertile agricultural land, e.g. around river deltas;
- increased salinity of water tables, with severe consequences for agriculture. For example, the aquifer of porous limestone underlying much of Florida could become increasingly saline. One study suggests that this could be avoided only if a dyke were constructed to create a barrier to seawater. To prevent water seeping underneath, the base of the dyke would need to extend to 50 m below the ground surface;
- destruction of coastal wetlands, which play a critical role in fisheries. Many economically important fish species spawn close to the shore. Nine of the 20 most valuable United States fisheries – including salmon, shrimp, lobster, flounder, oyster and various crabs – involve species that depend on coastal ecosystems for at least part of their lifecycle;
- inundation of oceanic islands. Coral atolls rise only a metre or two above sea level. Already there is a programme to redistribute part of the population of the Maldives to islands that are less low lying;
- large world increase in the number of environmental refugees displaced from coastal areas. One estimate is that 50 million people could be forced to move.

References

Blumberg AF, Di Toro DM (1990) Effects of climate warming on dissolved oxygen content in lake Erie. *Transactions of the American Fisheries Society* **119**, 210–23

Brown BE, Ogden JC (1993) Coral bleaching. *Scientific American* **268**, 44–50

Busch DE, Fisher SG (1981) Metabolism of a desert stream. *Freshwater Biology* **11**, 301–7

Chatters JC, Neitzel DA, Scott MJ, Shankle SA (1991) Potential impacts of global climate change on Pacific Northwest spring chinook salmon (*Oncorhynchus tshawytscha*): an exploratory case study. *Northwest Environmental Journal* **7**, 71–92

Cooter EJ, Cooter WS (1990) Impacts of greenhouse warming on water temperature and water quality in the southern United States. *Climate Research* **1**, 1–12

Coutant CC (1990) Temperature–oxygen habitat for freshwater and coastal striped bass in a changing climate. *Transactions of the American Fisheries Society* **119**, 240–53

Cushing DH, Dickson RR (1976) The biological response in the sea to climatic changes. *Advances in Marine Biology* **14**, 1–122

Fahrbach E, Trillmich F, Arntz W (1991) The time sequence and magnitude of physical effects of El Niño in the Eastern Pacific. In *Pinnipeds and El Niño. Responses to environmental stress. Ecological Studies* 88, eds F Trillmich and KA Ono. Springer-Verlag, Berlin, pp.8–21

Ferrier RC, Whitehead PG, Miller JD (1993) Potential impacts of afforestation and climate change on the stream water chemistry of the Monachyle catchment. *Journal of Hydrology* **145**, 453–66

Frank KT, Perry RI, Drinkwater KF (1990) Predicted response of Northwest Atlantic invertebrate and fish stocks to CO_2-induced climate change. *Transactions of the American Fisheries Society* **119**, 353–65

Goreau TJ, Hayes RL (1994) Coral bleaching and ocean 'hot spots'. *Ambio* **23**, 176–80

Healey MC (1990) Implications of climate change for fisheries management policy. *Transactions of the American Fisheries Society* **119**, 366–73

Jones R (1982) Ecosystems, food chains and fish yields. In *Theory and Management of Tropical Fisheries*, eds D Pauly and GI Murphy. International Center for Living Aquatic Resources Management, Manila, pp.195–239

Krogh A (1941) *The comparative physiology of respiratory mechanisms,* University of Pennsylvania Press, Philadelphia

Mandrak NE (1989) Potential invasion of the Great Lakes by fish species associated with climatic warming. *Journal of Great Lakes Research* **15**, 306–16

Matthews WJ, Zimmerman EG (1990) Potential effects of global warming on native fishes of the southern Great Plains and the southwest. *Fisheries* **15**, 26–32

Meisner JD (1990) Potential loss of thermal habitat for brook trout, due to climatic warming, in two southern Ontario streams. *Transactions of the American Fisheries Society* **119**, 282–91

Minns CK, Moore JE (1992) Predicting the impact of climate change on the spatial pattern of freshwater fish yield capability in Eastern Canadian Lakes. *Climatic Change* **22**, 327–46

Moore HB (1972) Aspects of stress in the tropical marine environment. *Advances in Marine Biology* **10**, 217–69

Roberts CM (1991) Larval mortality and the composition of coral reef fish communities. *Trends in Ecology and Evolution* **6**, 83–7

Ryther JH (1969) Photosynthesis and fish production in the sea. *Science* **166**, 72–6

Scheibling RE, Stephenson RL (1984) Mass mortality of *Strongylocentrotus droebachiensis* (Echinodermata: Echinoidea) off Nova Scotia, Canada. *Marine Biology* **78**, 153–64

Schindler DW, Beaty KG, Fee EJ, Cruikshank DR, DeBruyn ER, Findlay DL, Linsey GA, Shearer JA, Stainton MP, Turner MA (1990) Effects of climate warming on the lakes of the central boreal forest. *Science* **250**, 967–70

Shuter BJ, Post JR (1990) Climate, population viability and the zoogeography of temperate fish. *Transactions of the American Fisheries Society* **119**, 314–36

Smock LA, MacGregor CM (1988) Impact of American chestnut blight on aquatic shredding macroinvertebrates. *Journal of the North American Benthological Society* **7**, 212–21

Times Books (1985) *The Times Atlas of the World*, Times Books, London
Trippel EA, Eckmann R, Hartmann J (1991) Potential effects of global warming on whitefish in lake Constance, Germany. *Ambio* **20**, 226–31
Veron JEN (1992) Environmental control of Holocene changes to the world's most northern hermatypic coral outcrop. *Pacific Science* **46**, 405–25
Williamson P, Holligan PM (1992) Ocean productivity and climate change. *Trends in Ecology and Evolution* **5**, 299–303
Wright DG, Hendry RM, Loder JW, Dobson FW (1986) *Oceanic changes associated with global increases in atmospheric carbon dioxide: a preliminary report for the Atlantic coast of Canada.* Canadian Technical Report of Fisheries and Aquatic Sciences 1426

Further reading

Carpenter SR, Fisher SG, Grimm NB, Kitchell JF (1992) Global change and freshwater ecosystems. *Annual Review of Ecology and Systematics* **23**, 119–39

Good section on the effects of the likely increase in rare events.

Reid WV, Trexler MC (1992) Responding to potential impacts of climate change on US coastal biodiversity. *Coastal Management* **20**, 117–42

A wide-ranging review that considers species and habitats and proposes some possible responses.

7 Conservation in a changing environment

Introduction

In this final chapter we consider the effects of GEC on biological conservation. First we consider the conservation of biodiversity. This is relevant to all kinds of people – those who wish to use biodiversity in industry, agriculture or forestry, or to protect it for its own sake or because it has a right to exist. Then we consider the conservation of global processes. Though less fashionable than the conservation of Sumatran rhinos or rare orchids, water and nutrient cycling and ecosystem stability have implications for everyone.

Earlier chapters show why GEC will have major effects on plants, animals and communities. This chapter shows ways in which biologists can try to tackle some of the problems that GEC will create for the conservation of genes, species, habitats and processes.

Effects of GEC on biodiversity

Biodiversity is a fashionable word used in different ways by different people. Here we consider it to be the variety and variability of organisms. It has three components: genetic diversity (genetic variation within species), species diversity (the variety of species) and ecosystem diversity (the variety of ecosystems).

Some reasons for maintaining high biodiversity are given in Table 7.1. They range from the utilitarian to the philosophical but, whatever the reason, the current loss of biodiversity is so rapid that urgent action is necessary. There is a growing consensus about the present rate of extinction of species worldwide: 27 000 species per year is a considered estimate (Wilson 1992). It is harder to put a meaningful figure on the rate of loss of genetic or ecosystem diversity, but both are just as considerable. Reasons for these losses include:

Table 7.1 Some reasons for conservation. (In part from Myers (1981)

'to allow evolutionary processes to continue'
'to safeguard the role of ecosystems in regulating the biosphere, especially in maintaining climatic stability – local, regional, even global'
'to safeguard watersheds – preventing flooding and soil erosion and maintaining
water supplies'
'to provide a stock of organisms for research'
'to provide ecosystems for benchmark monitoring'
'to provide products like building materials and food'
'to conserve gene pools for future use by humans'
'to provide wild areas for recreation and education'
'to provide income through tourism'

* conversion of land to agriculture and forestry;
* careless commercial overexploitation of natural products (e.g. timber);
* unsustainable land use forced by population pressure (e.g. overgrazing,
  shifting cultivation with too little regeneration time);
* environmental pollution;
* development of new settlements and roads.

The underlying problems are population growth and increased human aspirations. GEC is rarely ever mentioned on such a list.

Most of these causes of biodiversity loss can be ameliorated, at least in
theory. One approach is the creation and protection of biological reserves
which, in theory, can be kept free from human influence. At present around
4% of the world land area is more or less protected in biosphere reserves,
national parks and local reserves, although this network cannot include all
habitats. Some reserves are large enough to be self-contained in terms of
hydrology and nutrient cycling and they contain sufficiently large populations of the great majority of plants and animals to maintain viable breeding
populations.

However, of all the causes of biodiversity loss, GEC is a unique problem
because:

* it cannot be excluded by fences or armed guards;
* its effects are gradual and will become clearer in future decades;
* its effects are permanent.

GEC will continue even if CO_2 emissions were to stop immediately (see
Chapter 1): an average warming of 1–2°C would still occur. At present there
are few reasons to believe that there will be any change in the pattern of
increasing CO_2 emissions.

Losses of biodiversity due to GEC

GEC due to human activity is a new phenomenon that will have an increasing impact in decades to come. Current losses of biodiversity have other causes, but future losses will be caused directly by GEC. Other factors, especially the fragmentation of natural habitats which has reduced abundances and genetic diversity, will increase the severity of these losses far beyond those of any similar climate changes in the past.

We have already shown that many species will not be able to move quickly enough across the landscape to keep up with changing climate because of their poor mobility and because of the fragmented landscape. An immediate result will be a reduction in species diversity. Schwartz (1991) considered 316 species of rare, threatened and endangered plants from forests of the southeastern United States. For 56 species, the distance from the north to the south of their distribution is <50 km. For a further 58 species it is <100 km. GEC models predict a northwards shift in climate of 500 km. Only 15 of the rare species have a continuous distribution of 500 km or more. This does not necessarily mean that the other species will become extinct. For some their limited distribution is probably due to factors other than climate (e.g. the need for a particular soil type) and a different climate might not be important. For others, their occurrence on mountain slopes means that suitable conditions will be present a short way up the mountainside.

A simple model has been created to predict the effects of temperature change on mammals of isolated mountain tops in the Great Basin of western North America. For each 1°C increase in temperature climatic zones are likely to be shifted 160 m up a mountainside, so that mountain-top habitats shrink or disappear completely. This is important, because the number of mammal species is closely correlated with the area of suitable habitat that is available (Figure 7.1(a)). The model suggests that a temperature increase of 3°C will lead to the loss of 9–62% of species, varying for different mountain ranges (Figure 7.1(b)). Only two of 14 species – a chipmunk and a woodrat – will continue to survive on all the mountains where they currently occur. Three species – the western jumping mouse, the white-tailed jack rabbit and Belding's ground squirrel – will become extinct in the region. The main factor leading to the loss of species is their isolation on 'islands' of suitable habitat.

Other extinctions are likely not because of problems with movement but because suitable habitats disappear completely. Kirtland's warbler is a bird species with precise habitat requirements. It occurs only in central Michigan in a small area of jack pine forest on coarse sandy soils. The last census in 1989 recorded a total population of 212 males. The habitat is managed for the warbler by periodic burning, which increases the area of young trees in which the warblers nest. Models of climate change predict a deterioration of the habitat at the earliest signs of change. Other tree species will rapidly dominate. A possible result of the habitat change is the extinction of the bird

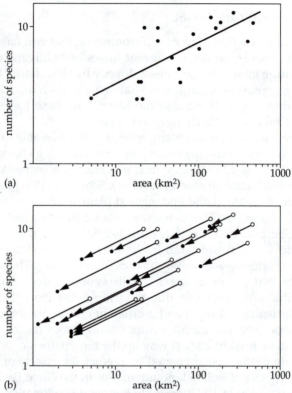

(a)

(b)

Figure 7.1   Possible effects of temperature change on small mammals of 19 isolated mountain ranges in the Great Basin of North America. The ranges are separated by desert valleys and dispersal from mountain to mountain is most unlikely. (a) The relationship between land area above 2280 m and the number of species of small mammals. Notice the close correlation. (b) Predicted changes in the number of species based on a model of climate and vegetation change. The model is based on a temperature rise of 3°C and no change in precipitation. Data for before (o) and after (•) climate change are given. (After McDonald and Brown 1992. Data on present distributions from Brown and Gibson 1983.)

within 30–60 years (Botkin *et al.* 1991). Leadbeater's possum could have a similar fate because suitable environmental conditions are likely to simply no longer exist (see Chapter 3).

It is possible to bring together factors such as dispersal ability and habitat requirements and use this set of criteria to indicate the vulnerability of species to climate change. Dennis and Shreeve (1991) have done this for British butterflies using seven factors (Table 7.2). This sort of indication of vulnerability focuses attention on species and ecosystems at particular risk.

Some special cases present a real challenge. In Chapter 3 we considered turtles and the fact that their sex is determined by the incubation tempera-

Table 7.2 Factors used to indicate the vulnerability of British butterflies to climate change. Each species is scored on a scale of 1 (most vulnerable) to 4 (least vulnerable) for each factor. Each factor is given the same weighting simply because it is not clear which matters most. According to this system, the most vulnerable British species is the swallowtail, a specialist restricted to vulnerable wetlands in the Norfolk Broads. It scores 9. The least vulnerable is the green-veined white, a widespread species of hedges and gardens. It scores 26. (From Dennis and Shreeve 1991)

Factor	Most vulnerable	Least vulnerable
Range in Britain	Latitude range <25% of Britain	Latitude range >75%
Distribution	Present in <24.5% of 10 km squares within its range	Present in >73.5% of 10 km squares
Feeding specificity	Monophagous	Polyphagous
Abundance of food plant	Depends on substrate	Cosmopolitan and ubiquitous
Habitat	Climax woodland or peat bog	Bare ground with short grasses and herbaceous plants
Range of semi-natural habitats occupied	<5	14–18
Dispersal ability	Closed populations with little evidence of dispersal outside colonies	Migrants and other species that make long-distance movements

ture of eggs in the sand. If the sand were 2°C warmer, all hatching green and leatherback turtles would be female, at least in parts of their range, which would surely lead to their local extinction. In theory the turtles could respond by selecting different nest sites, but sea turtles are faithful to their nest sites and other sites might be less suitable because of predation, distance from the sea or dense plant roots in the sand. Another possibility is to nest in a cooler season. However, sea turtles are at least 30 years old before they mature and it is unlikely that selection will act – and turtles change – fast enough. Conservation efforts will have to concentrate on protecting nest sites at the cooler northern edge of their range (Mrosovsky and Provancha 1989).

Another major conservation challenge is the likely disappearance of tsetse flies – carriers of trypanosomiasis – from large parts of central Africa if temperatures rise by 2°C. At present, 26% of Africa's human population but only 9% of Africa's livestock inhabits the areas in which tsetse flies are present. The absence of tsetse will open up parts of this vast area to domestic livestock, which is likely to devastate the environment in a way that has not been possible before. Thus the effect of GEC on a small group of flies could influence people, livestock and biodiversity in a spectacular way.

Fundamental problems with nature reserves

One problem with nature reserves is that their design is usually based on the assumption that the environment will stay more or less constant and contain the same assemblages of species as extinctions are offset by colonizations. During GEC it will not. As conditions change, species assemblages will also change as individual species respond in their own particular ways.

A range of management practices can be devised to ameliorate the effects of GEC in the small number of managed reserves that have resources available. For example, the Derwent Ings in Yorkshire, England, is an internationally important site that supports a range of wildfowl and waders. The Ings are flood meadows with a high plant species diversity and are traditionally maintained by flooding during the winter and cutting for hay and grazing in the summer. The likely impacts of GEC are (1) to encourage more rapid plant growth in the spring, stimulated by the increase in atmospheric CO_2 concentration, and (2) a change in the amount of water flowing in the Derwent river. The amount of plant growth can be regulated by allowing the floodwaters to remain longer in the spring and by cutting earlier for hay. Changes in river flow can be ameliorated by flood control works along the valley.

As another example, consider the observation in Chapter 3 that climate change will affect microclimate and that insects could respond by adjusting their use of the habitat. For grassland insects, a change in grass height of a centimetre or two makes all the difference (Figure 7.2). The land manager needs to know how the slightest change in grazing can affect the structure of

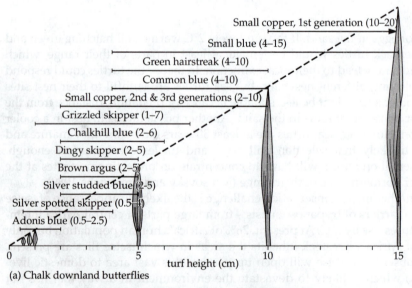

(a) Chalk downland butterflies

Figure 7.2   Preferred turf heights (cm) for some British butterflies. (Data from Fry and Lonsdale 1991.)

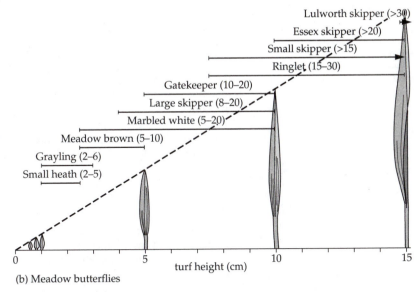

(b) Meadow butterflies

Figure 7.2   *continued.*

the vegetation, alter the microclimate and cause a spectacular change in butterfly abundance. Managers are able to use grazing by sheep or cattle – or
even mowing – as a powerful management tool. A response to GEC is to
maintain the heterogeneity of the environment by a diversity of grazing and
mowing regimes so that a diversity of habitats is available.

However, even if they are technically and financially feasible, attempts to
stabilize existing ecosystems by more intensive management, such as irrigation, drainage, culling of predators and weeding of invaders, can give only
a short-term solution. Whether or not a species survives will depend not on
the presence of nature reserves but on its ability to move, to tolerate change
or to adapt. This also presents a serious problem in conservation politics.
Land managers will be under considerable pressure to rewrite their management plans to try to retain the prized species for which many reserves
were created in the first place, even though this is an approach that does not
address the underlying problems that GEC will cause.

Some general rules for the design of nature reserves are listed in Table 7.3.
Several broad approaches are taken in the design of reserves that are suitable
for a time of environmental change. One approach is to site reserves in areas
where there is a range of climates in a small area. In mountain areas, for
example, heterogeneity would be maintained whatever the broad changes in
climate, and this would allow populations to move relatively short distances
to remain in suitable conditions. Another approach is to incorporate features
that increase the size of populations and allow species to disperse easily
across the landscape. This is more subtle, so it is dealt with in more detail
below. A third approach is to create a network of 'stepping stones' across the

Table 7.3   Some basic design rules for nature reserves. There are very many more (see, for example, Spellerberg *et al.* 1991 and references given there)

Design rule	Value during GEC
Large size	Number of species increases with increasing land area (each species tends to occur in habitat patches above a particular threshold size for that species) Larger patches have larger populations, reducing the risk of extinction
Large number of habitats	Allows species to adjust distribution within reserve in response to change Allows reserve to be effective for a long period Takes account of possible changes in the physical environment (e.g. river level, level of water table) that could be caused by GEC
Varied topography, aspect and soil type	Allows species to adjust distribution within reserve in response to change
Wide corridors should connect reserves	Allows species to adjust distribution by moving between large reserves. With increasing isolation the number of species decreases and there is a lower rate of colonization
Corridors should contain large number of habitats	Maximises diversity of species that move between reserves
Network of corridors should be extensive and complete. Even small gaps or occasional fences are enough to prevent dispersal	Maximises diversity of species that move between reserves
Maintain reserves across the whole distributions of species	Gives best chance of evolution in response to GEC because individuals at extremes of the distribution carry important genetic variability to tolerate stress
Selective, active management to promote some species and remove others according to stated goals	Especially important during GEC because equilibrium is unlikely
Studies on short-term responses of individual species to GEC, showing what factors determine range and abundance and how large an area is required for a population to persist	Required for effective land management inside and outside reserves

landscape – small habitat patches that are not necessarily connected. Needless to say, the three approaches are complementary.

The presence of 'corridors' linking reserves could increase movements between them. One benefit could be a greater number of species at each site because individuals more readily move into the site from outside. This could result in reduced natural variation in births and deaths, a process which can wipe out whole populations when populations are small. Another argument is that corridors increase gene flow, thereby reducing inbreeding depression. Another is that some species need a large home range (i.e. the area covered by an individual for foraging and other activities), which can only be provided by linking several reserves.

Movement corridors could also increase the speed of movement of plants and animals across the landscape as climate changes. Because many species move extremely slowly, corridors must themselves be reserves. River banks, hedges and ditches are important habitats in their own right, but also provide a network across the countryside and some of these are suitable corridors between larger patches of habitat. Hedges, for example, are similar in many ways to woodland edges, and so provide a continuous habitat for woodland edge species. However, there is a continuing decline in the extent and quality of hedges because barbed wire and electric fences are cheaper to maintain.

Another possibility is to use the verges of roads and railways, the routes of disused railways and the land below electrical power lines as corridors between fragmented habitats. Studies in the Netherlands have shown that ground beetles move considerable distances (tens, possibly hundreds, of metres) along road verges between reserves, and the Directorate General for Public Works and Water Management intends to improve road verges as habitats and corridors for threatened species based on these basic ecological studies. Hedges might have an uncertain future in many areas, but roads might be better for two reasons. First, roads will always criss-cross over the landscape. Secondly, a far wider diversity of habitats can be created on road verges, at least in theory. A disadvantage is that traffic pollution has major effects on plants and animals. Roads with high traffic density can pollute roadside ecosystems with more than 170 toxic compounds. This can change community structures, with a decrease in the abundance and diversity of predatory and parasitic insects, an increase in fungus feeders and outbreaks of plant feeders such as aphids (Butovsky 1990). Chemical changes stay consistently high for decades. For example, heavy metal concentrations in ground beetles collected near busy roads in the Netherlands were at least four times higher than around Moscow, where there are fewer cars, even though heavy metal pollution in the Netherlands stopped 20 years previously (Butovsky 1993).

Some have suggested creating national – even continental – corridors hundreds of metres wide, and many feel that corridors are the answer to all manner of conservation problems. However, Simberloff et al. (1992) show how little data there are to substantiate most claims. They use examples to show that:

- Many species persist in very small populations (e.g. large predators, or species on small islands) and the extinction of a small population is not inevitable. In other words, many species are rare, but not all of them are threatened.
- Many species do not show inbreeding depression and there is little evidence of it in the wild. Just one breeding individual moving from one population to another is enough to genetically link the populations as though they are breeding together as one.
- There is little good evidence that animals and plants use corridors. Many studies measure movements along corridors but not away from them.
- Even corridors that are several hundred metres wide are likely to be influenced by the surrounding habitats, so that they are not a true example of the habitat that is intended.
- Corridors could increase the spread of diseases, introduced species and fire.

Simberloff *et al.* show in a powerful way how features that conservationists take for granted are not necessarily based on good evidence.

A final option is to move species artificially. A simple example is the artificial reintroduction of individuals from a neighbouring population to a site where the species has become extinct. In Britain, more that 100 attempts at the introduction and reintroduction of butterflies were made in the 1980s and more than one-third of them succeeded. The main reason for failures was unsuitability of habitat.

At the other extreme, whole communities can be moved intact or created from individual components. There is already expertise in moving whole ecosystems. For example, an early attempt was to move part of a wood in southern England on to adjoining land when it was threatened by the extension of a quarry. After 5 years, all the trees and 75% of the ground plants had survived. So far the distances have been short – usually only a few kilometres – but long-distance movement of forests should be no more difficult. The problems are the large areas of land involved and the cost.

Habitat creation is also feasible. Arable land or regularly fertilized pasture can be returned to natural calcareous grassland communities over several years. The high nutrient levels in the soil must be reduced, and this can be done easily over 2 or 3 years by sowing grasses that require high nitrogen levels, then harvesting the grass and removing it from the site. A natural seed mix from a similar site locally can then be sown. The legal requirement in some European countries to reduce the area of agricultural land because of overproduction gives an opportunity to manage this spare land in imaginative ways. Creation of natural habitats is one possibility, and needs the same land management skills used by farmers, foresters and gardeners.

Responding to GEC by conserving genetic diversity

If species are to evolve in response to GEC, genetic variability must be conserved. Habitat fragmentation has reduced the size of many populations.

Human activities have also caused the population size of many species to fluctuate wildly. The effect of both is reduced genetic variability and a result is that species will be less adaptable. This is an important way in which GEC differs from historical climate change, and at present is a real unknown.

We need to know which populations contain genetic variation. One way to find out is by using electrophoresis (page 64) to indicate the degree of enzyme polymorphism. It is only necessary to look at a small number of enzymes, and they do not have to be ones with particular functions because the diversity of alleles at all loci is normally affected to a similar extent by processes such as inbreeding. A complementary approach is to look quantitatively at phenotypic traits for morphological or ecological characteristics, such as the ability to endure environmental stresses. This second approach may be more important at times of environmental change because at least it gives a feel for characteristics that may be particularly relevant.

The genetic variation most valuable in allowing species to persist is in populations at extremes of their distributions, where they must cope with stress (page 93). Because there is a metabolic cost to resisting stress, populations from more favourable environments are likely to have alleles that increase resistance to stress at low frequencies. This means that concentrating on conserving populations in locations where stress is less is not a good strategy from a genetic viewpoint, even though such populations might appear to be at less immediate risk (Parsons 1990).

To devise species recovery programmes we need to have genetic as well as population information. This has been done for an endangered fish from Arizona desert streams, the Sonoran topminnow. Quattro and Vrijenhoek (1989) examined three populations of the fish and found that the one with most genetic variation also had greatest growth, survival, early fecundity and developmental stability. Until this study, fish from the least variable population (homozygous at all 25 loci analysed!) had been used for reintroduction to the wild from a captive stock.

The species that should be most able to adapt genetically to climate change are those which are abundant, widespread, have a good dispersal ability and a short generation time. The problem is that these are least at risk of extinction in the first place. The rare species are those least able to evolve.

The situation is similar for economically important species such as forest trees, except that more time and money can be spent on establishing what genetic diversity is where. An immediate response to ensure that as much genetic diversity as possible is conserved is to collect and store material *ex situ* in seed banks or clone banks (see Chapter 5). A rule of thumb is that collecting 30 genotypes at random from a location will preserve 95% of common alleles. Populations and genotypes of potential value can then be tested for their suitability for forestry, selecting for characteristics that allow trees to take advantage of early springs, late autumns and increased rainfall without losing winter hardiness and drought tolerance (Fowler and Loo-Dinkins 1992). A complementary approach is to establish and preserve populations of important tree species *in situ* at the limit of their range, as they will already have some adaptation to stresses. During rapid change reserves for trees that have a long generation time will be of little use if they are intended to give species time to adapt. These are little more than a source of seed for elsewhere. Nevertheless, they will provide a biologically and architecturally diverse habitat in which organisms with shorter generations can maintain genetic diversity and evolve.

Biological indicators of GEC

Throughout this book we have shown how abiotic changes affect plants and animals. Measurements of physical and chemical changes are inevitably very coarse and very few. Furthermore, they are not necessarily relevant to plants and animals that are affected by these and other factors all acting together, but at present it is the best we can do when trying to predict the future.

However, physical and chemical parameters are not the only way to measure change as it is taking place. Plants and animals are better indicators because they respond to the effects of all these factors over long periods. Thus changes in the occurrence or abundance of plants and animals can be used to monitor environmental change.

Danks (1992) has proposed several different ways of monitoring change in the Arctic using insects. Reasons to use insects are that they are diverse, with around 2000 described species from north of the tree line in North America, and the ecosystem is complex enough to show interesting patterns.

Three of these patterns are shown in Figures 7.3 and 7.4. There is no doubt that the patterns are clear. That shown in Figure 7.4 for insect orders is just as distinct at other taxonomic levels. For example, within the flies the proportion of Chironomidae (midges) increases and of Asilidae (robber flies) decreases. Within the Muscidae (another family of flies), the proportion of *Spilogona* spp. increases and *Fannia* spp. decreases (Danks 1992). It takes no more than a basic list of species for a site to be able to compare it with other sites now or with assemblages of insects from the same site in future years.

If patterns are used instead of particular indicator species, there is less risk of choosing atypical indicators and less need to understand the taxonomy and ecology of all species in great detail. Even so, conspicuous well known species (e.g. solitary bees, mosquitoes, butterflies) are good indicators to show changes in distribution, abundance and phenology. Another interesting possibility is to monitor a series of physiological markers to see how populations change in traits such as cold hardiness and dormancy.

One prerequisite is a good understanding of the basic patterns of biodiversity across different environments. Another is sound taxonomic knowledge. We also need undisturbed sites in which monitoring can take place. Environments in which changes should be most visible at an early stage are:

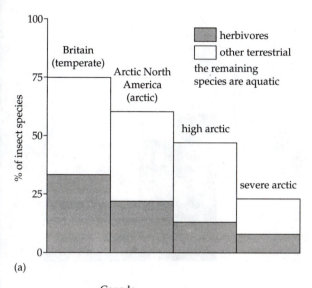

(a)

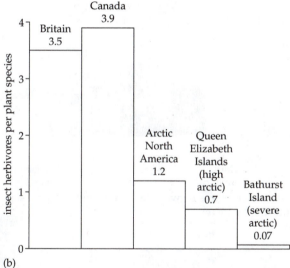

(b)

Figure 7.3 Differences in insect assemblages between temperate and Arctic sites: (a) by feeding behaviour; (b) by the ratio of plant-feeding insects to plants. (After Danks 1990, 1993.)

- the Arctic, where temperature changes will be greatest;
- mountains, where extinctions are especially likely;
- ecotones (transitions between habitats), where diversity will change especially rapidly;
- areas of human disturbance, where introductions of new species will be especially frequent.

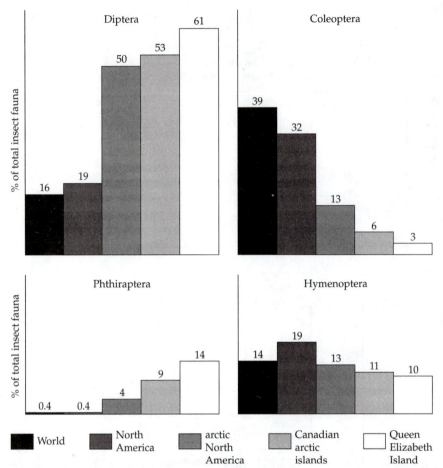

Figure 7.4   Differences in insect assemblages between temperate and arctic sites: by insect order. (After Danks 1990.)

Global processes

Although conservation is often associated with the care and protection of delineated reserves, or even single species, it also has much wider implications. The first aim of the World Conservation Strategy is to maintain 'essential ecological processes and life-support systems'. In a global context this means regulating processes such as the global carbon cycle, the nitrogen cycle or the hydrological cycle.

As discussed extensively in previous chapters, human disruption of the global carbon cycle is one of the principal causes of GEC. How can this be reduced? One of the best ways of understanding the complexity of the answer to this question is to consider how the IPCC approached predicting future CO_2 production. They projected future CO_2 emissions on the basis of several scenarios, which were generated by making assumptions in four key areas (Leggett *et al.* 1992):

• the rate of population increase;
• the rate of economic growth;
• the source of energy (coal, oil, natural gas, nuclear, solar etc.);
• the existence of international agreements or commitments to reduce pollutant emissions.

The decisions that will shape the future in each of these realms are in the political arena and beyond the scope of this book. But politicians should respond to the aspirations of their electorate. If sufficient people desire to preserve the natural heritage of our planet and understand the link between this and the regulation of global systems, then the correct decisions may be made.

Conclusion

Many different threats of extinction of many different species make the conservation of genetic, species and ecosystem diversity an urgent priority. The threat of GEC is less immediate than others, but strategic decisions made now must take it into account. We know that GEC can affect species in two ways: they may not be able to tolerate new conditions because of their physiology, and they may be affected by changing interactions with predators, parasites, competitors and mutualists. We need to know how CO_2 and climate and these interactions among species determine range size and abundance, the effects of small size on how populations persist, and why populations become small in the first place (Caughley 1994).

Because each species will respond in its own individual way, biologists – and those responsible for local, national and global conservation policies – must decide on the way forward. Is it more appropriate to try to maintain communities as we know them today, or to ensure that ecological processes continue – perhaps with a helping hand – and maintain biodiversity in its widest sense?

References

Botkin DB, Woodby DA, Nisbet RA (1991) Kirtland's warbler habitats: a possible early indicator of climatic warming. *Biological Conservation* 56, 63–78

Brown J, Gibson A (1983) *Biogeography*, C V Mosby Company, St Louis, Missouri

Butovsky RO (1990) Motorway pollution and entomofauna. *Agrochimija* 4, 138–50 (in Russian)

Butovsky RO (1993) The transition of heavy metals through trophic chains of roadside invertebrates. *Agrochimija* 8, 105–17 (in Russian)

Caughley G (1994) Directions in conservation biology. *Journal of Animal Ecology* **63**, 215–44

Danks HV (1990) Arctic insects: instructive diversity. In *Canada's missing dimension: science and history in the Canadian Arctic Islands*, ed. CR Harington. Canadian Museum of Nature, Ottawa, Volume 2, pp.444–70

Danks HV (1992) Arctic insects as indicators of environmental change. *Arctic* **45**, 159–66

Danks HV (1993) Patterns of diversity in the Canadian insect fauna. In *Systematics and entomology: diversity, distribution, adaptation and application*, eds GE Ball and HV Danks. *Memoirs of the Entomological Society of Canada* **165**, 51–74

Dennis RLH, Shreeve TG (1991) Climate change and the British butterfly fauna: opportunities and constraints. *Biological Conservation* **55**, 1–16

Fowler DP, Loo-Dinkins JA (1992) Breeding strategies in a changing climate and implications for biodiversity. *Forestry Chronicle* **68**, 472–5

Fry RE, Lonsdale D (eds) (1991) *Habitat conservation for insects. A neglected green issue*, Amateur Entomologists' Society, Hanworth

Leggett J, Pepper WJ, Swart RJ (1992) Emissions scenarios for IPCC: an update. In *Climate change 1992. The supplementary report to the IPCC scientific assessment*, eds JT Houghton, BA Callander and SK Varney. CUP, Cambridge

McDonald KA, Brown JH (1992) Using montane mammals to model extinctions due to global change. *Conservation Biology* **6**, 409–15

Mrosovsky N, Provancha J (1989) Sex ratio of loggerhead sea turtles hatching on a Florida (USA) beach. *Canadian Journal of Zoology* **67**, 2533–9

Myers N (1981) Conservation needs and opportunities in tropical moist forests. In *Biological aspects of rare plant conservation*, ed. H Synge. Wiley, Chichester, pp.141–54

Parsons PA (1990) The metabolic cost of multiple environmental stresses: implications for climatic change and conservation. *Trends in Ecology and Evolution* **5**, 315–17

Quattro JM, Vrijenhoek RC (1989) Fitness differences among remnant populations of the endangered Sonoran topminnow. *Science* **245**, 976–8

Schwartz MW (1991) Potential effects of global climate change on the biodiversity of plants. *Forestry Chronicle* **68**, 462–71

Simberloff D, Farr JA, Cox J, Mehlman DW (1992) Movement corridors: conservation bargains or poor investments? *Conservation Biology* **6**, 493–504

Spellerberg IF, Goldsmith FB, Morris MG (eds) (1991) *The scientific management of temperate communities for conservation*, Blackwell Scientific Publications, Oxford

Wilson EO (1992) *The diversity of life*, The Belknap Press of Harvard University Press, Cambridge, MA

Index

References which include the definition of a word are given in **bold**.
References to figures and tables are given in *italics*.